Thermal Engineering - I

AUTHOR

Dr. V. Raghavan
Professor,
Department of Mechanical Engineering
Indian Institute of Technology Madras,
Chennai 600036, Tamil Nadu, India

REVIEWER

Dr. Akhilendra Pratap Singh
Asst. Professor (Grade-I)
Department of Mechanical Engineering
IIT (BHU), Varanasi-221005, Uttar Pradesh, India

KHANNA BOOK PUBLISHING CO. (P) Ltd.
4C/4344, Ansari Road, Darya Ganj, New Delhi, India

All India Council for Technical Education
Nelson Mandela Marg, Vasant Kunj, New Delhi, India

Dear Readers,

To prevent the piracy, this book is secured with HIGH SECURITY HOLOGRAM on the front title cover. In case you don't find the hologram on the front cover title, please write us to at contact@khannabooks.com or whatsapp us at +91-99109 09320 and avail special gift voucher for yourself.

Specimen of Hologram on front Cover title:

Enlargement Of Overlay

Moreover, there is a SPECIAL DISCOUNT COUPON for you with EVERY HOLOGRAM.

How to avail this SPECIAL DISCOUNT:

Step 1: Scratch the hologram

Step 2: Under the scratch area, your "coupon code" is available

Step 3: Logon to www.khannabooks.com

Step 4: Use your "coupon code" in the shopping cart and get your copy at a special discount

Step 5: Enjoy your reading!

ISBN: 978-93-5538-901-5
Book Code: DIP444EN

Thermal Engineering - I

by Dr. V. Raghavan

First Edition: 2025

Originally Published by:
All India Council for Technical Education, Ministry of Education, GOI

Exclusively Published & Distributed by:
Khanna Book Publishing Co. (P) Ltd.
4C/4344, Ansari Road, Daryaganj,
New Delhi (INDIA)

Visit us at: **www.khannabooks.com**
Write us at: **contact@khannabooks.com**

To view complete list of books, Please scan the QR Code:

KPH

Printed in Bharat.

प्रो. टी. जी. सीताराम
अध्यक्ष
Prof. T. G. Sitharam
Chairman

सत्यमेव जयते

आज़ादी का अमृत महोत्सव

अखिल भारतीय तकनीकी शिक्षा परिषद्
(भारत सरकार का एक सांविधिक निकाय)
(शिक्षा मंत्रालय, भारत सरकार)
नेल्सन मंडेला मार्ग, वसंत कुंज, नई दिल्ली–110070
दूरभाष : 011–26131498
ई–मेल : chairman@aicte-india.org

ALL INDIA COUNCIL FOR TECHNICAL EDUCATION
(A STATUTORY BODY OF THE GOVT. OF INDIA)
(Ministry of Education, Govt. of India)
Nelson Mandela Marg, Vasant Kunj, New Delhi-110070
Phone : 011-26131498
E-mail : chairman@aicte-india.org

FOREWORD

Engineers are the backbone of any modern society. They are the ones responsible for the marvels as well as the improved quality of life across the world. Engineers have driven humanity towards greater heights in a more evolved and unprecedented manner.

The All India Council for Technical Education (AICTE), have spared no efforts towards the strengthening of the technical education in the country. AICTE is always committed towards promoting quality Technical Education to make India a modern developed nation emphasizing on the overall welfare of mankind.

An array of initiatives has been taken by AICTE in last decade which have been accelerated now by the National Education Policy (NEP) 2020. The implementation of NEP under the visionary leadership of Hon'ble Prime Minister of India envisages the provision for education in regional languages to all, thereby ensuring that every graduate becomes competent enough and is in a position to contribute towards the national growth and development through innovation & entrepreneurship.

One of the spheres where AICTE had been relentlessly working since past couple of years is providing high quality original technical contents at Under Graduate & Diploma level prepared and translated by eminent educators in various Indian languages to its aspirants. For students pursuing 2nd year of their Engineering education, AICTE has identified 87 books, which shall be translated into 12 Indian languages - Hindi, Tamil, Gujarati, Odia, Bengali, Kannada, Urdu, Punjabi, Telugu, Marathi, Assamese & Malayalam. In addition to the English medium, books in different Indian Languages are going to support the students to understand the concepts in their respective mother tongue.

On behalf of AICTE, I express sincere gratitude to all distinguished authors, reviewers and translators from the renowned institutions of high repute for their admirable contribution in a record span of time.

AICTE is confident that these outcomes based original contents shall help aspirants to master the subject with comprehension and greater ease.

T.G. Sitharam

(Prof. T. G. Sitharam)

ACKNOWLEDGEMENT

The author is grateful to the authorities of AICTE, particularly Prof. T.G Sitharam, Chairman; Prof. Rajive Kumar, Member-Secretary and Dr Amit Kumar Srivastava, Director, Faculty Development Cell for their planning to publish the book on *Thermal Engineering - I*. I sincerely acknowledge the valuable contributions of the reviewer of the book, Dr. Akhilendra Pratap Singh, Asst. Professor (Grade-I), Department of Mechanical Engineering, IIT (BHU), Varanasi-221005, Uttar Pradesh, India, for friendly comments and useful edits.

I am highly grateful to Dr. Alagani Harish, Scientist, Tribology and Combustion Division, CSIR-Indian Institute of Petroleum, Dehradun, P.O. Mohkampur - 248005, Uttarakhand, India, for carefully reading through the book, helping me in creating the illustrations, table of contents and index.

This book is an outcome of various suggestions of AICTE members, experts and authors who shared their opinion and thought to further develop the engineering education in our country. Acknowledgements are due to the contributors and different workers in this field whose published books, review articles, papers, photographs, footnotes, references and other valuable information enriched us at the time of writing the book.

Dr. V. Raghavan

PREFACE

Writing of this book titled "*Thermal Engineering -I*" has been possible due to the experience I gained during the teaching of basic thermal engineering courses in the Department of Mechanical Engineering at IIT Madras. This book is written to make the basics of thermal engineering clear to the diploma students. The main course objectives are:

- To provide a good understanding of and thorough insight into all important aspects of thermal systems, energy control and the general issue of energy.
- To understand the principles & working of various power producing & power absorbing devices.
- To study, analyse and evaluate the operation and the performance of I.C. engines, compressors and refrigerators, to apply pinch technology and to critically analyse and describe the global behaviour of integrated thermal systems.

This book introduces various energy sources; fossil and renewable fuels, their properties, followed by other non-conventional sources such as nuclear and fuel cells. The second chapter discusses the types of heat engines; diesel engine, petrol engine, their working principle, components and standard thermodynamic cycles. Chapter 3 provides insights of various systems in IC engines such as fuel injection system, ignition system, lubricating system and also briefly covers governing of IC engines. Where required examples and solved problems are included. The fourth chapter provides basic insights of the important parameters to evaluate the performance of I. C. Engines. These include wide range of measurable quantities such as brake power, indicated power, friction power and corresponding efficiencies. The final chapter presents useful discussions on the fundamentals of air compressors and their types, vapor compression refrigeration system, types of refrigerant, types of air conditioning, and seasonal air conditioning. This book also presents the method to conduct experiments for measuring important properties used in the analysis. Further, at the end of each chapter, multiple choice questions, short and long answer questions and exercise problems, as required, are provided for making the students to deepen their understanding. A student can further improve the understanding by referring to books and other online lectures of relevant courses, which are provided at the end of each chapter.

I sincerely hope that this book will inspire the diploma students to learn and discuss the ideas behind basic principles of Thermal Engineering. I would be grateful for all comments and suggestions contributing to the improvement of this book in the future editions.

Dr. V. Raghavan

OUTCOME BASED EDUCATION

For the implementation of an outcome based education the first requirement is to develop an outcome based curriculum and incorporate an outcome based assessment in the education system. By going through outcome based assessments, evaluators will be able to evaluate whether the students have achieved the outlined standard, specific and measurable outcomes. With the proper incorporation of outcome based education there will be a definite commitment to achieve a minimum standard for all learners without giving up at any level. At the end of the programme running with the aid of outcome based education, a student will be able to arrive at the following outcomes:

Programme Outcomes (POs) are statements that describe what students are expected to know and be able to do upon graduating from the program. These relate to the skills, knowledge, analytical ability, attitude and behaviour that students acquire through the program. The POs essentially indicate what the students can do from subject-wise knowledge acquired by them during the program. As such, POs define the professional profile of an engineering diploma graduate.

National Board of Accreditation (NBA) has defined the following seven POs for an Engineering diploma graduate:

PO-1. Basic and Discipline specific knowledge: Apply knowledge of basic mathematics, science and engineering fundamentals and engineering specialization to solve the engineering problems.

PO-2. Problem analysis: Identify and analyses well-defined engineering problems using codified standard methods.

PO-3. Design/development of solutions: Design solutions for well-defined technical problems and assist with the design of systems components or processes to meet specified needs.

PO-4. Engineering Tools, Experimentation and Testing: Apply modern engineering tools and appropriate technique to conduct standard tests and measurements.

PO-5. Engineering practices for society, sustainability and environment: Apply appropriate technology in context of society, sustainability, environment and ethical practices.

PO-6. Project Management: Use engineering management principles individually, as a team member or a leader to manage projects and effectively communicate about well-defined engineering activities.

PO-7. Life-long learning: Ability to analyse individual needs and engage in updating in the context of technological changes.

COURSE OUTCOMES

By the end of the course the students are expected to learn:

CO-1: Know various sources of Energy and their applications.

CO-2: Classify I.C. engines and understand their working and constructional features.

CO-3: Draw the energy flow diagram of an I.C. engine and evaluate its performance.

CO-4: Describe the constructional features of air compressor and working of different air compressors.

CO-5: Know the applications of refrigeration and Classify air-conditioning systems.

Mapping of Course Outcomes with Programme Outcomes to be done according to the matrix given below:

Course Outcomes	EXPECTED MAPPING WITH PROGRAMME OUTCOMES (1- Weak Correlation; 2- Medium Correlation; 3- Strong Correlation)						
	PO-1	PO-2	PO-3	PO-4	PO-5	PO-6	PO-7
CO-1	3	3	3	3	1	1	3
CO-2	3	2	2	2	1	1	3
CO-3	3	2	2	2	1	1	3
CO-4	3	2	2	3	1	1	3
CO-5	3	3	3	3	1	1	3

GUIDELINES FOR TEACHERS

To implement Outcome Based Education (OBE) knowledge level and skill set of the students should be enhanced. Teachers should take a major responsibility for the proper implementation of OBE. Some of the responsibilities (not limited to) for the teachers in OBE system may be as follows:

- Within reasonable constraint, they should manoeuvre time to the best advantage of all students.
- They should assess the students only upon certain defined criterion without considering any other potential ineligibility to discriminate them.
- They should try to grow the learning abilities of the students to a certain level before they leave the institute.
- They should try to ensure that all the students are equipped with the quality knowledge as well as competence after they finish their education.
- They should always encourage the students to develop their ultimate performance capabilities.
- They should facilitate and encourage group work and team work to consolidate newer approach.
- They should follow Blooms taxonomy in every part of the assessment.

Bloom's Taxonomy

Level	Teacher should Check	Student should be able to	Possible Mode of Assessment
Creating	Students ability to create	Design or Create	Mini project
Evaluating	Students ability to Justify	Argue or Defend	Assignment
Analysing	Students ability to distinguish	Differentiate or Distinguish	Project/Lab Methodology
Applying	Students ability to use information	Operate or Demonstrate	Technical Presentation/ Demonstration
Understanding	Students ability to explain the ideas	Explain or Classify	Presentation/Seminar
Remembering	Students ability to recall (or remember)	Define or Recall	Quiz

GUIDELINES FOR STUDENTS

Students should take equal responsibility for implementing the OBE. Some of the responsibilities (not limited to) for the students in OBE system are as follows:

- Students should be well aware of each UO before the start of a unit in each and every course.
- Students should be well aware of each CO before the start of the course.
- Students should be well aware of each PO before the start of the programme.
- Students should think critically and reasonably with proper reflection and action.
- Learning of the students should be connected and integrated with practical and real life consequences.
- Students should be well aware of their competency at every level of OBE.

ABBREVIATIONS AND SYMBOLS

Abbreviations

Abbreviation	Full form	Abbreviation	Full form
LPG	Liquified Petroleum Gas	NG	Natural Gas
CNG	Compressed Natural Gas	PV	Photovoltaic
USA	United States of America	U.S.	United States
KOH	Potassium Hydroxide	NAOH	Sodium Hydroxide
CV	Calorific Value	AHU	Air Handling Unit
IC	Internal Combustion	EC	External Combustion
TDC	Top Dead Centre	BDC	Bottom Dead Centre
MEP	Mean Effective Pressure	SI	Spark Ignition
CI	Compression Ignition	IV	Inlet Valve
EV	Exhaust Valve	SP	Spark Plug
FI	Fuel Injector	EVO	Exhaust Valve Opens
IPO	Inlet Port Open	IVC	Inlet Port Closes
HP	High Pressure	LP	Low Pressure
AC	Alternating Current	GP	Gross Power
BP	Brake Power	PP	Pumping Power
IP	Indicated Power	IMEP	Indicated Mean Effective Pressure
FP	Friction Power	SFC	Specific Fuel Consumption
BMEP	Break Mean Effective Pressure	BSFC	Brake Specific Fuel Consumption
ISFC	Indicated Specific Fuel Consumption	CO_2	Carbon Dioxide
CO	Carbon Monoxide	NO_2	Nitrogen Dioxide
NO	Nitrogen Oxide	NO_x	Nitrogen Oxides
N_2O	Nitrous Oxide	CR	Clearance Ratio
AF	Air-Fuel Ratio	COP	Coefficient of Performance
CF	Clearance Factor	FC	Fluorocarbon
HC	Hydrocarbon	HCFC	Hydrochlorofluorocarbons
HFC	Hydrofluorocarbon	HVAC	Heating Ventilation and Air-Conditioning
CFC	Chlorofluorocarbons		

List of Symbols

Symbols	Description	Symbols	Description
ν	Kinematic viscosity	t	Time
ρ	Density	μ	Dynamic viscosity
m	Mass	U	Internal energy
T	Temperature	c	Heat capacity
H	Enthalpy	V	Volume
p	Pressure	n	Number of moles
R_u	Universal gas constant	$\dot{m}_{fuel}$	Mass flow rate of fuel
$\dot{m}_w$	Mass flow rate of water	h_{wo}	Specific enthalpy of water at outlet
$\dot{m}_c$	Mass flow rate of the condensate	h_{fv}	Latent heat of vaporization
h_{wi}	Specific enthalpy of water at inlet	T_{wo}	Outlet temperature
T_{wi}	Inlet temperature	c_w	Specific heat of water
q_H	Heat gained by water	w_T	Turbine work produced
q_C	Heat loss in the condenser	w_P	Pump work
V_C	Clearance volume	V_{max}	Maximum volume
W_{cycle}	Work done in a cycle	V_{BDC}	Volume of air at BDC
V_{TDC}	Volume of air at TDC	T_H	Maximum temperature of the cycle
T_C	Minimum temperature of the cycle	S	Entropy
R	Specific gas constant	u	Specific internal energy
c_v	Specific heat at constant volume	c_p	Specific heat at constant pressure
γ	Ratio of specific heats	s	Specific entropy
v	Specific volume	T_2	Temperature at state 2
T_1	Temperature at state 1	V_1	Specific volume at state 1
V_2	Specific volume at state 2	p_2	Pressure at state 2
p_1	Pressure at state 1	$Q_{1\text{-}2}$	Heat interaction in process 1-2
$W_{1\text{-}2}$	Work interaction in process 1-2	U_1	Internal energy at state 1
U_2	Internal energy at state 2	$Q_{2\text{-}3}$	Heat interaction in process 2-3
$W_{2\text{-}3}$	Work interaction in process 2-3	T_3	Temperature at state 3
V_3	Volume at state 3	$Q_{3\text{-}4}$	Heat interaction in process 3-4
$W_{3\text{-}4}$	Work interaction in process 3-4	p_3	Pressure at state 3
p_4	Pressure at state 4	V_4	Volume at state 4
U_3	Internal energy at state 3	U_4	Internal energy at state 4
T_4	Temperature at state 4	$Q_{4\text{-}1}$	Heat interaction in process 4-1
$W_{4\text{-}1}$	Work interaction in process 4-1	W_{net}	Net work done in the cycle
S_2	Entropy at state 2	S_3	Entropy at state 3
S_4	Entropy at state 4	V_1	Volume occupied at state 1
V_2	Volume occupied at state 2	r	Compression ratio

Symbols	Description	Symbols	Description
r_c	Cut-off ratio	η_{th}	Thermal Efficiency
D	Bore diameter	L	Stroke length
z	Distance between the liquid level in the main jet and the nozzle exit	$\dot{m}_a$	Theoretical mass flow rate of air
A_1	Area at section 1	A_2	Area at section 2
C_p	Specific heat at constant pressure	C_d	Coefficient of discharge
ρ_f	Density of fuel	p_3	Vent pressure
p_1	Atmospheric pressure	V_{f2}	Velocity of fuel at nozzle exit
g	Acceleration due to gravity	$\dot{m}_f$	Mass flow rate of fuel
A_j	Jet exit area	C_{dj}	Coefficient of discharge
W	Total weight of masses	T	Torque
N	Revolutions per minute	r	Distance of the load from the centre of the drum or the length of the load bar
S	Reading weight	d_f	Diameter of flywheel
d_r	Diameter of rope	D	Effective diameter
R_1, R_2, R_3, R_4	Strain gauges	k_i	Spring constant
h_i	Height of indicator diagram	A_{ni}	Net area of indicator diagram
L_d	Length of the indicator diagram	θ	Crank angle
x	Piston displacement	R	Crank radius
l	Length of connecting rod	V	Corresponding volume
y	y coordinate	IP_1	Indicated power of 1st cylinder
BP_i	Break power of ith cylinder	IP_i	Indicated power of ith cylinder
I	Moment of inertia	α	Angular acceleration
ω_1, ω_2	Angular speed	t_1	Time at no load condition
T_f	Frictional torque	t_2	Time at load conditions
T_L	Torque due to load	W_{cycle}	Net work of the cycle
W	Net power output	ip	Indicated net work per cycle
V_{BDC}	Volume at BDC	V_{TDC}	Volume at TDC
n	Number of power strokes	K	Total number of cylinders
L	Length of stroke	A	Piston cross-sectional area
η_{ith}	Indicated thermal efficiency	$\dot{m}_f$	Mass flow rate of fuel
η_{bth}	Brake thermal efficiency	η_m	Mechanical efficiency

Symbols	Description	Symbols	Description
η_{rel}	Relative efficiency or efficiency ratio	$\dot{Q}_s$	Rate of heat supplied to the engine
CV	Calorific value of fuel	$\dot{Q}_w$	Rate of heat carried by cooling water
$\dot{m}_w$	Mass flow rate of cooling water	C_w	Specific heat of cooling water
T_{wo}	Temperature of cooling water at outlet	T_{wi}	Temperature of cooling water at inlet
T_{gi}	Inlet temperature of the exhaust gas mixture	T_{go}	Outlet temperature of the exhaust gas mixture
$\dot{m}_1$	Mass flow rate of air entering the control volume	$\dot{m}_2$	Mass flow rate of air exiting the control volume
p_1	Pressure of air at point 1	p_2	Pressure of air at point 2
v_1	Specific volume of air entering the control volume	v_2	Specific volume of air exiting the control volume
h_1	Specific enthalpy of air entering the control volume or point 1	h_2	Specific enthalpy of air exiting the control volume or at point 2
m_{cv}	Mass of air in the control volume	$\dot{Q}$	Rate of heat interaction
$\dot{W}_c$	Rate of work interaction	$\dot{m}$	Mass flow rate of air
p	Pressure of gas	v	Specific volume of gas
T	Temperature	R	Specific gas constant
γ	Ratio of specific heat	c_p	Specific heat at constant pressure
c_v	Specific heat at constant volume	T_1	Temperature of entering air (point 1)
T_2	Temperature of air leaving the control volume at point 2	w_c	Specific compression work or refrigerator pump work
p_c	Pressure at the end of first stage compression	p_d	Pressure at the exit of intercooler
p_3	Pressure after air discharge (point 3)	p_4	Pressure at the end of expansion stroke or at point 4
V_3	Clearance Volume	V_1, V_2, V_3, V_4	Volume of the air at the respective states
η_{vol}	Volumetric efficiency	W_{cycle}	Work for the cycle
m_c	Mass of air in clearance volume	m_i	Mass of air inducted
m_g	Mass of air inducted & delivered	m_1, m_4	Mass of air at point 1 and 4
T_{2s}	Isentropic temperature at point 2	η_{isen}	Isentropic efficiency
N	Compressor speed	T_C	Cooling space temperature
Q_C	Heat interaction from cold space	W	Work per cycle to the refrigerator

Symbols	Description	Symbols	Description
Q_H	Heat rejected	T_H	Temperature of hot reservoir
p_L	Low Pressure	p_H	High Pressure
w_e	Work in the expansion stroke	h_3	Specific enthalpy at point 3
h_4	Specific enthalpy at point 4	T_3	Temperature at point 3
T_4	Temperature at point 4	$\eta_{isen,c}$	Isentropic efficiency during compression
$\eta_{isen,e}$	Isentropic efficiency	h_{1s}	Isentropic specific enthalpy at point 1
h_{3s}	Isentropic specific enthalpy at point 3	q_C	Specific heat received by the evaporator
s_1, s_2, s_3, s_4	Specific entropy at points different state points 1, 2, 3, 4 respectively	s_{1s}	Specific entropy at the end of isentropic process at state 1
s_{3s}	Specific entropy at the end isentropic process at state 3	T_{sat}	Saturation temperature at a given pressure
h_f	Specific enthalpy of the saturated fluid	h_g	Specific enthalpy of the saturated vapor
p_a	Partial pressure of dry air	p_v	Partial pressure of dry vapor
p_{sat}	Saturation pressure at a given temperature	φ	Relative humidity
ω	Specific humidity	W_{cycle}	Work for the cycle
η_{vol}	Volumetric efficiency of the compressor	m_i	Mass of air inducted into the compressor
m_c	Mass of air in the clearance volume	m_1, m_4	Mass of air at point 1 and 4
m_g	Mass of air inducted and delivered	η_{isen}	Isentropic efficiency
T_{2s}	Isentropic temperature at point 2	T_C	Cooling space temperature
N	Compressor speed	c_{pg}	Specific heat of exhaust gas mixture at constant pressure

LIST OF FIGURES

LIST OF TABLES

CONTENTS

1 Sources of Energy

UNIT SPECIFICS

Through this unit, the following aspects are discussed:

- Classification of energy sources;
- Non-renewable energy sources;
- Fossil fuels: CNG, LPG, Gasoline, and Diesel;
- Renewable energy sources;
- Solar energy and its applications;
- Wind, tidal, ocean thermal and geothermal energies;
- Biomass, Biogas, Bio-diesel;
- Nuclear energy;
- Fuel cell.

This unit introduces various energy resources, their classifications and characteristics. Naturally available, but non-renewable fossil energy sources, such as Liquified Petroleum Gas (LPG), Natural Gas (NG) and derivatives of crude oil such as gasoline and diesel, are described with their properties in detail. Methods to evaluate the properties are also discussed.

Features of nuclear energy, and its advantages and disadvantages, are systematically explained. Solar energy is a much more useful naturally available renewable energy source. This has been described. Its applications in the fields such as water heating, power production using a photovoltaic cell and solar distillation process are briefly explained. Other naturally available energy resources such as wind, tidal, ocean thermal and geothermal energy are discussed with pros and cons.

Man-made or processed energy sources are alternative renewable energy sources, such as biogas and bio-diesel, which are subsequently explained along with their properties. A brief description of the working concept of a fuel cell is also included in this init. Finally, a comprehensive summary of the topics discussed in this unit is provided. Multiple choice questions, and short and long answer subjective questions are also provided towards the end of this unit to make the students test themselves and understand the concepts in a better manner.

RATIONALE

This first unit of this book helps students to get an overall idea about energy resources. Each energy resource has its defined properties and applications. A student going through this unit will be able to select an energy source based on its properties and application. Important properties of a few fossil energy sources are discussed to enable a student to understand them and also know the method to measure those properties. Renewable energy sources are explained along with its applications to make the student conceptualize a device using that energy source. This unit also enables the student to derive alternative fuels from biomass, plant and animal wastes. The usefulness of waste to energy will be understood by going through this unit. Students will also be able to understand the working principle of a fuel cell by going through this unit.

PRE-REQUISITES

Basic Mechanical Engineering (MEPC102)

UNIT OUTCOMES

List of outcomes of this unit is as follows:

U1-O1: Know various sources of Energy and their applications.

U1-O2: Differentiate between renewable and non-renewable energy sources

U1-O3: Understand the advantages and disadvantages of energy sources

U1-O4: Know the applications of solar energy

U1-O5: Know the method of production of alternative renewable fuel sources

Unit-1 Outcomes	EXPECTED MAPPING WITH COURSE OUTCOMES (1- Weak Correlation; 2- Medium Correlation; 3- Strong Correlation)				
	CO-1	CO-2	CO-3	CO-4	CO-5
U1-O1	3	2	-	-	-
U1-O2	3	-	-	-	-
U1-O3	3	-	-	-	-
U1-O4	3	-	-	-	-
U1-O5	3	2	-	-	-

1.1 ENERGY AND ITS RESOURCES

Energy is defined as the capacity to do work. It may be available in a thermodynamic system (fixed mass) or in a control volume (fixed volume), using which work may be done. The energy is of various forms; kinetic and potential energy (mechanical form), internal energy (molecular level), chemical energy (as stored in fuel or battery), electrical energy, nuclear energy (atomic level), and so on. Internal energy, a microscopic form of energy, is normally evaluated using basic properties such as temperature and pressure. This is used in the conservation of energy, defined by the first law of thermodynamics.

There are different ways of harnessing each of these forms of energy. For example, the potential energy of stored water can be used to produce electricity by using it to run a Pelton wheel turbine. Chemical energy in a fuel can be brought out by burning it with an oxidizer such as air in a furnace. During this process, which is called combustion, heat is released that can be used to produce steam and run a steam turbine or produce hot gas, which can be used to run a gas turbine. A steam or gas turbine is connected to a generator (electro-magnetic device) to generate electricity. Chemical energy is also available in a battery or fuel cell, which can be used as electrical energy directly. Nuclear energy produces electrical power through nuclear fission reaction.

Therefore, it is clear that various sources of energy are available to primarily produce electricity, to meet various energy needs of a country. A country is also ranked based on its energy resources. The standard of living of the citizens in a country depends upon its energy usage. However, there are several factors to be taken into account, when utilizing energy resources. They are the environmental aspects and continuous availability of energy resources (sustainability). For example, utilizing sources having chemical energy, such as fuels (hydrocarbons), leads to the production of greenhouse gases, such as carbon dioxide, and emissions such as nitric oxides, which are harmful to the environment. Based on the energy consumption, there may be notable depletion of the energy source; usage being more than the production. Especially, naturally occurring fuels may deplete at a faster rate based on their utilization, as observed in the case of petroleum (crude oil). These energy sources are therefore called non-renewable. Even, nuclear energy is primarily non-renewable. Therefore, considering the environmental and sustainability factors, renewable (made available anytime or in a cyclic manner) and alternative (newer) sources of energy are required. Scientists and engineers are working toward these energy sources and significant improvements are happening, especially in the fields of solar energy and wind energy as a result. The classification of energy resources and discussion on various aspects of these are presented in the following sections.

1.2 CLASSIFICATION OF ENERGY SOURCES

Energy sources are classified in different ways. Customarily, they are classified as non-renewable or renewable, based on whether they deplete on usage or they are available for usage within a time period or in a cyclic manner. Further, energy sources are classified as conventional or non-conventional. Energy sources such as fossil fuels (coal, crude oil, natural gas and so on), nuclear energy, and hydro energy, are being used for several decades. These are called conventional energy sources. Renewable counterparts such as solar, wind, and tidal energy, have been used in the past in a large scale, especially when conventional energy sources had scarcity. Therefore, these sources are often called non-conventional energy sources. Fig. 1.1 presents the chart listing the different types of energy resources.

Conventional or non-renewable energy sources are formed under the earth over millions of years. The plant and animal residues, buried under the earth over millions of years undergo several chemical processes under high pressure and high temperature under the earth and form fuels of different kinds. Liquid, solid and gaseous fuels are obtained from underground. However, these fuels are not available in all places and are available only in certain regions. The word "petroleum" means rock oil or oil under the earth. This is the primary liquid fossil fuel, available in different regions of the world, and is called crude oil. The crude oil cannot be used in its original form and it has to be processed to derive various types of fuels such as heavy diesel oil, kerosene, light diesel oil, and gasoline (petrol). A solid residue, called paraffin, is also obtained during the distillation process. Similarly, coal is a solid fossil fuel obtained under the earth. It is a heterogeneous solid that has moisture (water vapor) and volatiles (gaseous fuel) trapped in it apart from fixed carbon and ash (mineral) contents. These contents vary based on the location of the earth from where coal is obtained. Coal is ranked based on its carbon content. Anthracite is the name given to coal having carbon in the range of 92% to 98%. This depends upon the number of years the plant and animal residues have been processed under the earth. As the carbon content decreases, semi anthracite (90% to 95% carbon), bituminous (80% to 90% carbon), semi-bituminous (70% to 80% carbon) and lignite (60% to 72% carbon) are got. Natural gas, which primarily has 90% to 95% methane, is the gaseous fossil fuel got under the earth. Wood is the unprocessed biomass fuel directly got from trees. This is also a fossil fuel (natural resource); however, once used, it can be replaced within a few years, as compared to millions of years required to get coal, and therefore it is considered renewable. Nuclear energy is obtained when a uranium atom is split into two smaller nuclei and energy is released during that process. This energy is used to produce steam, run a steam turbine and produce power.

Non-conventional or renewable energy resources include biomass, solar energy, wind energy, hydro energy, tidal energy, geothermal energy, ocean thermal energy and so on. Biomass is an organic matter that contains chemical energy. It is considered renewable and is an alternative form of energy. It has also four components listed for coal, namely, moisture, volatiles, fixed carbon and ash. In general, biomass has a high percentage of volatiles than fixed carbon. Examples of biomass are wood, wheat straw, wheat husk, rice straw, rice husk, sugarcane bagasse and so on. These can be directly burned to produce heat or can be subjected to chemical processes to derive liquid and gaseous fuels. For example, from sugarcane bagasse, ethanol, an alcohol fuel, can be produced. Similarly, vegetable seed can be processed to get vegetable oil and it can be further processed to get bio-diesel. Gasification of biomass and coal yields synthetic gas, which is primarily composed of carbon monoxide, carbon dioxide, hydrogen, methane and nitrogen. Energy radiated from the Sun is called solar energy. This energy is used for heating purposes as well as to produce power. Similarly, energy from the kinetic energy of the wind can be used to rotate the rotors in windmills, which in turn is used to produce electricity. Hydroelectric energy is obtained when the potential energy of stored water is used to make water fall on a Pelton wheel turbine in a controlled manner and rotate it to produce electricity. Harnessing heat under the earth is called geothermal energy. Under the earth, there are several hot spots, which can be utilized for heating purposes. For example, geysers are formed naturally when water seeps into the earth and contacts these hot spots. Ocean thermal energy can be harnessed using the temperature difference between the surface of the seawater, which is hotter, and the colder deep seawater. Tidal energy is the one that can be trapped from the sea using tides produced due to gravitational force between the earth and the moon.

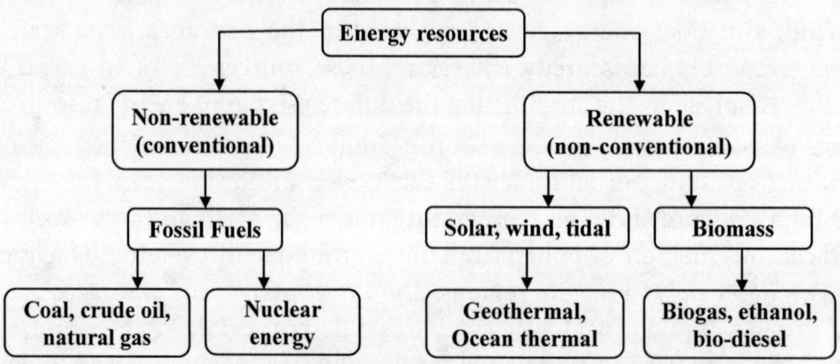

Fig. 1.1: Classification of energy sources

1.2.1 Properties of a Few Fossil Fuels

In this section, important properties of selected fossil fuels are discussed. The main property of a fuel is its *calorific value*, which is also called the *heating value*. It is the amount of energy that is released when one kg of the fuel is completely burnt and the products are cooled to standard reference temperature (298 K). Calorific value of a solid or liquid fuel is determined by using an instrument called *Bomb Calorimeter*. Calorific value of a gaseous fuel is measured using a *Gas Calorimeter*. Viscosity of a liquid fuel is measured using a *viscometer*. Other than that, a few more properties such as *molecular weight*, *density* and so on are usually considered when a burner is designed.

Natural gas is a colourless and odourless gas, consisting primarily of methane (CH_4) by around 95% on a volume basis. Traces of higher order hydrocarbons (C_2H_2, C_2H_4, etc.), carbon dioxide, water vapor and nitrogen are also usually present in natural gas. Some amount of sulfur may also be present. It is available underground over crude oil deposits. It is extracted, compressed and stored in huge storage tanks. When the natural gas is compressed to pressure in the range of 200 bar and 250 bar, a good energy density is obtained. This is called *Compressed Natural Gas (CNG)*. It is lighter than air, having a molecular mass of around 16 kg/kmol, and it has a calorific value between 50000 kJ/kg to 55000 kJ/kg.

Liquid Petroleum Gas (LPG) is a mixture of various hydrocarbons, with butane and propane as its primary constituents. This evolves during the refining of petroleum. When the gas mixture is pressurized to over six times the atmospheric pressure, it liquefies. The liquid is stored in steel cylinders and distributed to homes and industries. Once released through a pressure regulator into the atmosphere, the liquid instantly vaporizes into its gaseous components. LPG has a molecular mass of over 50 kg/kmol and is heavier than air. Commercial LPG has a synthetic odorant added for easy leak detection. It has a calorific value between 45000 kJ/kg to 50000 kJ/kg.

Crude oil or *petroleum* consists of a large number of hydrocarbon compounds, namely, paraffins, isoparaffins, olefins, naphthene and aromatics. Crude oil as a whole has by weight 80% to 85% C, 10% to 15% H and traces of S, O and N for the remaining proportion. When crude oil is subjected to a fractional distillation process, several components are obtained as products. Gasoline (petrol), kerosene and diesel are the primary components used in automotive and aerospace industries. Components heavier than diesel cannot be used in these applications unless processed further. These fuels are multi-component (have more than one liquid component) and as a result, their density, boiling and freezing points vary across a range. Gasoline has a density in the range of 710 – 730 kg/m^3 and its boiling point is in the range of 30°C to 80°C. On the other hand, diesel has a density in the range of 880 – 900 kg/m^3 and its boiling point is in the range of 220°C to 280°C. Properties of kerosene will be intermediate to those of gasoline and diesel. Other than *density* and *boiling point*, a few more properties are important for liquid fuels. These are discussed subsequently.

Flash point of a liquid fuel is the minimum temperature of the liquid at which sufficient vapors are produced. The vapor mixes with atmospheric air and produces a flash or an instantaneous flame when a pilot flame (for example, a flame from a matchstick) is introduced over the liquid surface. When the pilot flame is removed, the flame disappears.

Fire point is a temperature higher than the flash point, at which sufficient vapors are generated. When a pilot ignition source is introduced, a flame is established over the liquid surface and this flame sustains even after the removal of the pilot flame.

Boiling point is a temperature higher than the fire point and it is the saturation temperature (at which phase change occurs at constant temperature) of the liquid at a given pressure. Normal boiling point is the saturation temperature at atmospheric pressure. When the liquid reaches its boiling point, there will be no further increase in the temperature as a result of heat addition and all the heat that is added is used to provide the latent heat of vaporization.

Freeze point is the temperature at which the liquid freezes. This property is uniform in cold regions, where the fuel may freeze at low temperatures. Anti-freezing additives are usually added to prevent the freezing of liquid fuels.

The *latent heat of vaporization* is the energy that is required for converting the liquid to its vapor. A higher value of latent heat would indicate that a higher amount of heat is required for the phase change at a given pressure and that the liquid may be less volatile.

The liquid fuel is usually at a temperature less than the boiling point, to begin with. Heat is required to increase its temperature to the boiling point. The heat supplied for this process is termed *sensible heat*. This depends on the specific heat of the liquid. Then for the phase change, the latent heat has to be supplied. Therefore, the *volatility* of the liquid fuel is generally governed by the liquid-phase *specific heat*, boiling point and the latent heat of vaporization.

The *viscosity* of the liquid plays an important role in the *atomization* process, which leads to disintegration of liquid jet or liquid sheet into small droplets. Atomization helps in increasing the surface area so that the evaporation rate is increased.

1.2.2 Applications of Solar Energy

Solar energy, obtained as the radiation from the Sun can be utilized in several applications. Most of the solar radiation reaching the earth consists of wavelengths in the range of 315 nm to 1400 nm, 45% of this radiation is in the visible region (400 nm to 700 nm). The earth absorbs radiation mainly in the visible region and emits radiation in the infrared region. Solar energy is an almost limitless source of energy available with negligible pollution. For example, the average value of solar irradiation (incoming radiation) is approximately in the range of 5.5 to 7 kWh per square meter area per day in India. However, the limitations are: (1) At present, it is expensive to produce power at a large scale using solar energy, (2) it is possible to harness this only when the sun shines; the output varies with a change in irradiation and (3) it needs energy storage devices to store and supply the energy when the sun is not available, making it complex and expensive. Research works are still going on to improve the utilization of solar energy effectively. Solar energy is used in several applications. It is used to produce heat or electricity directly.

Solar heating: In cold regions, solar energy is used to heat buildings. Sunspaces, which act as heat absorbers, are used for this purpose. These are tiles or some form of bricks, which can absorb energy incident on that during the daytime and release the heat during the night. Solar energy can be used to heat water in a roof tank. The collector heats the water, which then flows to a well-insulated pipe into a well-insulated storage tank. The flow of water is due to natural circulation for small-scale applications. In larger-scale applications, pumps are used to circulate the water. A schematic of a typical solar water heater with natural circulation of water is shown in Fig. 1.2.

Similarly, solar energy can be used in cooking. The solar radiation is reflected into a metal vessel, which is coated in the black color inside, to absorb the heat effectively. The lid, when open, can reflect the sun ray into the box, where food to be cooked is kept. Further, solar energy is also used in the desalination of seawater. In one of the methods, solar energy is directly used to heat water, evaporate it and allow it to condense over an inclined surface to collect fresh water. Such devices are called solar stills. In the indirect method, first solar energy is used to produce power and that is used to desalinate using membranes.

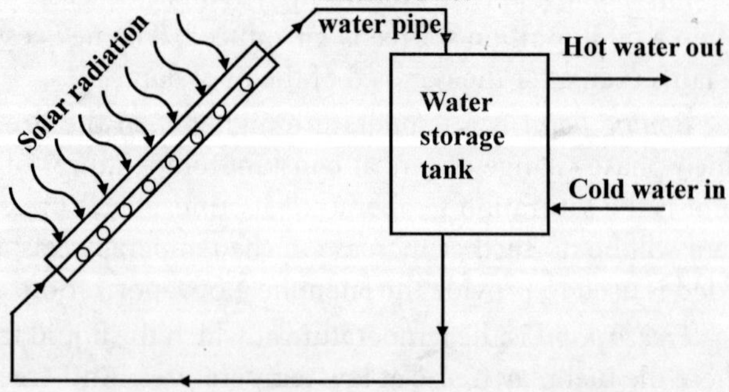

Fig. 1.2: Schematic of a solar water heater

Solar photovoltaic cell: Photon is the smallest unit of radiant energy, which is invisible. Its energy is equal to the frequency of radiation multiplied by Planck's constant. Photons can be viewed as particles, which carry solar radiation at a speed of 3×10^5 km/s. When photons of sufficient energy are incident on special semiconductor materials made of silicon, the photons are absorbed and electrons are generated. This is called the photoelectric effect. When an electron leaves an atom, a vacant space (positively charged, termed a hole) is created and the electrons randomly move toward another vacant space. Electrons can be made to flow in one direction, completing a loop, two types of silicon layers are used. One layer of silicon is doped with phosphorus that has one more electron than silicon. This is called n-type. The other layer is doped with boron that has one electron less than silicon. This is called p-type. A p-n junction is formed using these two layers formed as a sandwich. Above this sandwich layer, a glass plate with an anti-reflective coating is provided. Metal strips are also provided beneath the glass plate to provide electrical contact. At the bottom of the sandwich layer, another metal layer is provided to provide electrical contact. When photons are incident on an n-type layer, electrons are excited and they move to the n-side by an electric field. Similarly, the holes drift to the p-side. The electrons and holes are directed to the electrical contacts applied to both sides before flowing to the external circuit in the form of electrical energy. This produces a direct current. The efficiency of a solar PV is around 15% and the materials are costly. Research works are going on to reduce the price and improve efficiency. A schematic of a photovoltaic (PV) cell is shown in Fig. 1.3. Many PV cells are used to construct a PV module. In a PV system producing solar electricity, many PV modules are used.

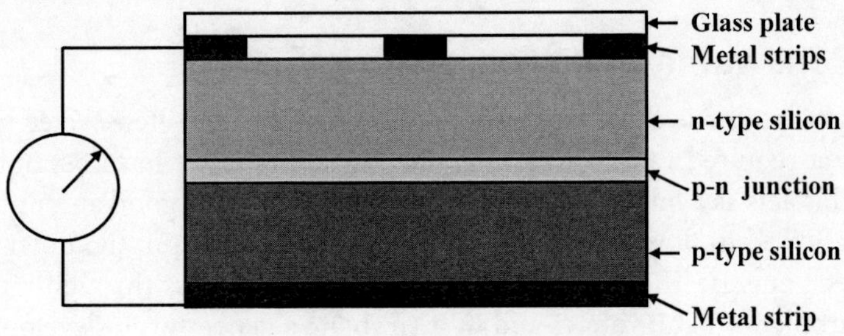

Fig. 1.3: Schematic of a photovoltaic cell

Solar power plant: Solar energy can be collected using a flat plate (non-focussing) collector and using concentrating collectors, depending upon the application. Flat plate collector, as schematically shown in Fig. 1.2, has an absorption plate coated in black in contact with tubes through which water or air flows. The base and lateral sides are well insulated. A non-reflective glass plate is placed above the plate. Any reflections on the black-coated plate surface eventually are absorbed after multiple reflections between glass and the plate. The plate absorbs the incident radiation to the maximum extent and transfers it to the tubes. Both plate and tubes are made of materials having high thermal conductivity. Concentrating collectors are classified as reflective and refractive types. Parabolic dish collector and parabolic trough collector are examples of reflective type concentrators. Refractive type collectors use Fresnel refractors or lenses.

A typical large-scale solar power plant can be constructed using parabolic trough collectors. An array of these collectors are used to exchange heat and produce steam. This array is called a solar field. The steam produced is used to run a steam turbine to produce electrical power. After exiting the turbine, the steam passes through a condenser. Liquid water coming out of the condenser (operating at low pressure), is pumped to high pressure. At that pressure, water is heated to steam and this cycle continues.

The block, consisting of boiler, turbine, condenser and pump, is the same as in a conventional steam power plant and is called the power block. Usually, a single tracking mechanism is used to track the parabolic collector by keeping it normal to the incident solar radiation as the Sun moves. A schematic of this power plant is shown in Fig. 1.4.

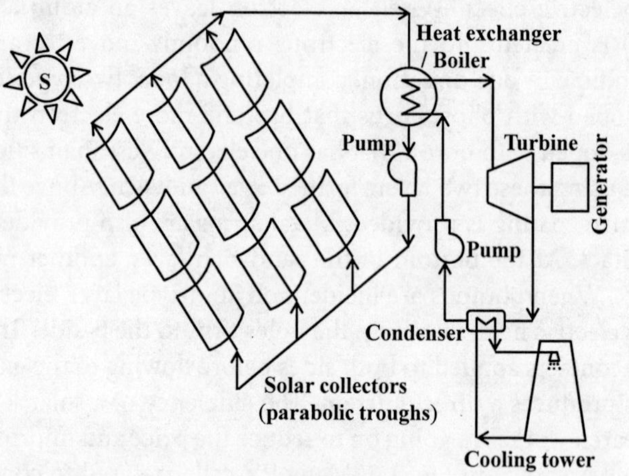

Fig. 1.4: Schematic of solar power plant with parabolic trough collectors

1.2.3 Other Renewable Energies

Hydro energy or hydropower is the energy obtained from flowing water. Water in rivers is stored in dams and is let out at required rates for various purposes. The water level behind a dam is generally several meters and this acts as a huge reservoir. This stored water has a good amount of potential energy. When the water is allowed to flow through a given opening in the dam, the potential energy of water is converted to kinetic energy. The flowing water can be made to pass through a rotating device such as a Pelton wheel turbine so that it rotates and in turn rotate a generator to develop electrical power. In some possible cases, the flowing water in a river can be diverted to another passage, where it is made to pass through a special turbine to generate power. Hydropower has advantages such as it is a very clean, renewable source, quick starting and so on. However, it has disadvantages such as it needs a large area to construct the dam, high initial and maintenance costs, problems with fisheries and so on. Further, in some areas, the construction of huge dams can create seismic problems.

Wind (airflow) is generated globally due to the rotation of the earth and differential solar heating of the earth and its atmosphere. It is also generated locally due to differential heating of ground and water surfaces. The kinetic energy of the wind is used to rotate a single blade or set of blades. This in turn rotates a generator, through a set of gears, and produces electricity. The wind speed should be in a given range (2 m/s to 15 m/s) for convenient operation of a windmill. A set of anemometers is used to estimate the speed and direction of the wind, and the blades are oriented in windward direction suitably, to enable optimized operation of the windmill. Thus, a feedback control loop is used. Based on a detailed survey, regions are identified to set up windmills. The wind movement may be seasonal and therefore, the windmill may not operate throughout the year. Wind turbines are classified mainly with respect to their axis of rotation - as wind axis (horizontal axis) and crosswind (vertical axis) turbines. There are several configurations in each of these. The orientation of blades (called steering) is done by active (feedback-based) or passive (using tail) methods. Windmills are available in capacities in the ranges of 0.5 kW to 15 kW (small), 15 kW to 150 kW (medium) and 250 kW to 1000 kW (large). There are installations of more than 1 MW in some countries including the USA. Even though wind energy is relatively inexpensive to generate and it produces no pollutants, windmills may be set up only in certain areas, where sufficient wind speed is available and the power generation may also be seasonal.

Geothermal energy is obtained from the underground, sub-surface of the earth. Geothermal energy is a renewable energy source as heat is continuously produced inside the earth. This can be used for heating purposes as well as for power generation. It is available in a few countries such as New Zealand, the Philippines, Kenya and so on, where a good contribution to power production by geothermal energy is obtained. However, on the disadvantages side, the cost is much high, it can contaminate the water, reservoirs should be properly maintained and so on. Further, it is not available in all places and is location-specific. Researchers mention that natural calamities such as an earthquake can result due to the harnessing of geothermal energy in some places.

Ocean thermal energy utilizes the natural temperature difference between the ocean surface and the deep ocean. The hot surface temperature is used to heat and vaporize a liquid and run a turbine. The heat is rejected to the cold temperature of the deep sea. For example, Hawaii in the USA has much warmer surface water and very cold water in the deep ocean. The U.S. National Science Foundation has funded an ocean thermal energy conversion facility in this area. This source is fuel free, has no significant pollution, produces pure water during the cycle, has low maintenance, is reliable and so on. However, it can be used only in a few locations. It has a high initial cost, moderate efficiency and can be harmful to marine life.

Tidal energy is obtained from tides, which are formed by gravitational forces between the moon and the earth. The ocean water level changes during the rise or fall of the tide and this is a form of kinetic energy. The resulting movement of water can be used to run a turbine and generate power. The turbine is designed such that it is rotated in one direction both during increasing or decreasing water levels. This is renewable energy with no pollution. It is also reliable. However, it has high construction and maintenance costs and has an environmental impact. Further, it is not available at all locations.

Biomass is a renewable energy source. It is also called a carbon-neutral energy source. It is an organic matter obtained from plants (wood, rice straw, wheat straw), plants derived materials (vegetable seeds, rice husk, wheat hush, sugarcane bagasse) and animal wastes such as cow dung. It primarily consists of hemicellulose, cellulose, and lignin. Biomass fuels can be directly burnt in furnaces to generate heat. Wood is currently used for heating and cooking purposes in several countries. In rural places in India, wood stoves are primarily used for cooking. There are several types of biomass fuels, which can be burnt directly to produce power. Presently, biomass is used as a fuel blend along with coal in several power plants. Biomass can also be used in several processes to produce various types of fuels. Biomass can be subjected to processes such as pyrolysis, anaerobic digestion and gasification, to convert biomass into gaseous fuels such as producer gas, synthetic gas and biogas. Synthetic gas is primarily a mixture of carbon monoxide, hydrogen, methane, carbon dioxide and nitrogen. Biogas mainly consists of methane (50% to 60%) and the rest of carbon dioxide. These gaseous fuels can be used in furnaces for heating purposes as well as for power generation. Vegetable seeds are used to produce vegetable oils. When the vegetable oil is processed in the transesterification process, its glycerine content is removed, and bio-diesel is got. Bio-diesel has features closer to fossil diesel. It can be used in diesel engines by blending some proportion of it with diesel. Sugarcane bagasse can be processed to get ethanol, a cleaner alcohol fuel. The advantages of bio-diesel and ethanol are that they are oxygenated fuels and their combustion performance is better. Also, several other chemical processes are available to convert biomass into useful chemicals. The main advantage of biomass is that it is renewable and closes the carbon cycle within a few years. However, it is available only in certain locations and the whole energy demand cannot be met by biomass as per the present scenario. Further, the variations in the properties of biomass are extensive and it is not easy to design a reactor for biomass for optimal operating conditions and performance. Research works are ongoing to address these issues.

1.3 NUCLEAR ENERGY

Nuclear energy is got from the nucleus of an atom. When the nucleus of relatively unstable heavy atoms such as uranium 235 ($_{92}U^{235}$), for example, is split into two smaller nuclei using neutrons, heat is released. The reaction is written as follows:

$$_{92}U^{235} + {}_0n^1 \rightarrow {}_{92}U^{236} \rightarrow {}_{56}Ba^{141} + {}_{36}Kr^{92} + 3\ {}_0n^1 + 177 \text{ MeV (energy)}$$

This reaction yields Barium, Krypton, three neutrons and 177 Mega electric volts of energy. When the neutrons produced react further with uranium atoms, more energy is produced. This reaction proceeds as a chain reaction and if not controlled would lead to excessive energy liberation and disaster, as in the case of an atom bomb. However, in nuclear reactors, the reaction is carried out in a controlled manner, by allowing only one neutron to react further and by absorbing other neutrons. Control rods, made of hafnium or boron, in a nuclear reactor serve the purpose of absorbing neutrons, thereby reducing the rate of the chain reaction. The products are radioactive. Disposal of these wastes has not been planned yet. They are kept underground. Uranium reserves are not very high. Thus, the usage of nuclear energy will also deplete. Thus, this cannot be considered as renewable energy. These are the few disadvantages of nuclear energy. However, one kg of uranium can produce energy generated by burning approximately 200 kg of oil or 4000 kg of coal. The energy from the nuclear fission reaction can be used to heat water, produce steam and run a steam turbine to produce power. A schematic of a nuclear reactor is shown in Fig. 1.5.

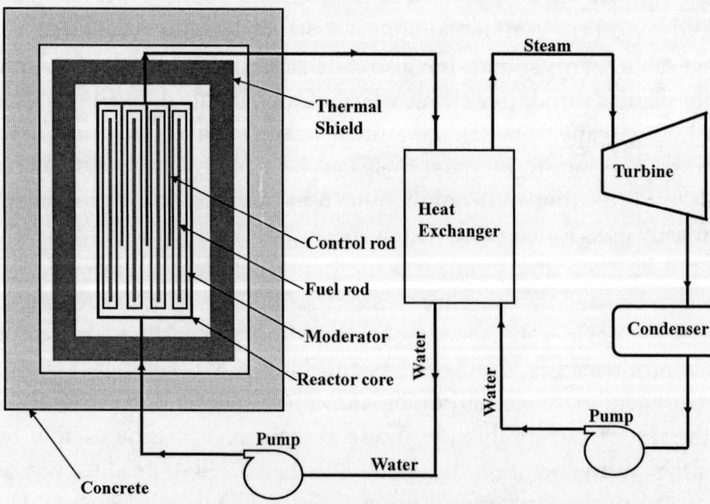

Fig. 1.5: Schematic of a nuclear power plant

The reactor core has fuel rods, a moderator surrounding it and control rods to control the chain reaction rate. The core is enclosed in a thermal shield. A concrete structure is used to barricade the nuclear reactor core along with a thermal shield. The heat from the nuclear reaction is transferred to water or sodium, which in turn heats water to produce steam in a heat exchanger. The steam runs a turbine and produces electricity.

On the other hand, nuclear fusion reaction, written as, ${}_1H^2 + {}_1H^3 \rightarrow {}_2He^4 + {}_0n^1 + 17.6$ MeV, can also be used to produce a significant amount of energy. This process will not produce radioactive products. However, the technology for this process has not yet been available.

1.4 FUEL CELLS

A fuel cell is a device used to produce electricity by converting the chemical energy of a fuel directly to electrical energy. Here, a fuel and oxidizer undergo a series of reactions. If hydrogen is used as fuel, products are only water and electrons (electricity), with some amount of heat release. If a hydrocarbon fuel is used, then carbon dioxide will also be present in the products. A fuel cell consists of two electrodes, which are an anode (negative electrode) and a cathode (positive electrode), kept in an electrolyte. There are layers of catalysts attached to both anode and cathode. A fuel, for example, hydrogen, is fed into the anode chamber. The oxidizer, air, is fed into the cathode chamber. Fuel gas is continuously fed and a part of it diffuses into the catalyst layer of the anode, and the rest of it is recycled back. The catalyst at the anode separates hydrogen molecules into protons (for example, H^+) and electrons (e^-). Electrons flow through an external circuit connecting anode and cathode, producing electricity. The protons flow through the electrolyte to the layer of catalyst at the cathode, where it reacts with electrons and oxygen to produce water vapor (and carbon dioxide, in the case of a hydrocarbon fuel) and heat. A schematic of a fuel cell is shown in Fig. 1.6.

There are various types of electrolytes used depending upon the type of fuel cell. Aqueous alkaline solution, acids and polymer membranes are used in several fuel cells. For example, in hydrogen–oxygen fuel cell, KOH (potassium hydroxide) or NaOH (sodium hydroxide) is used. This is typically an alkaline fuel cell. Here, the water vapor is produced on the anode side and left along with recycling hydrogen. The other types of fuel cells are acid fuel cells (example, phosphoric acid fuel cell), solid acid fuel cell (uses H+ conducting oxyanion salt, solid acid), solid oxide fuel cell (uses a special ceramic material as electrolyte), direct ethanol fuel cell (uses polymer membrane) and so on. Catalysts are made from materials such as platinum and platinum alloys, supported on carbon. Research is going on for finding cheaper materials to be used as catalysts.

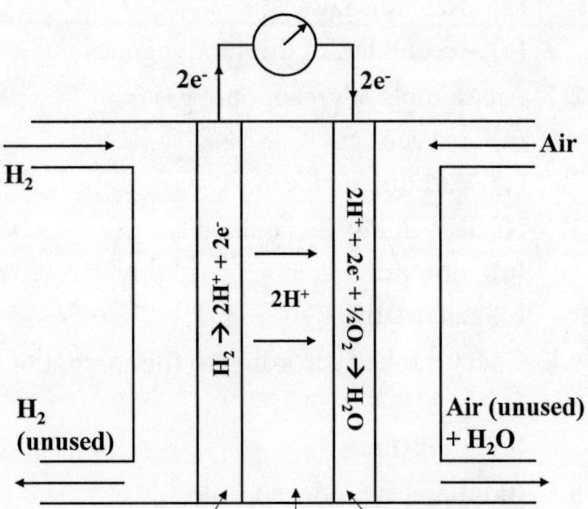

Fig. 1.6: Schematic of a fuel cell

The advantages of a fuel cell are that it directly produces electricity, has high energy density and lower pollution (especially when hydrogen is used as fuel). The disadvantages are its cost, efficiency and less durability.

UNIT SUMMARY

This unit starts with an introduction to energy and its various resources. Systematic classification of energy such as conventional (non-renewable) and non-conventional (renewable) has been made with an appropriate listing of corresponding energy resources in each classification. Properties of important gaseous and liquid fuels, used widely in several applications are discussed subsequently. A brief discussion on solar energy and its applications is included in a separate section. Aspects of solar electricity using photovoltaic cells, solar heating and solar thermal power plant have been reported. Important characteristics of other renewable and alternative energy resources such as hydropower, wind, geothermal, ocean thermal, tidal and biomass, are briefly discussed to bring out their usefulness, advantages, and disadvantages. Nuclear energy is then discussed in a separate section. Nuclear fission reaction, controlled chain reaction, nuclear power production, radioactive products, and limitations have been briefly presented. Finally, a brief presentation on fuel cells is included in the last section. The working principle of a fuel cell and various types of electrolytes and catalysts used are discussed.

EXERCISES

Multiple Choice Questions

1. Conservation of energy is defined by
   (a) Newton's laws (b) First law of thermodynamics
   (c) second law of thermodynamics (d) Third law of thermodynamics
2. An example of greenhouse gas is
   (a) oxygen (b) nitrogen
   (c) carbon dioxide (d) water vapor.
3. Nuclear energy is classified as
   (a) non-renewable (b) renewable
   (c) alternative (d) none of these
4. Coal is ranked according to the content of its
   (a) ash (b) volatiles
   (c) moisture (d) carbon
5. Bio-diesel is produced from
   (a) vegetable oil (b) bagasse
   (c) wood (d) rice straw
6. A bomb calorimeter is used to determine
   (a) viscosity (b) heating value
   (c) specific heat (d) thermal conductivity
7. The fire point of liquid fuel is
   (a) more than boiling point (b) lesser than flash point
   (c) lesser than boiling point (d) none of these

8. From vegetable oil, bio-diesel is produced by removing
   (a) glycerine (b) water
   (c) alcohol (d) none of these
9. Nuclear fission is
   (a) forming a single nucleus from two nuclei
   (b) splitting of a nucleus into two nuclei
   (c) forming two neutrons
   (d) none of these
10. Fuel cell supplies fuel gas into
   (a) cathode (b) electrolyte
   (c) catalyst (d) anode

Answers to Multiple Choice Questions									
1. (b)	2. (c)	3. (a)	4. (d)	5. (a)	6. (b)	7. (c)	8. (a)	9. (b)	10. (d)

Short and Long Answer Type Questions

1. What is a fossil fuel?
2. What is meant by an alternative source of energy?
3. List the four main constituents of coal.
4. Give the names of five fuels derived from biomass.
5. What is the definition of calorific value?
6. List the categories of hydrocarbons in crude oil.
7. What are the advantages and disadvantages of wind energy?
8. Briefly discuss the energy conversion in hydropower plants.
9. Discuss ocean thermal and tidal energies.
10. With a sketch, describe the working of a solar water heater.
11. Draw a neat sketch of a solar photovoltaic cell and briefly explain its working principle.
12. Name the type of collectors used in solar applications.
13. With a neat diagram, briefly explain the components of a solar power plant.
14. What are the advantages and disadvantages of nuclear energy?
15. Explain in a paragraph, the working principle of a fuel cell.

PRACTICAL

From this unit, there are contents for practical learning. They are the determination of flash and fire points of liquid fuels, determination of the calorific value of solid, liquid and gaseous fuels, and determination of viscosity of liquids. There are various apparatus used for determining the above properties. In this section, the basic working principles of apparatus used for measurement of flash point, fire point, calorific value and viscosity are briefly discussed.

Flash point and fire point apparatus: In section 1.2.1, definitions for flash and fire points have been presented. In order to determine the flash and fire points, controlled and uniform heating of liquid fuels from a low initial temperature is carried out and temperature as a function of time is monitored. Further, a pilot flame (like a flame from a candle) is kept close to the liquid surface and the occurrence of a flash (or a momentary flame) is monitored. The minimum temperature at which the flash is produced is called flash point. Upon removal of the candle flame, the flash disappears. On further heating, the liquid reaches temperatures higher than the flash point. At a particular temperature, when the candle flame is brought near the surface, ignition occurs and a flame is formed over the liquid surface. This flame continues to burn even when the candle flame is removed. The minimum temperature at which a continuous sustained flame forms over the liquid fuel surface is called the fire point.

Flash point and fire point apparatus are designed to heat the liquid fuel in a controlled manner. For this, a water bath is used. The water bath is heated either using a Bunsen burner or an electric heater. The liquid fuel is kept in a copper (or any high thermal conductivity material) crucible and the crucible is kept in the water bath so that it is gradually heated in a controlled manner. The liquid fuel (and water bath) is also stirred so that the temperature is uniform within the liquid. Thermometers are used to record the temperatures of water as well as the liquid fuel at regular time intervals. Also, a candle/pilot flame is brought near the surface of the liquid fuel at various time instants to monitor if a flash is formed. The minimum temperature at which a flash is formed is carefully recorded. Then, heating is continued and the temperature is monitored continuously. In regular time intervals, a candle flame is brought near the liquid fuel surface to monitor if the ignition occurs and a continuous flame is formed over the surface. When a flame is formed over the liquid surface, the candle flame is removed to see if the flame is put-off or not at each time instant, noting the corresponding temperature. If the flame sustains, the temperature is noted as the fire point. A schematic of this apparatus, which is completely manually operated, is shown in Fig. 1.7.

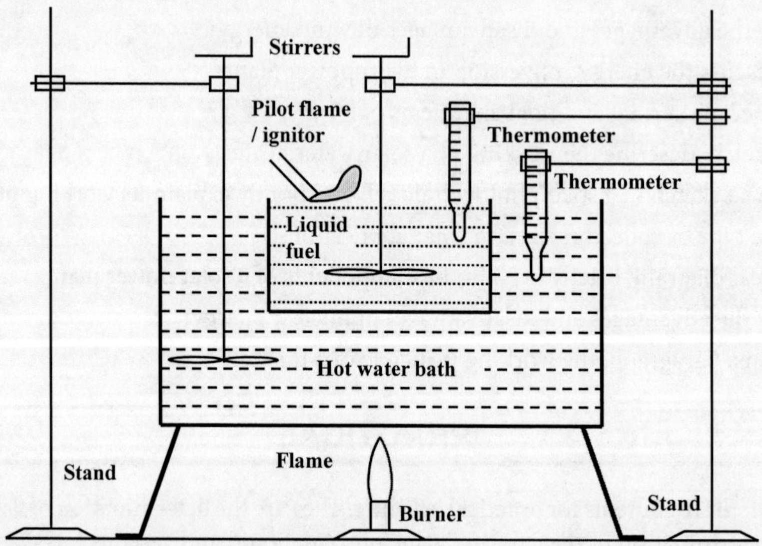

Fig. 1.7: Schematic of apparatus used to measure flash and fire points

There are several commercially available apparatus for determining flash and fire points. Some of them are open cup or open vessel types, as shown in Fig. 1.7. Example of this is the automatic Cleveland open cup tester produced by Anton Paar. This is a fully automated, electrically heated apparatus. There are semi-automatic versions also. Some of the flash point apparatus are closed cup type. In this, the liquid and its vapor are heated with its container or lid closed. Then at regular time intervals, the temperature is noted. Simultaneously, the lid is opened allowing air to go inside and an ignition source is also provided. A minimum temperature at which a flash is observed is designated as the flash point. The main difference between the closed cup and open cup apparatus is that the liquid and vapor are in equilibrium in the open cup type and it may not be in the closed cup type. Value of flash point will be lesser as determined by the closed cup type apparatus. Pensky Martens closed cup flash point tester is an automated apparatus. Another commercial product is by Abel, which is also a closed cup type apparatus.

Viscometer: An apparatus used to measure the viscosity of liquids is called a viscometer. Based on the value of viscosity, under a certain force, fluid travels a certain distance in a given time. If the value of viscosity is higher, then the viscous stresses are higher and more time is required to transport the liquid through the same distance. A simple viscometer measures the time taken by a liquid to descend through a distance or fill a given volume and correlates that time with the viscosity value. Saybolt viscometer is one such type. This viscometer is similar in its operation to a capillary tube viscometer, where the time taken for the liquid to descend through a given distance in a capillary tube is correlated to the viscosity.

Saybolt viscometer contains a vessel or a cup to hold liquid, which has an orifice at its bottom to restrict the flow through it. The types of orifices used are named universal, furol and asphalt. The orifices have different dimensions. For example, the universal orifice has a diameter of 0.176 cm and a length of 1.225 cm and is the most commonly used. The cup and orifice combination can be selected such that the flow time is set in the range of 20 to 100 seconds. First, 60 ml of liquid is weighed and poured into the cup keeping the exit of the orifice at the bottom closed with a help of a cork. The cup and orifice setup is placed in a hot water bath so that the oil is gradually heated to a required temperature at which viscosity value is to be measured. When oil reaches the desired temperature, the cork is opened so that oil is gradually allowed to flow through the oil and get collected in another vessel. The time taken for the given mass of oil in the cup to completely flow out is measured. The collected oil is again weighed to ensure the completeness of the collection. The time taken is correlated to viscosity. The experiment is carried out for a number of trials and at different temperatures. A schematic of the Saybolt viscometer is shown in Fig. 1.8.

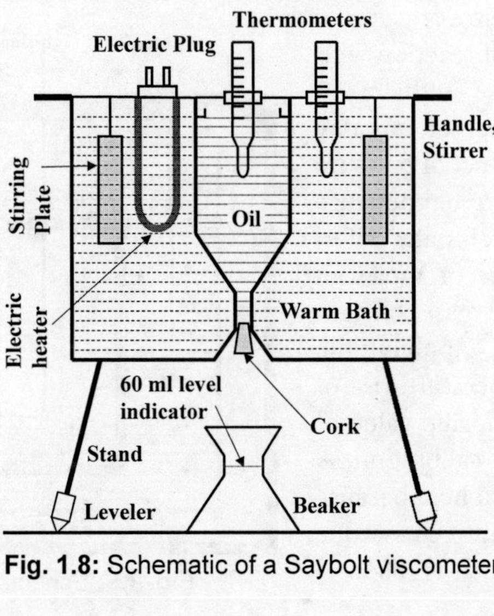

Fig. 1.8: Schematic of a Saybolt viscometer

The time (t) measured in seconds to collect the oil in the beaker is carefully recorded and is related to the kinematic viscosity (ν) as:

$$\nu = 0.226 \times t - 195/t \text{ Centistokes, if } t \leq 100 \text{ s}$$

$$\nu = 0.220 \times t - 135/t \text{ Centistokes, if } t > 100 \text{ s}$$

Here, one centistoke is equal to 1×10^{-6} m^2/s. Dynamic viscosity (μ) is calculated by multiplying the kinematic viscosity and density (ρ) of the oil, measured at the same temperature, ($\mu = \nu \times \rho$). There are other types of viscometers available commercially. Some of these measure the time taken by a spindle to rotate inside a layer of oil at a given temperature with a set force. Based on the viscosity of the oil, for a given force and spindle dimension, the time taken by the spindle to rotate through a given angle will vary. This is correlated to the viscosity of the oil. These apparatus are semi-automatic. The Saybolt viscometer is used in fields to check the viscosity of various types of oils.

Bomb calorimeter: An apparatus used to measure the calorific value of liquid and solid fuels is called a bomb calorimeter. A schematic of the bomb calorimeter is shown in Fig. 1.9. Bomb calorimeter has a rigid container made up of stainless steel, called a bomb. It has a lid with an opening for a valve to inject oxygen. An igniting system, which is a pair of electrodes with a fuse, also passes through the lid of the bomb. A crucible containing a solid (powdered form) or a liquid fuel is placed inside the bomb. The bomb itself is kept inside a water bath as shown in Fig. 1.9.

A known mass of fuel is kept in the crucible and kept inside the bomb. Oxygen is injected into the bomb up to a known pressure. When electricity passes through the electrodes, the fuse heats up, burns and ignites the reactants. Combustion (or burning) occurs at constant volume. Since it is exothermic, heat is released. This heat is transferred to the water bath and its temperature increases. In order to facilitate faster heat transfer and to have water temperature maintained uniform, a stirrer operates continuously on the water bath. First, a fuel of known calorific value (CV), such as benzoic acid, is burned in the bomb calorimeter and the temperature rise of water is recorded as it burns inside. Since the bomb is a rigid closed vessel, and the vessel containing the water is also insulated, the combined system of bomb and water bath is isolated. Therefore, the net change in the internal energy, ΔU, is zero during the process: $\Delta U_{reaction} + \Delta U_{surr} = 0$. Here, $\Delta U_{surr} = (m \times c) \times \Delta T$, where $m \times c$ is the combined heat capacity. The value of $\Delta U_{reaction}$ is called heat of reaction at constant volume. This is a negative quantity. Heat of combustion is the heating or calorific value and is the same as heat of reaction with opposite sign. For finding the enthalpy of reaction, $\Delta H_{reaction}$, the definition of enthalpy ($H = U + pV$) is used. The product of pressure and volume, pV is related to temperature using the ideal gas equation of state: $pV = nR_uT$, where n is the number of moles of products, R_u is the universal gas constant and T is the temperature in K. Applying the energy conservation, the temperature rise of water can be related to the calorific value of the fuel. This process is called calibration. A small correction is also required here because there is a given amount of heat release due to the burning of the fuse, which is made of

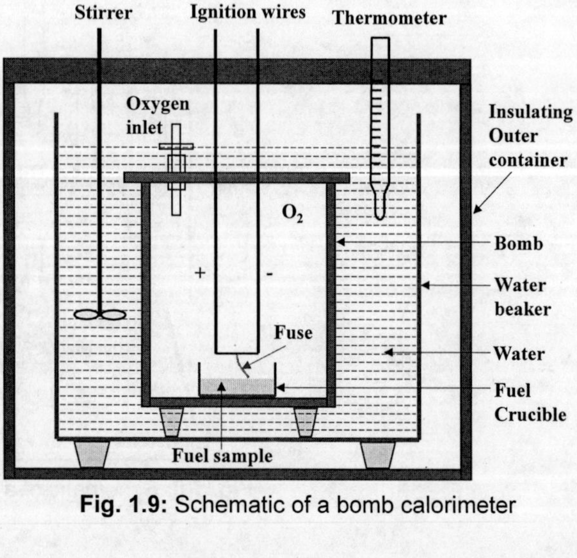

Fig. 1.9: Schematic of a bomb calorimeter

a material like nickel, used for igniting the reactant mixture. Incorporating all these, the temperature difference of the water is directly used to determine the heating value of the fuel. Fully automated digital bomb calorimeters are commercially available for the accurate measurement of calorific values of solid and liquid fuels.

Gas calorimeter: A device called Junkers calorimeter is used to measure the calorific or heating value of a gas fuel. A schematic of this device is shown in Fig. 1.10. It consists of a typical burner, through which the fuel gas is supplied at a known mass flow rate. A fuel meter and regulator are used to control the fuel flow rate. Air from the atmosphere naturally entrains and mixes with the gas fuel. Upon ignition, a flame (similar to a Bunsen burner flame) is formed over the burner as shown in Fig. 1.10. After ignition, the burner along with the flame is clamped to a heat exchanger, which has a series of tubes with water flowing through it. The burnt gases exchange the heat with the water flowing through the tubes and come out through a port at the bottom, as shown in Fig. 1.10. The water is supplied through a tank, with its level maintained constant in the tank. This ensures a steady supply of water through a given head. Burning occurs at a constant pressure of 1 atm. After a given time of around 15 minutes, a steady state is reached. This is indicated by the temperatures of incoming water, outgoing water and exhaust gas. The exhaust gas is left after it cools sufficiently so that its temperature is very close to the atmospheric temperature. Water vapor in the products condenses and the condensate is collected from the bottom, and its flow rate is also measured. The heat exchanger is insulated so that the hot combustion products heat the water flowing through the tube without significant losses.

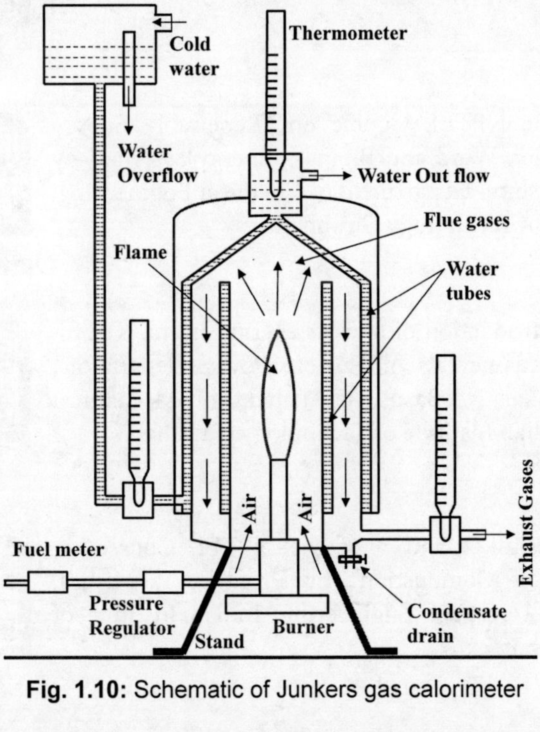

Fig. 1.10: Schematic of Junkers gas calorimeter

Considering a simple control volume around the heat exchanger, there is an inlet for the cold water and outlets for the hot water and the condensate. Exhaust gas heats the water. Energy conservation is written as,

$$\dot{m}_{fuel} \times CV = \dot{m}_w \times h_{wo} + \dot{m}_c \times h_{fv} - \dot{m}_w \times h_{wi} = \dot{m}_w \times c_w \times (T_{wo} - T_{wi}) + \dot{m}_c \times h_{fv}$$

Here, $\dot{m}_{fuel}$ is the mass flow rate of the fuel in kg/s and CV is its higher calorific value in J/kg, $\dot{m}_w$ is the mass flow rate of the water flowing through the pipes, $\dot{m}_c$ is the mass flow rate of the condensate, T_{wo} and T_{wi} are the outlet and inlet temperatures of water in K, respectively, c_w is the specific heat of the water in J/kg-K, and h_{fv} is the latent heat of vaporization of water at atmospheric pressure. Using energy conservation, the calorific value of the fuel, CV, is determined.

REFERENCES AND SUGGESTED READINGS

1. Vaughn Nelson, Introduction to Renewable Energy, CRC Press, 2011.
2. P. L. Ballaney, Thermal Engineering (Engineering Thermodynamics & Energy Conversion Techniques), Khanna Publishers, 2002.
3. V. Raghavan, Combustion Technology, Springer, 2016.
4. John Twidell and Tony Weir, Renewable Energy Resources, Routledge, 2015.

Dynamic QR Code for Further Reading

1. Lectures 1-3 of the NPTEL Course on "Fuels Refractory and Furnaces", by Prof. S. C. Koria, Department of Material Science and Engineering, Indian Institute of Technology Kanpur.

Scan Me

2. Lecture 1 of the NPTEL Course on "Renewable Energy Engineering: Solar, Wind and Biomass Energy Systems", by Prof. Anandalakshmi, Department of Chemical Engineering, Indian Institute of Technology Guwahati.

Scan Me

3. A lecture on "Introduction of nuclear energy" in the NPTEL Course on "Fundamentals of Nuclear Power Generation", by Prof. Dipankar N. Basu, Department of Mechanical Engineering, Indian Institute of Technology Guwahati.

Scan Me

4. A Lecture notes of 2 and 3 of the NPTEL Course on "Fundamentals of Combustion", by Prof. D. P. Mishra, Department of Aerospace Engineering, Indian Institute of Technology Kanpur.

Scan Me

2 Internal Combustion Engines

UNIT SPECIFICS

Through this unit, the following aspects are discussed:

- Difference between internal and external combustion engines;
- Classification of IC engines;
- Components in IC engines and their functions;
- Working of four-stroke and two-stroke petrol engines;
- Working of four-stroke and two-stroke diesel engines;
- Comparison of petrol and diesel engines;
- Comparison of two-stroke and four-stroke engines;
- Air standard cycles to understand the ideal operation of internal combustion (IC) engines;
- Valve and port timing diagrams.

This unit starts with listing the differences between internal and external combustion engines. Then, it presents an introduction to reciprocating engines and the nomenclature used in these engines.

Main components in a single-cylinder IC engine are described using simple sketches, along with their functions. These include, Cylinder, crank case, crank pin, crank, crank shaft, connecting rod, wrist pin, piston, cooling pin, cylinder head, exhaust valve and inlet valve. Working principles of petrol engines are discussed considering two-stroke and four-stroke modes of operation. Similarly, working principles of two-stroke and four-stroke diesel engines are also presented.

A comparison of two-stroke and four-stroke engines, with their respective advantages and disadvantages is presented subsequently. Similarly, a comparison of petrol and diesel engines along with their pros and cons is discussed.

Analysis using a simple thermodynamic cycle, which is called an air standard cycle, is presented next. Air standard cycle helps in understanding the ideal performances of three cycles. A comparison of these cycles with the Carnot cycle is briefly presented.

Finally, systematic procedures to draw valve timing diagrams and port timing diagrams are presented with simple sketches.

RATIONALE

The second unit of this book helps the students to get an overall idea about the energy conversion using reciprocating internal combustion (IC) engines. In power plants, fuel is burnt externally in a furnace and the flue gases supply heat to a boiler to produce steam, which runs a turbine to produce power. In contrast to this, in IC engines, fuel is burnt inside a cylinder and power is produced by displacing the piston. This unit also presents the classifications of IC engines. This unit also presents systematic descriptions of components used in IC engines. By reading this unit, students will be able to understand the working principles of two-stroke and four-stroke petrol engines and their diesel counterparts. Through this unit, students will be able to perform basic thermodynamic analyses of reciprocating engine processes. Finally, this unit discusses the procedures to draw valve and port timing diagrams.

PRE-REQUISITES

Basic Mechanical Engineering (MEPC102)

UNIT OUTCOMES

List of outcomes of this unit is as follows:

U2-O1: Know the differences between internal and external combustion engines

U2-O2: Understand the components in IC engines with their applications

U2-O3: Know the working principles of petrol and diesel engines operating in two and four-stroke modes

U2-O4: Perform air standard cycle analysis of reciprocating engines

U2-O5: Understand valve and port timing diagrams

Unit-2 Outcomes	EXPECTED MAPPING WITH COURSE OUTCOMES (1- Weak Correlation; 2- Medium Correlation; 3- Strong Correlation)				
	CO-1	CO-2	CO-3	CO-4	CO-5
U2-O1	-	2	-	-	-
U2-O2	-	3	2	-	-
U2-O3	2	3	-	-	-
U2-O4	-	3	2	-	-
U2-O5	-	3	-	-	-

2.1 HEAT ENGINES

A heat engine is a device that operates in a thermodynamic cycle and converts heat to work. Here, the chemical energy of a fuel is converted into thermal energy by burning it and subsequently thermal energy is converted into a mechanical form of energy or electrical energy. Heat engines are classified as internal combustion (IC) engines and external combustion (EC) engines. As the name suggests, in IC engines, combustion occurs within the engine that develops power. On the other hand, in EC engines, combustion occurs in a separate combustion chamber, and power is developed by another device. EC engines employ heat exchangers to transfer the heat to the working fluid from the combustion products. The working fluid then passes through another device such as a turbine to generate power.

In both of these categories, engines are further classified as rotary type or reciprocating type. Popular IC engines such as gasoline (petrol) and diesel engines, are of reciprocating type. These are used primarily in automobile and generator set applications. Examples of rotary type of IC engines are the open cycle gas turbine and the Wankel engine. The former is used in aircraft engines and the latter is used selectively in automobile applications. Closed cycle gas turbines and steam turbines are examples of rotary type external combustion engines. Of these EC engines, steam turbine power plants contribute to power production to a major extent. Steam engines and Stirling engines are examples of reciprocating type EC engines. Steam engines are not used much in the present scenario and Stirling engines have selective applications in cryogenic cooling systems. Fig. 2.1 shows the chart of heat engine classifications.

A reciprocating type of IC engine primarily consists of a cylinder and a piston moving through a certain distance within the length of the cylinder in a reciprocating manner. The linear movement of the piston is converted into continuous rotary movement of a shaft by using suitable mechanisms. The shaft in turn is connected to either a generator to produce electricity or to the wheels of an automobile to run the vehicle. The first IC engine for commercial use was built by J. J. E. Lenoir in 1860. In 1867, N. A. Otto and E. Langen developed an IC engine with improved efficiency. Again in 1876, N. A. Otto built a four-stroke engine using the principles laid down by Beau de Rochas, which gave much higher efficiency. D. Clerk, J. Robson and K. Benz developed two-stroke IC engines in 1880s. In 1892, R. Diesel developed an IC engine with a high compression ratio, which worked with diesel. Several advances and updates have happened to the IC engines and several engines have been available in the market with various capacities. The rotary type of IC engine, Wankel engine, was developed by F. Wankel. It is presently used in automotive and marine applications. Its thermal efficiency is relatively lower than reciprocating IC engines. In this course, the main focus will be on the reciprocating type of IC engines, which have automotive applications.

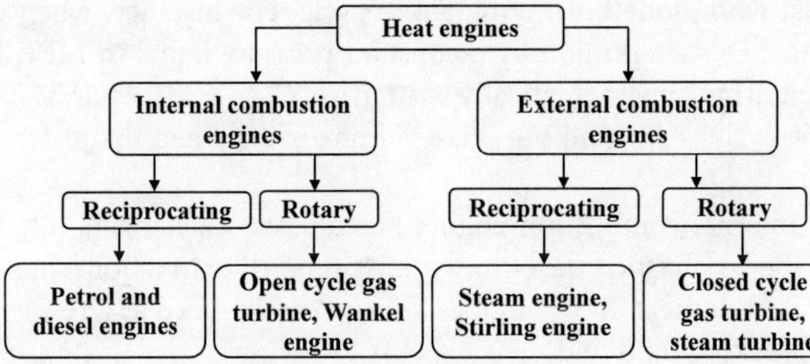

Fig. 2.1: Classification of heat engines

2.1.1 External Combustion Versus Internal Combustion Engines

From the discussions presented in the previous section, it is apparent that mostly used IC engines are reciprocating type petrol and diesel engines. Similarly, mostly employed EC engine is the steam power plant. The relative advantages and disadvantages of these engines are discussed in this section.

A steam power plant has four major components. They are boiler, steam turbine, condenser and pump. A schematic layout of a steam power plant is shown in Fig. 2.2. In the boiler, fuel such as coal is burnt and the hot product gases exchange heat with water (q_H). The liquid water is heated to superheated steam in stages. The superheated steam expands in the steam turbine producing power (w_T). The expanded steam further losses its heat in a condenser (q_C) such that liquid water exits the condenser. The liquid water is pumped (w_P) to the boiler pressure and this cycle continues. Here, combustion and heat exchange for producing high enthalpy fluid to expand in a turbine occurs separately. Thus, this engine is called external combustion (EC) heat engine.

The advantage of an EC engine is that more control is available for combustion in a separate chamber. Auxiliary devices such as reheaters, regenerators and so on, can be added to improve the overall efficiency. The main disadvantages are the lower efficiency and requirement of heat exchangers.

Considering a reciprocating IC engine, it is necessary to understand a few terminologies with respect to piston-cylinder configuration. A schematic of this is shown in Fig. 2.3. The diameter of the piston is called bore. The distance travelled by the piston in one direction is called stroke. When the piston is at the possible top-most point in the cylinder, which is called the top dead centre (TDC), the volume occupied by the air in the cylinder is the minimum. This volume is called the clearance volume (V_C). When the piston moves to the possible bottom-most point in the cylinder, called the bottom dead centre (BDC), the air inside the cylinder occupies the maximum volume (V_{max}). The difference between the maximum volume and the clearance volume is called the displacement volume. The ratio of the clearance volume to the displacement volume is called percent clearance. The ratio of the volume occupied by the air at BDC (maximum volume) to the volume occupied by the air at TDC (clearance volume) is called compression ratio, r (= V_{max}/V_C). The mean effective pressure (MEP) is the theoretical average pressure that is expected to produce an amount of work equal to the actual work done during the entire cycle. For instance, when the piston undergoes expansion from TDC to BDC acted upon by a constant pressure equal to MEP, it produces the same work as done by the cycle. This is mathematically written as: $W_{cycle} = MEP \times (V_{BDC} - V_{TDC})$, where W_{cycle} is work done during the cycle, V_{BDC} and V_{TDC} are volume of air when the piston is at BDC and TDC, respectively.

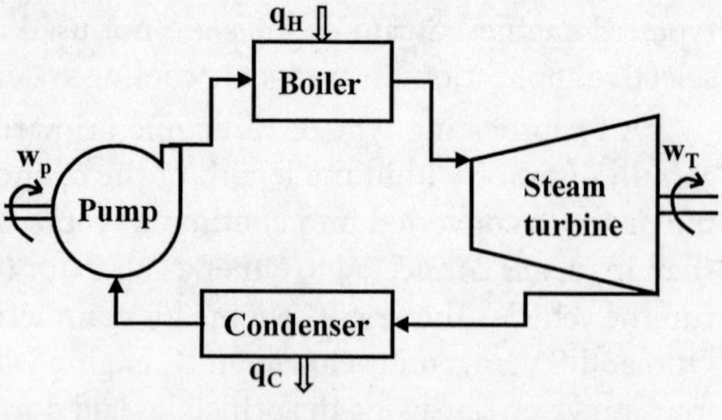

Fig. 2.2: Layout of a steam power plant

The reciprocating internal combustion engine has no heat exchangers like in an EC engine, for transferring heat from the combustion gases to working fluid (like in a boiler) and from working fluid to the ambient (like in a condenser). In IC engines, flue gases produced as a result of combustion of fuel and air, are part of the working fluid and their exhaust to atmosphere constitutes the heat rejection from the engine. Therefore, IC engines have simplicity, compactness and higher efficiency.

Reciprocating IC engines operate at a much lower average temperature (average calculated over the entire cycle), since combustion (heat release) happens only in a small fraction of the entire cycle. This average temperature can be increased by suitable methods to obtain higher thermal efficiency. Similarly, IC engines operate at moderate values of average pressure. Thus, the weight to power ratio is much less in IC engines when compared to that of a steam power plant. On the other hand, temperatures and pressures at the inlet of a steam turbine are already quite high. The scope of increasing them to obtain higher efficiency is low.

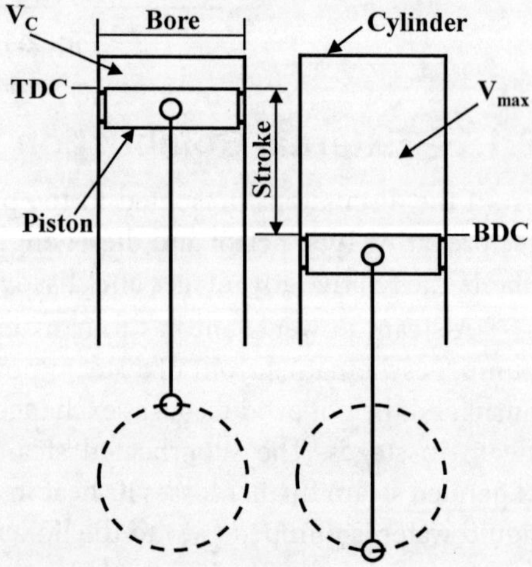

Fig. 2.3: Nomenclature of reciprocating IC engine

One of the main disadvantages of reciprocating IC engines is the resulting vibration due to reciprocating components. The power production is also limited. Further, fuel flexibility is much lower in IC engines. Only liquid or gaseous fuels of standard specifications can be used. Biofuels such as ethanol and bio-diesel can be blended only to a limited percent to the fossil fuels and used in IC engines. When compared to the coal used in steam power plants, the fuels such as gasoline and diesel used in IC engines are relatively costly.

2.2 CLASSIFICATION OF IC ENGINES

Classification of IC engines is done with respect to different parameters such as type of fuel used, method of heat addition, method of charging, type of ignition, type of cooling and configuration of cylinders.

(1) Several types of fuels are used in IC engines, even though commercially available liquid fuels such as petrol and diesel are the two common fuels used in several automotive vehicles of different capacities (two, three and four wheelers and so on). Usually, the engines are classified as petrol and diesel engines.

Basically, if the liquid fuel is highly volatile (easily evaporative) such as petrol, kerosene and alcohol, then it can be vaporized almost instantly and mixed with air in a device called carburettor. This homogeneous reactant mixture can be charged to the engine and after compression, it can be ignited by a spark. Thus, a petrol engine is also called spark-ignition (SI) liquid fuel engine. Similarly, gaseous fuels such as CNG, LPG and biogas can be used in SI engines and they are called spark-ignition gas engines.

If the liquid fuel is less volatile, that is, if it cannot vaporize easily, then it is subjected to a process called atomization. Atomizers of different types produce small droplets of the liquid fuel in required size ranges. These small droplets easily evaporate in hot and high pressure turbulent air environment established inside the cylinder. The fuel vapor and hot air mixture is auto ignited (without using a spark) and combustion takes place. Therefore, a diesel engine is also called compression-ignition (CI) engine.

Engines have also been using two fuels (one volatile and another relatively less volatile). These are called dual-fuel engines.

(2) The heat addition in petrol and diesel engines due to combustion occurs differently. An engine may be classified based on the process in which heat is added (or released during combustion). In petrol engines, heat addition occurs nearly at a constant volume. In diesel engines, heat addition occurs nearly at a constant pressure.

(3) On the method of charging, engines are classified as naturally aspirated and supercharged. In naturally aspirated engines, air or fuel-air mixture is charged into the engine almost under atmospheric pressure condition. In supercharged engines, the engine is charged at a pressure higher than the atmospheric pressure.

(4) Type of ignition is also used to classify the engine. Under this, spark-ignition (SI) and compressed-ignition (CI) are the two main categories, as discussed earlier. In SI engines, method of producing a spark (called the ignition system) can be a battery ignition system or a magneto ignition system, based on the primary source of energy producing the spark. In CI engines, where no external ignition system is required, a fuel injection system (atomizer) is required.

(5) An engine has to be cooled due to material constraints. Type of cooling also classifies the engine. There are two types of cooling methods. Based on this, there are air-cooled engines (for example, a two-wheeler engine) and liquid-cooled engines (for example, a car engine). In air-cooled engines, fins or extended surfaces are used on cylinder walls and in heat transfer areas. In water-cooled engines, water is circulated through all the engines parts, which are required to dissipate heat. The hot water coming out of the engine is cooled in a radiator using air stream. There are natural convection based and forced convection based water circulation systems used in water-cooled engines.

(6) Often multiple cylinders are used in an engine system to meet the required power capacity. In this context, engines are classified as in-line engine, V-engine, opposed cylinder engine, opposed piston engine, radial engine (an extension of V-engine) and so on. Schematics of a few multi-cylinder engine configurations are shown in Fig. 2.4.

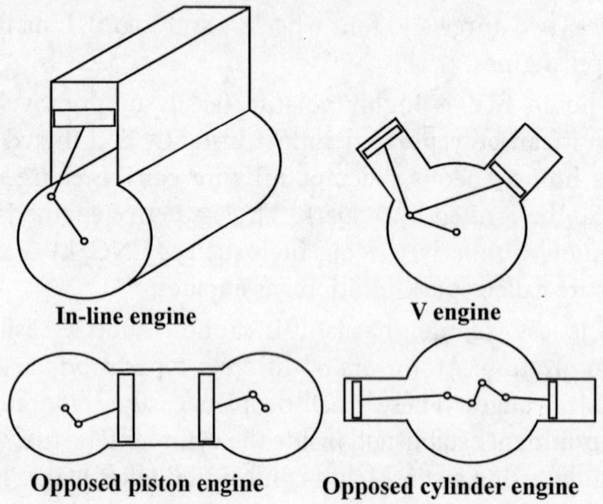

Fig. 2.4: Schematics of a few multi-cylinder engine configuration

2.3 COMPONENTS IN IC ENGINES

There are several components present in an IC engine assembly. In this section, some of the important components of an IC engine are explained. A simple schematic of a single cylinder SI engine is shown in Fig. 2.5.

Cylinder block and cylinder: The main component of an engine that supports various components is called cylinder block. Usually, a cylinder block is made of casting. Even multiple cylinders are housed in a cylinder block. Required water jackets or cooling fins are provided in this block.

The bottom portion of the cylinder block is called the crankcase. This acts as a vessel or sump for the lubricating oil. Inner surfaces of the cylinder block are accurately machined to obtain cylindrical surfaces of high-level finish. These cylinders house piston assemblies. These are called bores. The cylinder head, which houses valves, manifolds, spark plug and so on, is assembled in the cylinder block with the help of a gasket and several fasteners.

Piston: It is a cylindrical component that operates inside a cylinder to provide time varying space within the cylinder by its reciprocating motion. Even though it is free to move inside the cylinder, it is made leak proof by using piston rings, which are connected to the slots provided in the circumference of the piston. This is connected to a connecting rod that transmits the movement of the piston further to a crankshaft. Combustion occurs in the space enclosed in the cylinder between the upper surface of the piston and the bottom of the cylinder head.

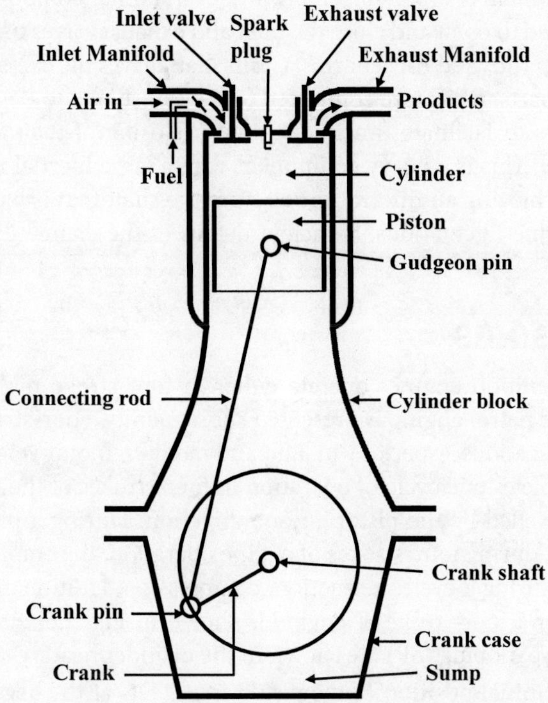

Fig. 2.5: A schematic of different parts typically present in an SI engine

Inlet manifold: This is a pipe that connects the intake system to the inlet valve. For SI engines, this has a carburettor that mixes fuel (petrol) vapor and air. In CI engines, only air is drawn into the cylinder through the inlet manifold.

Exhaust manifold: Exhaust valve is connected to the exhaust system through a pipe called exhaust manifold.

Valves: Inlet and exhaust valves are present either in the cylinder head or on the side of the cylinder to regulate the flow of incoming charge and outgoing exhaust gases, respectively. They open and close periodically depending upon the set timings during a cycle of operation.

Spark plug (or fuel injector): This component facilitates ignition. In SI engines, as shown in Fig. 2.5, a spark plug is present on the cylinder head to provide a spark of required strength at an appropriate time instant for a given small time duration. In the case of CI engine, an atomizer or a fuel injector is connected to the cylinder head instead of a spark plug, which injects fuel into the hot air around the end of the compression stroke.

Connecting rod: The main link that connects the piston and the crank shaft to transmit the power is called the connecting rod. Two ends of the connecting rods are called small and big ends. The small end is connected to the piston using a gudgeon pin and the big end is connected to the crank using a crank pin. The gudgeon pin is also called wrist pin or piston pin. Connecting rod has an I-shaped cross section with varying area along its length.

Crankshaft: As the piston moves linearly in a reciprocating motion, a mechanism is required to convert this linear motion into a rotary motion. Crankshaft is enclosed in the crankcase. It is connected to the crank that rotates by the movement of the connecting rod.

Apart from the above main components, there are several other components not shown in Fig. 2.5. Camshaft and cams are used to open and close the inlet and exhaust valves using associated parts such as tappets, valve springs, push rods and rocker arms. Crankshaft drives the camshaft through a gear system. Cams are specially made parts, which are connected to the camshaft and engage with components such as push rods, tappets, etc., to facilitate timely opening or closing of the valves. One more important component is the flywheel. This is a heavy component with a large inertial mass that is attached to the output shaft. It helps in achieving a uniform torque from the shaft that is having changes in its angular velocity as a result of engine fluctuations. Sufficient details of the engine components are available in literature.

2.4 PETROL ENGINES

Petrol engines or spark ignition engines operate either in four-stroke mode or in two-stroke mode. Operation of a four-stroke petrol engine is presented subsequently. Four-stroke petrol engines are used in several automotive applications, especially in light and medium motor vehicles. As the name suggests, a four-stroke engine completes one cycle of operation in four-strokes of the piston. A stroke, as defined earlier, is the distance travelled by the piston in one direction. During a piston stroke, the crankshaft rotates by 180°. Therefore, during four-strokes of engine operation, the crankshaft rotates through 720°. The processes occurring during a cycle are suction, compression, ignition and combustion, expansion, and exhaust. Schematic of a four-stroke SI engine is shown in Fig. 2.6, where an inlet valve (IV), an exhaust valve (EV) and a spark plug (SP) are shown in the cylinder head.

Suction Stroke: The initial position of the piston is at TDC at the beginning of suction or intake stroke. When the piston starts moving down from TDC, the inlet valve opens. The exhaust valve is kept closed. As the piston move downwards, a suction is created in the cylinder space above the piston. Charge, which is the premixed fuel-air mixture, flows into the cylinder. When the piston reaches the BDC, the inlet valve is closed and the suction stroke ends. This is shown in Fig. 2.6(a).

Compression stroke: The fuel-air mixture taken into the cylinder is now compressed as the piston starts moving upwards from BDC to TDC. In this stroke, both inlet and exhaust valves remain closed. The reactant mixture is compressed from maximum volume to clearance volume. This stroke is illustrated in Fig. 2.6(b).

Ignition and combustion process: As the piston reaches TDC, the spark plug produces a spark igniting the fuel-air mixture. The reaction of premixed petrol vapor and air is much rapid. Therefore, the combustion reaction is assumed to be completed at a much rapid rate and the heat is also released when the piston momentarily stays at TDC. Therefore, the heat addition is theoretically modelled as constant volume heat addition.

Expansion or power stroke: As a result of combustion, heat is released and temperature increases to a value of around 2200 K. Product gas mixture at very high pressure is formed in the clearance volume (ideally). The high pressure product gases push the piston downwards from TDC to BDC. Both inlet and exhaust valves remain closed. This is also sketched in Fig. 2.6(c). As a result of the expansion process, pressure and temperature decrease. In the ideal cycle, there is no heat loss and the process is isentropic.

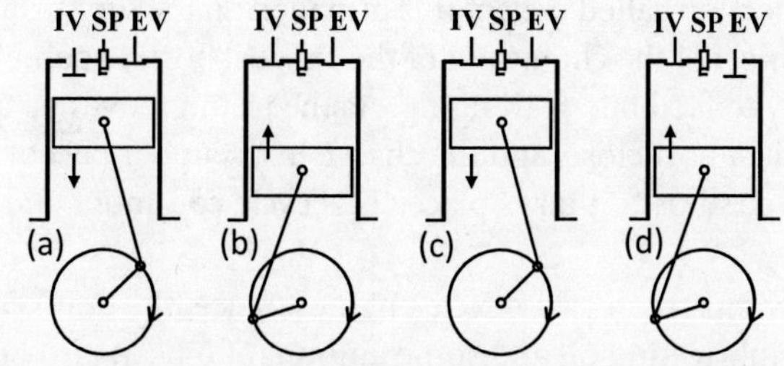

Fig. 2.6: Schematics of four-strokes in a petrol engine

Exhaust stroke: When the piston reaches BDC, the exhaust valve opens and the inlet valve remains closed. Product gases leave through the exhaust valve. The piston moves up and reaches TDC, pushing all the product gases through the exhaust valve. The subsequent cycle starts when the piston is at TDC. This stroke is shown in Fig. 2.6(d).

D. Clark in 1878 invented an engine that completes one cycle in two-strokes, that is, 360° of crankshaft rotation. This engine produces power once in one rotation of crankshaft, as compared to once in two rotations in a four-stroke engine. Compression and power strokes are productive strokes in a four-stroke engine and the other two-strokes are mainly used for intake of charge and exhaust of product gases. In two-stroke engines, the productive strokes (compression and expansion) themselves take care of intake of charge and exhaust of product gases. Fig. 2.7 presents a simple schematic of a two-stroke engine. There is a spring loaded inlet valve. Instead of an exhaust valve, there is an exhaust port. In addition, there is a transfer port, as shown in Fig. 2.7.

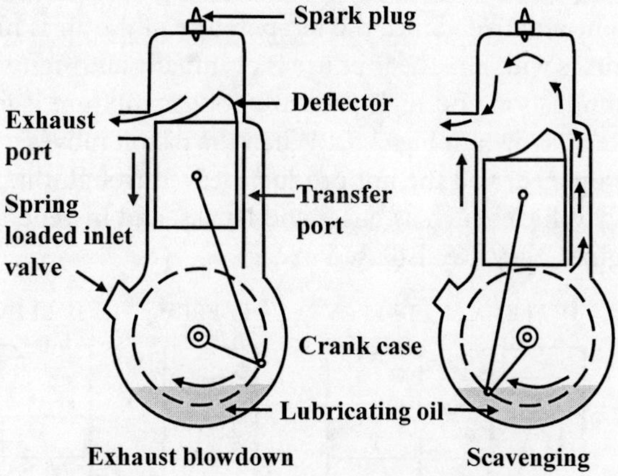

Fig. 2.7: Schematic of a two-stroke SI engine

Here, the reactant mixture (fresh charge) is taken into the crankcase through an inlet valve. As the piston moves up, the pressure in the crankcase reduces and the charge flows in. When the piston moves down during the expansion or power stroke, it compresses the charge in the crankcase. When the piston crosses the exhaust port and opens it, exhaust gases flow out of the exhaust port. This is called exhaust blowdown (Fig. 2.7, left). The charge in the crankcase, which is at higher pressure, flows to the top part of the cylinder through the transfer port. As the charge is transferred to the top, it also expels the remaining exhaust gases out through the exhaust port. This is called cross-flow scavenging (Fig. 2.7, right). To facilitate scavenging, a projection called deflector is provided on the top surface of the cylinder. Deflector also avoids the direct transport of the charge out of the exhaust port. In some engines, the transfer port is also designed appropriately to facilitate scavenging. As the piston moves up again, first the transfer port, and subsequently, the exhaust port close, and the charge in the upper part of the cylinder is compressed. Spark ignition occurs and combustion takes place. This cycle continues and power is produced once in two-strokes.

There are a few disadvantages in two-stroke engines. Since, the crankcase is filled with lubricating oil, the charge mixes with lubricating oil and some amount of oil can also be transferred along with the charge and burn. During scavenging, some fresh charge can also leave through the exhaust port without burning. Two-stroke petrol engines have been used in two-wheeler and small generator set applications. Now, the two-stroke engines are slowly replaced by four-stroke engines.

2.5 DIESEL ENGINES

Diesel engines are compression-ignition engines. A four-stroke diesel engine is similar to a four-stroke petrol engine, but it operates at a higher compression ratio in the range of 15 to 22. Due to this, the construction of a diesel engine is sturdier than a petrol engine. Fig. 2.8 presents a schematic of a four-stroke diesel engine, where an inlet valve (IV), an exhaust valve (EV) and a fuel injector (FI) are shown in the cylinder head. The main change is that the spark plug of the petrol engine is replaced by a fuel injector or an atomizer in the diesel engine. A high pressure fuel pump is connected to the injector to supply the required amount of fuel. Air is taken into the cylinder during the suction stroke, as the piston moves down and the inlet valve only is open (Fig. 2.8a). In the compression stroke, both inlet and exhaust valves are closed and the air is compressed to high pressure (Fig. 2.8b). Diesel is sprayed as small droplets through the atomizer. Since the temperature of the air is high, small droplets instantly evaporate and the vapor mixes with air. The mixture is eventually auto-ignited due to high temperature. Heat is released during combustion and high pressure hot gas mixture is formed. Piston moves down delivering the power stroke as shown in Fig. 2.8c. When the piston moves up in the exhaust stroke (Fig. 2.8d), the exhaust valve is opened, and the hot products leave through that. Four-stroke diesel engines are primarily used in heavy vehicles such as buses and trucks, and in generator sets. Presently, with the invent of lighter diesel engines, they are also used in cars.

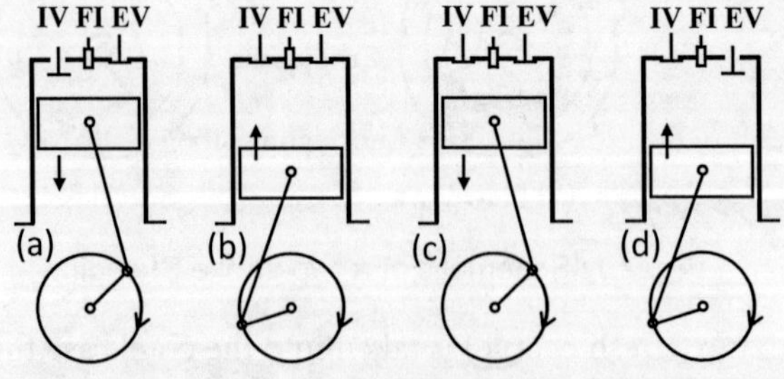

Fig. 2.8: Schematics of four-strokes in a compression-ignition engine

Two-stroke diesel engines are similar to two-stroke petrol engines with two main differences, as discussed before. The spark plug is replaced with a fuel injector and air alone is taken into the cylinder through the inlet port or valve. The crankcase is filled to some level with lubricating oil like in the petrol engine. A slightly different construction of a two-stroke diesel engine is shown in Fig. 2.9. Here, inlet ports are used and exhaust valves are present. As the piston moves down during power stroke, inlet ports as well as exhaust valves are opened. Air is taken into the cylinder through inlet ports and hot product gases go out through the exhaust valves. This is called uniflow scavenging. During the second stroke, as the piston moves upwards, both inlet port and exhaust valves are closed. Air is compressed and when the piston reaches TDC, diesel is injected through the fuel injector and combustion occurs. Hot products are formed, power stroke takes place and the cycle repeats. Two-stroke engines of very high power are used in marine applications for ship propulsion.

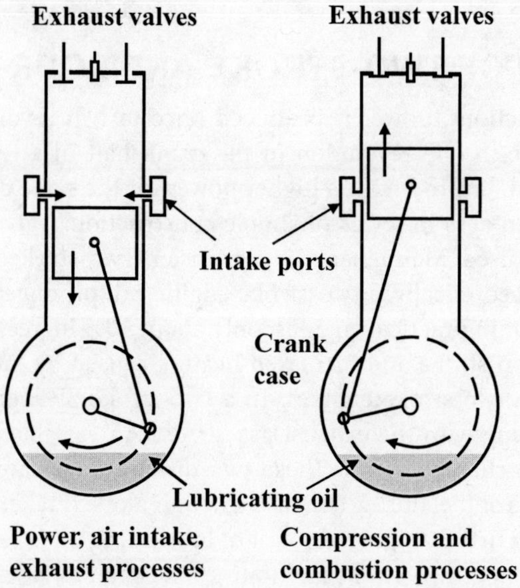

Fig. 2.9: Schematic of a two-stroke diesel engine

2.6 COMPARISON OF PETROL AND DIESEL ENGINES

A comparison of petrol and diesel engines is presented in this section. As discussed earlier, petrol is more volatile than diesel and its auto-ignition temperature is high. A mixture of petrol vapor and air is taken into the petrol engine and an external ignition source such as a spark is used for ignition. Therefore, the petrol engine is also called a spark-ignition engine. On the other hand, only air is taken into the CI engine and diesel is sprayed into the hot compressed air to cause rapid vaporization and auto-ignition. No external ignition source is used. Important differences between petrol and diesel engines are tabulated in Table 2.1.

Table 2.1: Comparison of petrol and diesel engines

Petrol Engine	Diesel Engine
Works on Otto cycle. Constant volume heat addition takes place. Moderate compression ratio.	Works on Diesel cycle. Constant pressure heat addition takes place. High compression ratio.
Carburettor and ignition system are used. Modern engines have incorporated direct petrol injection.	A fuel pump and injection system are required.
Throttle valve controls the intake of fuel-air mixture to handle the engine load.	Fuel injection rate is controlled to handle engine load and not the air quantity.

Petrol Engine	Diesel Engine
Requires an ignition system consisting of a spark plug and battery or magneto.	Ignition system not needed.
Light weight and high speed engines.	Relatively heavier and low speed engines.
Due to lower compression ratio, the thermal efficiency is lower.	Due to higher compression ratio, the thermal efficiency is higher.

2.7 COMPARISON OF TWO-STROKE AND FOUR-STROKE ENGINES

As discussed in previous sections, power is produced once in two revolutions of the crankshaft in a four-stroke engine and once in one revolution of the crankshaft in a two-stroke engine. Two-stroke engines have been developed for producing a higher power for the same engine size. Ports used in two-stroke engines provide advantages in terms of simple construction. Valves and actuating mechanisms are not required if ports are used. Maintenance is also easier. Two-stroke engines also provide uniform torque on the crankshaft. Theoretically, a two-stroke engine can produce double the power of its four-stroke counterpart. However, in practical engines, only about 30% increase in power is realized. This is a result of reduced expansion stroke and increased heating caused by more power strokes. Therefore, more cooling is required in two-stroke engines. In a two-stroke SI engine, during scavenging, some fresh charge may be lost along with the exhaust gases. Also, in variable loads, a two-stroke SI engine displays irregular operation characteristics. These two disadvantages are not present in a two-stroke diesel engine. There is no loss of fuel during exhaust, since air alone is taken in. Under variable loads, fuel injection can be controlled. Further, higher amount of lubricating oil is required for both two-stroke SI and CI engines. A comparison of two-stroke and four-stroke engines is reported in Table 2.2.

Table 2.2: Comparison of two-stroke and four-stroke engines

Two-stroke Engine	Four-stroke Engine
Power stroke is obtained in one revolution of the crankshaft. Lighter engine for the same power.	Power stroke is obtained in two revolutions of the crankshaft. Heavier engine for the same power.
More uniform torque distribution and a lighter flywheel is enough.	Relatively non-uniform torque distribution and a heavier flywheel is needed.
Higher cooling and lubricating requirements. Higher rate of wear and tear.	Lower cooling and lubricating requirements. Lower rate of wear and tear.
Other than conventional exhaust valve or reed valve used in some two-stroke diesel engines, no valves are required.	Valves and actuation mechanisms are required.
Thermal efficiency is lower and part load efficiency is poor.	Thermal efficiency is higher and part load efficiency is better.
Lower volumetric efficiency due to lower time for charge intake.	Higher volumetric efficiency because of higher time for charge intake.
Used where low-cost vehicles and light weight are important. Examples are mopeds and scooters. Also used in heavy marine applications.	Used when efficiency is important. Examples are cars, buses, trucks and generator sets.

2.8 AIR STANDARD CYCLES

The operation of a gas engine operating in a thermodynamic cycle may be analysed in a simplified manner by assuming that the working fluid is a homogeneous pure substance such as air. The complexities of considering chemical reactions and the mixture of gases involved before and after the reactions are eliminated in this analysis. Here, air undergoes the thermodynamic cycle constituted by four processes. These are compression process, heat addition process, expansion process and heat rejection process. The nature of these processes differs between different engines. The cycle is called an air standard cycle. This cycle is analysed as a system (fixed mass), which exchanges heat and work with the surroundings. There are different types of reciprocating IC engines, which operate with a piston-cylinder arrangement. These can be analysed thermodynamically using the air standard cycle approach.

An ideal cycle that is shown to have maximum efficiency is the Carnot cycle. This cycle consists of four reversible processes. Process 1-2 is an adiabatic compression process, where the working substance (air) is slowly compressed and its temperature increases from initial temperature, T_C, which is also the temperature of the low-temperature thermal reservoir, to the maximum temperature of the cycle, T_H. A high-temperature thermal reservoir is also at the same temperature of T_H. In the process 1-2, work is done on the system. Process 2-3 is an isothermal expansion process, where heat is added from the thermal reservoir at T_H to the air isothermally, under negligible temperature difference. Process 3-4 is an adiabatic expansion process, where the system performs work on the surroundings. Here, the temperature drops from T_H to T_C. Finally, process 4-1 is an isothermal compression process, where heat is rejected to the thermal reservoir at T_C and this heat transfer also occurs isothermally at negligible temperature difference. The volume of air decreases during this process. The state diagrams of this cycle in p-V and T-S coordinates are shown in Fig. 2.10.

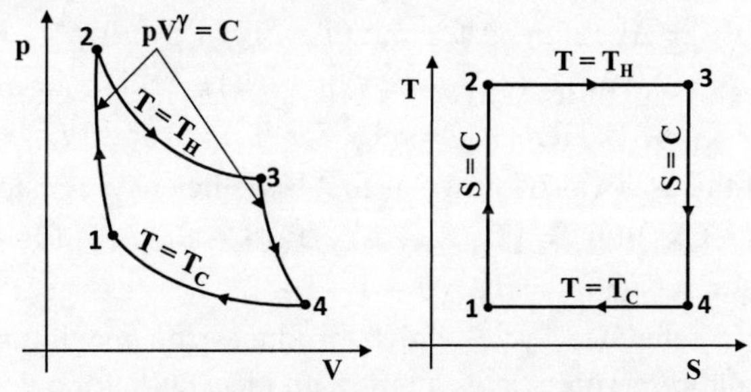

Fig. 2.10: Carnot cycle in p-V and T-S diagrams

Air is treated as an ideal gas. Thus, it obeys the equation of state given by $pV = nR_uT$, where p is pressure in Pa, V is volume in m^3, n is number of moles of air in the system in kmol, R_u is universal gas constant (8314 J/kmol-K) and T is temperature in K. Equation of state is also written in terms of specific gas constant of air (R = 287 J/kg-K) as, $pV = mRT$, where m is the mass of the air in the system in kg. Therefore, for isothermal process undergone by air in a fixed mass of a system obeys the process pV = constant. The caloric equations of state for air are written as $du = c_v dT$ and $dh = c_p dT$, where u is specific internal energy in J/kg, h is specific enthalpy in J/kg, c_v is the specific heat at constant volume in J/kg-K and c_p is specific heat at constant pressure in J/kg-K. For air, the ratio of specific heats ($c_p/c_v = \gamma$) is equal to 1.4. For reversible adiabatic process, change in entropy is zero; it is an isentropic process (S = constant). Using one of the Gibbs (or Tds) equations,

$$Tds = du + pdv, \text{since } ds = 0, du = c_v dT = -pdv.$$

$$pV = mRT \text{ or } pv = RT \Rightarrow p = \frac{RT}{v}.$$

Using this,

$$c_v dT = -RT\left(\frac{dv}{v}\right).Or, \left(\frac{c_v}{R}\right)\left(\frac{dT}{T}\right) = -\frac{dv}{v}.$$

The quantity, $c_v/R = 1/(\gamma-1)$. If air is treated as a perfect gas, then c_v is a constant, else, c_v depends on the temperature. Assuming air to be a perfect gas, integration of the above equation yields,

$$\frac{T_2}{T_1} = \left(\frac{v_1}{v_2}\right)^{\gamma-1}.$$

Using the equation of state, the above relation is written in terms of pressure and volume as,

$$\frac{p_2}{p_1} = \left(\frac{v_1}{v_2}\right)^{\gamma}.$$

Therefore, the isentropic process undergone by an ideal gas is written as pv^γ = constant. All the processes in the Carnot cycle are shown clearly in both p-V and T-S diagrams. The heat added to the cycle is obtained by integrating the area below the line 2-3 in the T-S diagram. Similarly, the heat rejected by the cycle is obtained by integrating the area under the line 4-1 in the T-S diagram. The net work output of the cycle is the area bounded by the rectangle in the T-S diagram. Applying the first law of thermodynamics for all processes,

Process 1-2: Here, $Q_{1-2} = 0$. $W_{1-2} = (p_1V_1 - p_2V_2)/(\gamma - 1) = U_1 - U_2 = mc_v(T_1 - T_2)$.

Process 2-3: $Q_{2-3} - W_{2-3} = \Delta U$. Here, $\Delta U = mc_v(T_3 - T_2) = 0$ and $W_{2-3} = p_2V_2 \times \ln(V_3/V_2)$.

Process 3-4: Here, $Q_{3-4} = 0$. $W_{3-4} = (p_3V_3 - p_4V_4)/(\gamma - 1) = U_3 - U_4 = mc_v(T_3 - T_4)$.

Process 4-1: $Q_{4-1} - W_{4-1} = \Delta U$. Here, $\Delta U = mc_v(T_1 - T_4) = 0$ and $W_{4-1} = p_4V_4 \times \ln(V_1/V_4)$.

Thermal efficiency of the cycle (also known as first law efficiency) is calculated as:

$\eta = W_{net}/Q_{2-3} = (Q_{2-3} - Q_{4-1})/Q_{2-3} = [T_H(S_3 - S_2) - T_C(S_4 - S_1)]/ [T_H(S_3 - S_2)]$

Since $S_3 - S_2 = S_4 - S_1$, $\eta = (T_H - T_C)/T_H = 1 - T_C/T_H$.

The Carnot cycle is a reference cycle, which produces the maximum efficiency for the given temperatures of hot and cold reservoirs. Subsequently, an ideal cycle for a petrol engine, called the Otto cycle, and an ideal cycle for a diesel engine, called the Diesel cycle, are presented.

Otto cycle also consists of four processes like the Carnot cycle. These are displayed in the p-V and T-S diagrams in Fig. 2.11. Air is the working fluid in this cycle. The piston is located at BDC at state 1 and air occupies the maximum volume, V_1 at this state. Pressure and temperatures are the lowest, p_1 and T_1, respectively. Piston rises upwards from BDC, compresses the air and reaches TDC. This is designated as state 2. The volume occupied by the air, V_2, is equal to the clearance volume, V_c (the minimum volume for the cycle). It is noted that the ratio, V_1/V_2, is the compression ratio (r). Pressure and temperature increases to p_2 and T_2, respectively. This compression process 1-2 is adiabatic. Since this cycle is ideal, all the processes are considered reversible. Therefore, process 1-2 is isentropic. T-S diagram in Fig. 2.11 indicates that the process 1-2 occurs at constant entropy. Quantities at state 2 can be arrived at using the isentropic relations for an ideal gas. As discussed, in a petrol engine, a mixture of petrol and air is taken inside the cylinder and they are compressed during the compression process. When a spark plug is activated, the spark ignites the mixture. Combustion occurs at a much faster rate since premixed petrol and air mixture is highly reactive. So, it is assumed that the reaction is complete within the time the piston starts to descend from TDC. The chemical reaction in an actual engine is modelled as heat addition in an air standard cycle. Therefore, heat is added when the piston remains at TDC. Process 2-3 represents the heat addition in a constant volume process. Moreover, in the ideal cycle, the heat addition is assumed to be reversible (negligible temperature difference). Due to the heat addition, the temperature and the pressure reach their maximum values, p_3 and T_3, respectively, increasing the enthalpy of air to its maximum. The high-enthalpy air expands pushing the piston down from TDC to BDC, doing a positive displacement work (representing the power stroke that does the work in an actual engine). The expansion process 3-4 is reversible and adiabatic, therefore, isentropic, as clearly shown in Fig. 2.11. The pressure and temperature decrease to p_4 and T_4, respectively. State 4 quantities can be calculated using the isentropic relations for an ideal gas. When the piston is at BDC, heat is lost to the surroundings, as the volume remains constant. In fact, in an actual engine, the piston moves up to TDC, pushing the hot gases out through the exhaust valve and subsequently returns to BDC, where the fresh charge of petrol and air mixture is taken inside. The exhaust and intake processes are not modelled in the air standard cycle. Process 4-1 is a constant volume heat rejection process, by which the cycle returns to its initial state.

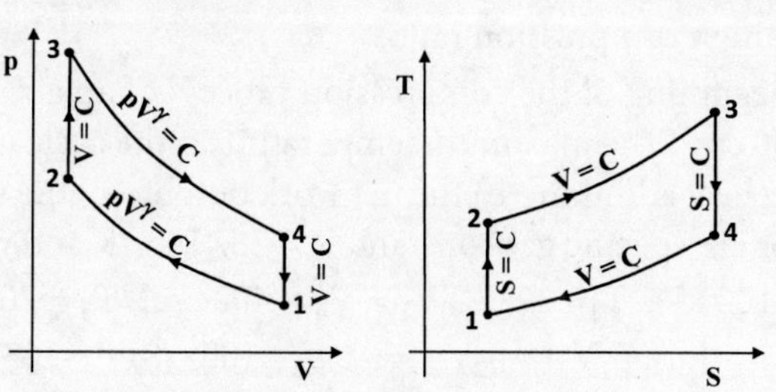

Fig. 2.11: Otto cycle in p-V and T-S diagrams

The first law analysis of Otto cycle is presented below:

$$Q_{2-3} = mc_v (T_3 - T_2)$$

$$Q_{4-1} = mc_v (T_4 - T_1)$$

$$\eta = 1 - \left(\frac{Q_{4-1}}{Q_{2-3}}\right) = 1 - \frac{T_4 - T_1}{T_3 - T_2} = 1 - \frac{T_1\left(\dfrac{T_4}{T_1}\right) - 1}{T_2\left(\dfrac{T_3}{T_2}\right) - 1} \quad (2.1)$$

From isentropic relations applied to processes 1-2 and 3-4,

$$\frac{T_2}{T_1} = \left(\frac{V_1}{V_2}\right)^{\gamma-1}$$

$$\frac{T_3}{T_4} = \left(\frac{V_4}{V_3}\right)^{\gamma-1} = \left(\frac{V_1}{V_2}\right)^{\gamma-1}$$

$$\Rightarrow \frac{T_3}{T_4} = \frac{T_2}{T_1}$$

$$\Rightarrow \eta = 1 - \frac{T_1}{T_2} = 1 - \left(\frac{V_2}{V_1}\right)^{\gamma-1} = 1 - \frac{1}{r^{\gamma-1}} \tag{2.2}$$

It may be noted that in the above analysis, c_v is assumed to be constant. This analysis can also be carried out using properties of air varying as a function of temperature, by referring to the air tables or by employing correlations.

From equation (2.2), the efficiency of the Otto cycle clearly depends on the compression ratio, r. The variation of efficiency as a function of compression ratio, r, is shown in Fig. 2.12. As the compression ratio increases, the efficiency sharply increases initially. When compression ratio exceeds a value of around 5, the rate of increase of efficiency decreases. In practice, the compression ratio of a petrol engine is kept in the range of 8 to 10. This is due to the variation trend of efficiency with compression ratio and further due to a phenomenon called 'knocking', which occurs at high compression ratios.

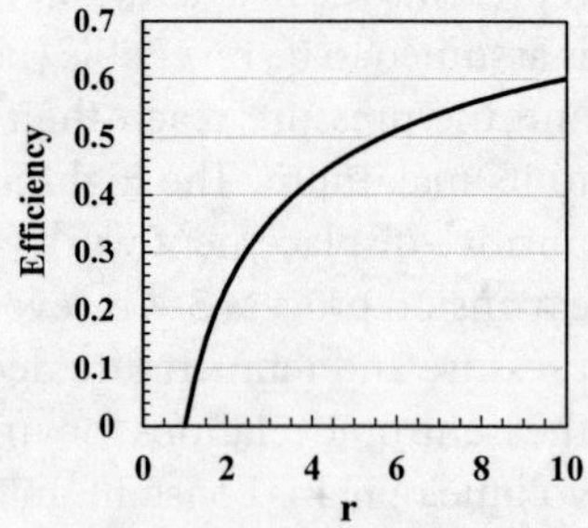

Fig. 2.12: Variation of efficiency of Otto cycle with compression ratio

Example 2.1: At the beginning of the compression process of an air standard Otto cycle, $p_1 = 100$ kPa, $T_1 = 298$ K and $V_1 = 400$ cm³. The maximum temperature in the cycle is 2000 K and the compression ratio is 8. Determine (a) the heat addition, (b) the net work output, (c) the thermal efficiency and (d) the mean effective pressure. For air, specific gas constant, R = 287 J/kg-K and ratio of specific heats, $\gamma = 1.4$.

Solution: Given: $p_1 = 100$ kPa, $T_1 = 298$ K, $V_1 = V_4 = 400$ cm³. $T_3 = 2000$ K, $V_1/V_2 = V_4/V_3 = 8$.

Process 1-2 is isentropic, thus, $p_1V_1^\gamma = p_2V_2^\gamma \Longrightarrow p_2 = 100\times(8)^{1.4} = 1837.92$ kPa.

Using the equation of state (pV = mRT), $m = 100 \times 10^{-3} \times 400 \times 10^{-6}/(287 \times 298) = 0.000468$ kg.

Using equation of state, (T = pV/mR), $T_2 = 1837.92\times50\times10^{-3}/(0.000468\times287) = 684.18$ K.

For constant volume process 2-3, $V_3 = V_2 = 50$ cm³.

Given that $T_3 = 2000$ K. So, using equation of state (p = mRT/V), $p_3 = 5372.64$ kPa.

Process 3-4 is isentropic, thus, $p_3V_3^\gamma = p_4V_4^\gamma \Longrightarrow p_4 = 5372.64 \times (1/8)^{1.4} = 292.322$ kPa.

Using equation of state, $T_4 = 870.55$ K.

Specific heat at constant volume, $c_v = R/(\gamma - 1) = 717.5$ J/kg-K.

Heat addition during constant volume process 2-3, $Q_H = m \times c_v \times \Delta T$

$= 0.000468 \times 717.5 \times (2000 - 684.18) = 441.84$ J.

Work done during isentropic expansion 3-4 = $W_{3-4} = -(U_4 - U_3) = m \times c_v \times (T_3 - T_4) = 379.26$ J.

Isentropic compression work, $W_{1-2} = m \times c_v \times (T_1 - T_2) = -129.675$ J.

Net work output, $W_{net} = 379.26 - 129.675 = 249.58$ J.

Thermal efficiency, $\eta_{th} = W_{net}/Q_H = 56.5\%$.

As per the definition of MEP, $W_{net} = MEP \times (V_1 - V_2) \Longrightarrow MEP = 713.085$ kPa.

Air standard diesel cycle consists of four processes as displayed in p-V and T-S diagrams in Fig. 2.13. In a diesel engine, during the suction stroke, air is taken in as the piston moves down from TDC to BDC. This process is not included in the air standard diesel cycle. In the diesel cycle, the initial state is fixed when the piston is at BDC with a maximum volume of air (V_1) available inside the cylinder. Pressure and temperature are at their minimum values (p_1 and T_1, respectively). Like the Otto cycle, process 1-2 is an adiabatic reversible compression process, where air is compressed to a pressure of

p_2 and temperature increases to T_2. As the piston reaches TDC, the volume occupied by the air is at its minimum value (V_2). Compression ratio (r) is defined as usual as V_1/V_2. However, the compression ratio of a diesel engine (15 to 22) is much higher than that of gasoline engine. As discussed earlier, in the actual diesel engine, at this state, diesel is sprayed through a fuel injector into the cylinder having hot and pressurised air. The diesel droplets vaporize almost instantaneously and diesel vapor mixes with the air. This reactant mixture is usually above a temperature called auto-ignition temperature because of high compression ratio, so that it ignites without a need of an external ignition source such as a spark plug. As the diesel is sprayed and reaction occurs, the heat is released gradually when compared to that in a petrol engine. During this, the piston starts moving down equilibrating the pressure inside the cylinder. Thus, in the air standard diesel cycle, the heat addition is modelled as a constant pressure heat addition as shown by the process 2-3 in Fig. 2.13. The volume at the end of the constant pressure heat addition is called expansion volume (V_3). It may be noted that during heat addition some amount of displacement work occurs due to piston movement. One more ratio, called the cut-off ratio, r_c, is defined for diesel cycle as the ratio of the expansion volume to the clearance volume ($r_c = V_3/V_2$). The cut-off ratio also signifies the volume increase due to heat release. It also denotes the volume when the fuel injection is cut-off. Process 3-4 is reversible adiabatic (isentropic) process, where the piston moves further to reach the BDC. Finally, to complete the cycle, process 4-1, which is the heat rejection at constant volume occurs, as seen in the Otto cycle.

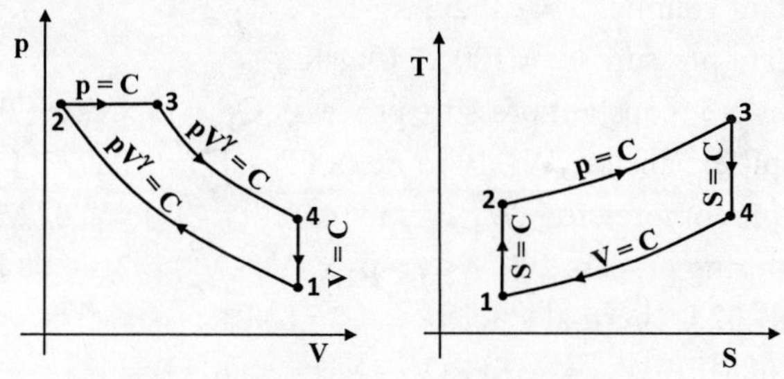

Fig. 2.13: State diagrams for Diesel cycle

Considering c_p and c_v as constants, first law analysis of diesel engine is carried out as follows:

$$Q_{2-3} = mc_p\left(T_3 - T_2\right)$$

$$Q_{4-1} = mc_v\left(T_4 - T_1\right)$$

$$\eta = 1 - \left(\frac{Q_{4-1}}{Q_{2-3}}\right) = 1 - \frac{c_v\left(T_4 - T_1\right)}{c_p\left(T_3 - T_2\right)} = 1 - \frac{T_1\left(T_4/T_1\right) - 1}{\gamma T_2\left(T_3/T_2\right) - 1}$$

Using the isentropic relations for T_2/T_1, T_4/T_3 and using cut-off ratio, the efficiency of diesel engine is written in terms of compression and cut-off ratios. This derivation is left as an exercise to the readers. Finally, the thermal efficiency is written as,

$$\eta = 1 - \frac{1}{r^{\gamma-1}}\frac{r_c^{\gamma} - 1}{\gamma\left(r_c - 1\right)} \tag{2.3}$$

From equations (2.2 and 2.3), it is clear that, for a given compression ratio, r, efficiency of the diesel cycle is less than that of an Otto cycle. For example, if r = 10 and $r_c = 2$, the Otto cycle has an efficiency of 60.2 percent and the diesel cycle has an efficiency of 53.4 percent. As r_c increases, the efficiency of the diesel cycle decreases. As mentioned earlier, a diesel engine operates at much higher compression ratio. Using $r = 20$ and $r_c = 2$, the efficiency of the diesel engine is 64.7 percent. Therefore, due to higher compression ratios, a diesel engine typically operates at a higher efficiency than a gasoline engine.

There is another air standard cycle, called the dual cycle. In this, the heat addition process is split into two processes. Part of the heat is added in a constant volume process and remaining heat is added in a constant pressure process. This cycle has five processes. This cycle resembles the performance of an actual diesel engine more closely. Analysis of this cycle is left as an exercise to the reader.

Example 2.2: At the beginning of the compression process of an air standard Diesel cycle, $p_1 = 100$ kPa, $T_1 = 298$ K and $V_1 = 0.016$ m^3. The maximum temperature in the cycle is 1290 K and the compression ratio is 15. Determine (a) the heat addition, (b) the net work output, (c) the thermal efficiency and (d) the mean effective pressure. For air, specific gas constant, R = 287 J/kg-K and ratio of specific heats, $\gamma = 1.4$.

Solution: Given: $p_1 = 100$ kPa, $T_1 = 298$ K $= T_0$ and $V_1 = V_4 = 0.016$ m^3. $T_3 = 1290$ K, $V_1/V_2 = 15$.

Isentropic compression 1-2: $p_1V_1^\gamma = p_2V_2^\gamma$ ==> $p_2 = 100\times(15)^{1.4} = 4431.26$ kPa.

Using equation of state, m = 100000 × 0.016/(287×298) = 0.0187 kg.

Using equation of state, $T_2 = 4431.26\times10^3 \times 0.001067/(0.0187\times287) = 880.7$ K.

For process 2-3: $p_3 = p_2$. $T_3 = 1290$ K, Thus, using equation of state, $V_3 = 0.00156$ m^3.

Isentropic expansion 3-4: $p_3V_3^\gamma = p_4V_4^\gamma$ ==> $p_4 = 4431.26 \times 10^3 \times (0.00156/0.016)^{1.4} = 170.268$ kPa.

$V_4 = V_1$, thus, using equation of state, $T_4 = 507.61$ K.

Specific heat at constant volume, $c_v = 717.5$ J/kg-K.

Specific heat at constant pressure, $c_p = 1004.5$ J/kg-K.

Heat added in process 2-3 (constant pressure process), $Q_H = m \times c_p \times (T_3 - T_2) = 7688.35$ J.

Work during isentropic expansion, $W_{3\text{-}4} = m \times c_v \times (T_3 - T_4) = 10497.7$ J.

Work during isentropic compression, $W_{1\text{-}2} = m \times c_v \times (T_1 - T_2) = -7822.26$ J.

Displacement work during process 2-3, $W_{2\text{-}3} = p_2 \times (V_3 - V_2) = 2186.08$ J.

Net work, $W_{net} = 4861.52$ J. Thermal efficiency, $\eta_{th} = 63.2\%$.

Using the definition of MEP, $W_{net} = MEP\times(V_1 - V_2)$ ==> MEP = 325.548 kPa.

2.9 VALVE AND PORT TIMING DIAGRAMS

Valve timing is the regulation of the time instants when intake and exhaust valves open and close. Theoretically, it is assumed that the valves open or close instantly. However, there is a finite time required for the opening or closing of a valve. Cams provided on camshafts are designed carefully to achieve smooth operation of the valves, starting at a given time instant (or crank angle) and completing within a given time period. For example, theoretically, the intake valve is expected to open instantly at the TDC, at the end of the exhaust stroke. In practice, to accommodate the time required for valve operation, the intake valve is made to open a few degrees (10° to 25°) of the crank angle before TDC on the exhaust stroke. This will facilitate the complete opening of the intake valve as soon as the piston reaches the TDC and fresh charge flows into the cylinder during the suction stroke. Similarly, theoretically, the inlet valve is expected to close exactly at BDC and the compression stroke should start. In practice, the charge coming into the cylinder has some inertia (momentum) due to pressure difference and this is dependent on the engine speed. Therefore, the rapidly moving piston may run away from the incoming charge. As a result of this, when the piston reaches the BDC, enough time will not be available for the required charge to come into the cylinder. This will reduce the volumetric efficiency of the engine. Therefore, the inlet valve is closed a few degrees (25° to 50°) after BDC, depending on the engine speed. The intake valve setting is done considering the low to high speed range of the engine. The theoretical and actual valve timing diagrams of a four-stroke engine with respect to TDC and BDC are shown in Fig. 2.14.

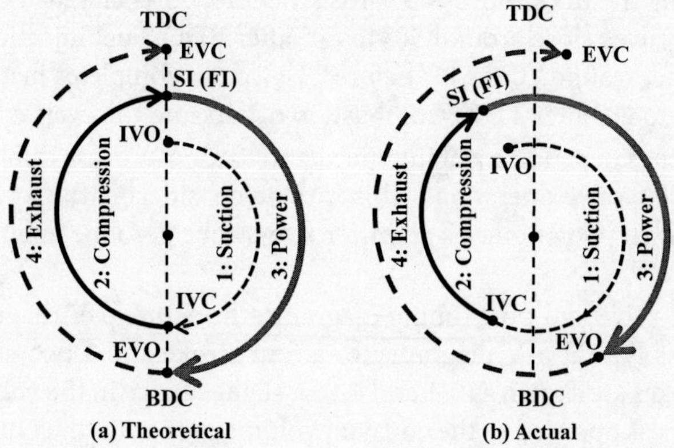

Fig. 2.14: Theoretical and actual valve timing diagrams of four-stroke engines

It can be noted that the spark ignition (SI), in the case of SI engine, or fuel injection (FI) in the case of CI engine, starts at TDC, at the end of the compression stroke. Similar to the time requirement of a valve operation, actuating a spark or injecting the fuel requires some finite time period. To facilitate this, the initiation of the spark (30° to 40°) or the injection of the fuel (5° to 10°) is started a few degrees of crank angle before the TDC on the compression stroke as shown in Fig. 2.14. Similarly, the exhaust valve opening and closing are not done exactly at the BDC and the TDC, respectively, as shown in the theoretical valve timing diagram. The timing of exhaust valve operation also affects the volumetric efficiency. The exhaust valve is opened a few degrees (30° to 35°) before the BDC on the power stroke. This may slightly decrease the work done during the expansion process. However, it reduces the flow work required to expel the exhaust gases during the subsequent exhaust stroke. Similarly, the exhaust valve is closed a few degrees (10° to 15°) after the TDC on the exhaust stroke. This will facilitate better scavenging of the exhaust gases remaining in the clearance volume.

Similar to the valve timing diagram of four-stroke engines, port timing diagrams are drawn for two-stroke engines, indicating the times when the ports are opened and closed. Considering the two-stroke diesel engine discussed in Fig. 2.9, the port timing diagram is drawn as in Fig. 2.15.

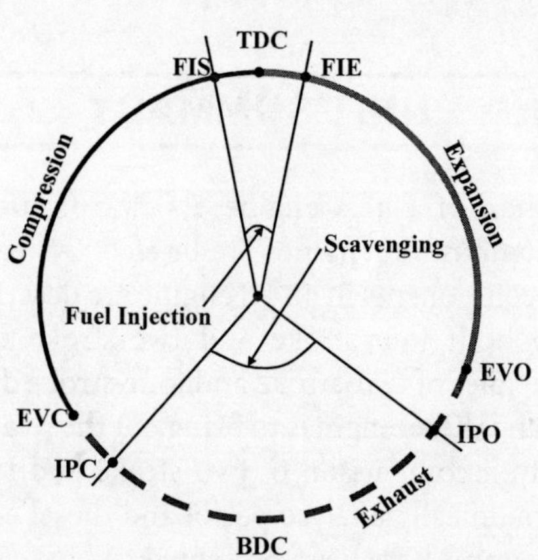

Fig. 2.15: Typical port timing diagram of a two-stroke diesel engine

As the piston moves down during the power stroke, the exhaust valves open (EVO) around 50° to 60° before BDC. Subsequently, the inlet ports open (IPO) around 40° to 45° before BDC, as shown in Fig. 2.15. Piston after reaching the BDC moves upwards. The inlet ports close (IVC) around 40° to 45° after BDC and then exhaust valves close around 50° to 60° after BDC. Fuel injection starts towards the end of the compression stroke, around 10° to 15° before TDC and it completes just after the pistons starts to come down, around 15° to 20° after TDC. Combustion occurs and the cycle continues.

Valve and port timings depend on engine speed and load. A process called tuning is carried out to set appropriate timings for valve operations. This is done considering the low to high speed range (or load) of the engine. Drawing port time diagram for two-stroke gasoline engine is left as an exercise to the readers.

With respect to the valve and port timing diagrams, the actual p-V diagram for an engine can be drawn. Fig. 2.16 presents typical p-V diagrams for a four-stroke and a two-stroke petrol engines. The suction and exhaust strokes are shown as 0-1 and 4-0. A slight change in the volume during heat addition and heat rejection occurs as opposed to the constant volume process in the Otto cycle. The compression and expansion processes are not isentropic. These processes may be approximated as polytropic processes. In the two-stroke engine, suction and scavenging occurs during 0-1. Ignition occurs before the end of compression stroke. Process line 4-0 represents the exhaust stroke. These p-V diagrams are also called indicator diagrams.

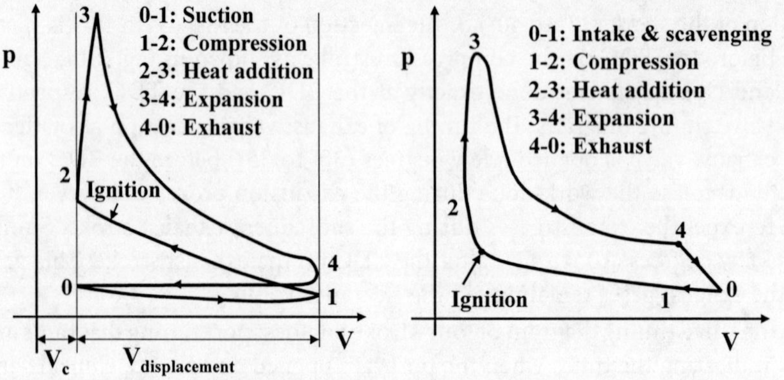

Fig. 2.16: Typical p-V diagrams for four-stroke and two-stroke petrol engines

UNIT SUMMARY

This unit starts with the definition of a heat engine, its classifications and applications. Differences between internal and external combustion engines are briefed. Systematic classifications of IC engines have been presented. Important components in an IC engine are described after this. Working principles of a petrol engine considering both four-stroke and two-stroke modes are reported with simple sketches. Similarly, working principles of two-stroke and four-stroke diesel engines are briefly discussed. Tabulated comparison of petrol and diesel engines to bring out the relative advantages and disadvantages are presented next. Subsequently, a comparison of two-stroke and four-stroke engines is made. Ideal air standard cycles to thermodynamically analyse petrol and diesel engine cycles are reported. Finally, typical valve and port timing diagrams have been presented.

EXERCISES

Multiple Choice Questions

1. Heat engine is a device that converts
   (a) work to heat (b) chemical energy to heat
   (c) heat to work (d) potential energy to work

2. Advantage of reciprocating IC engines over steam power plant is
   (a) higher average temperature (b) improved efficiency
   (c) mechanical construction (d) none of the above

3. Heat transfer to the Carnot cycle occurs in
   (a) an isothermal process (b) a constant volume process
   (c) a constant pressure process (d) a polytropic process

4. Typical range of the compression ratio of a diesel engine is
   (a) 8 to 12 (b) 15 to 22
   (c) 10 to 14 (d) none of the above

5. A two-stroke engine completes a cycle when crankshaft rotates by
   (a) 360° (b) 720°
   (c) 180° (d) 270°

6. Intake charge of a diesel engine is
   (a) fuel + air (b) air alone
   (c) air + lubricating oil (d) air + Fuel + lubricating oil

7. Gudgeon pin links
   (a) piston and small end of connecting rod
   (b) piston and big end of connecting rod
   (c) big end of connecting rod and crank
   (d) small end of connecting rod and crank

8. Thermal efficiency of a diesel engine is higher than that of a petrol engine due to
   (a) the type of the fuel used (b) higher weight of diesel engine
   (c) higher compression ratio (d) constant pressure heat addition

9. Total volume of the cylinder in an IC engine of bore D and stroke L is
   (a) $\pi D^2 L/4$ + clearance volume (b) $\pi D^2 L/4$ - clearance volume
   (c) $\pi D^2 L/4 \times$ clearance volume (d) $\pi D^2 L/4$

10. In four-stroke petrol engine, the inlet valve is closed
   (a) at BDC (b) a few degrees before BDC
   (c) at TDC (d) a few degrees after BDC

Answers to Multiple Choice Questions										
1. (c)	2. (b)	3. (a)	4. (b)	5. (a)	6.	(b)	7. (a)	8. (c)	9. (a)	10. (d)

Short and Long Answer Type Questions

1. Tabulate the main differences between internal and external combustion engines.
2. Draw the state diagrams of an Otto cycle in p-V and T-S coordinate.
3. Define the following terms (a) bore (b) stroke (c) compression ratio and (d) clearance ratio.
4. Draw the typical variation of thermal efficiency of Otto cycle as a function of the compression ratio.
5. Define cut-off ratio of the diesel cycle.
6. Write an expression for the thermal efficiency of air standard diesel cycle in terms of compression and cut-off ratios.
7. Classify IC engines based on ignition.
8. With neat sketches, explain various configurations of multi-cylinder engines.
9. Draw a neat schematic of a spark-ignition engine with all major components.
10. Write briefly about the function of the cylinder head.
11. How reciprocating motion of a piston is converted to a rotary motion?
12. With the help of neat sketches, explain the working principle of a four-stroke petrol engine.
13. With the help of neat sketches, explain the working principle of a four-stroke diesel engine.
14. With the help of neat sketches, explain the working principle of a two-stroke petrol engine.
15. With the help of neat sketches, explain the working principle of a two-stroke diesel engine.
16. Write briefly about uniflow and cross-flow scavenging.
17. Tabulate the important differences between petrol and diesel engines.
18. Tabulate the main differences between two-stroke and four-stroke engines.
19. Draw typical valve timing diagram of a four-stroke petrol engine.
20. Draw typical port timing diagram of a two-stroke diesel engine.

Numerical Problems

1. A Carnot engine operates between two reservoirs of 450 K and 300 K. The cycle using air has an initial state pressure of 100 kPa and volume of 0.1 m^3. During the isothermal expansion, the volume increases to three times the initial volume. Determine the net work done and the thermal efficiency. For air, R = 287 J/kg-K and c_v = 717.5 J/kg-K.
2. Consider an air standard Otto cycle with a compression ratio of 10. At the beginning of the compression process, pressure and temperature are 100 kPa and 300 K, respectively. The maximum temperature in the cycle is 2000 K. Determine the thermal efficiency and the mean effective pressure. For air, R = 287 J/kg-K and c_v = 717.5 J/kg-K.
3. Consider an air standard diesel cycle that has a compression ratio of 15 and a cut-off ratio of 2. At the start of the compression process, the pressure and temperature are 2 bar and 473 K, respectively. Calculate the thermal efficiency and the mean effective pressure. For air, R = 287 J/kg-K and c_p = 1004.5 J/kg-K.

PRACTICAL

Carbon residue test using Conradson apparatus

In IC engines, commonly petroleum products are used. These oils (fuel and lubricating) are subjected to various thermal conditions during the operation of an engine. To qualify the low volatile oils such as diesel and kerosene, carbon residue test is carried out. The carbon residue test indicates the tendency of the oil to form a carbon based residue, usually called coke or thermal coke, when subject to high temperatures. Carbon residues can deposit over fuel injector, ports and valves and deteriorate the engine performance. An apparatus used for determining the carbon residue is called Conradson apparatus. In this apparatus, 5 grams of fuel sample is taken in a crucible, made of iron. This crucible is kept within another crucible, called the Skidmore crucible, which is also a part of the apparatus. Both the crucibles are closed using a lid having holes for the vapours to escape. An electric oven is used to heat the fuel sample in a controlled manner. A heating rate of 10°C per minute is usually used to increase the temperature of the oven up to 500°C and maintain it for 15 minutes. During this period, pyrolysis of the fuel occurs, where gaseous products escape from the fuel sample. Inert gas, nitrogen, is used to purge the pyrolysis products at a certain flow rate. The oven is shut-off and nitrogen flow is allowed such that the sample cools to 150°C. The crucible is taken out and the sample is further cooled temperature to 30°C in a desiccator. Finally, the weight of the carbon residue is measured using a precision weighing balance. The percent of weight of carbon residue with respect to the weight of the fuel sample is calculated. This should be below a certain value for smooth operation of the engine.

Instead of the electric oven, a Bunsen burner is also used for heating the sample in some versions of the apparatus. In this case, an additional nickel or iron crucible is used to hold the Skidmore crucible within a sand bath for uniform heating. The Skidmore apparatus in turn holds the porcelain crucible. A schematic of a typical Conradson apparatus is shown in Fig. 2.17. This type of apparatus is usually manually controlled based on the visual observation and temperature measurement. Instructions of use will be available in the manual of the apparatus.

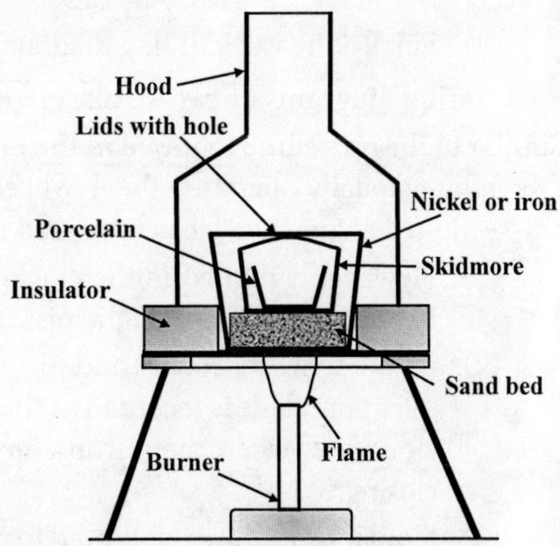

Fig. 2.17: Schematic of a typical Conradson apparatus

Assembling and disassembling of I.C. Engines

In section 2.3, important components of an IC engine have been presented. An IC engine consists of several parts and its assembly is quite complex. It is not easy to understand them by just reading the theory from a book. In a typical lab unit, usually a single cylinder IC engine will be available for thorough study. This engine can be disassembled and each part therein can be studied carefully. Based on the type of the engine, a manual will be provided to explain the procedure for disassembling and assembling the engine back to shape.

Valve timing diagrams of four-stroke engines

In section 2.9, valve timing diagrams have been presented. The actual valve timing diagram for a four-stroke engine can be measured and drawn from an engine installed in a lab. The engine may be a cut-sectioned engine or with an openable top cover, which facilitates visual observation. This is done by manually rotating the flywheel and observing the movement of the piston along with opening and closing of the inlet and the exhaust valves. Following steps are followed.

(1) In the flywheel of the engine, a circumferential scale with markings is attached. This scale can directly indicate the angle of rotation or used to measure the arc length between two marked points for the corresponding movement of the flywheel.

(2) Flywheel is slowly rotated in the clockwise direction such that the piston moves up and reaches the TDC. At this point, an indication is made in the scale for TDC with respect to a reference location called indicator.

(3) Flywheel is rotated further in the clockwise direction to enable the movement of the piston towards BDC until the piston reaches BDC. The corresponding angle is marked in the scale as BDC. In fact, BDC will be 180° away from the TDC.

(4) The opening and closing of inlet valves are then carefully noted by further rotating the flywheel gradually in the clockwise direction. The angle at which the inlet valve just opens is marked on the scale with respect to TDC or BDC, which is observed to be nearer. Similarly, the angle corresponding to the complete closing of the inlet valve is indicated in the scale. Whether the given event happens before or after TDC or BDC is also noted.

(5) In the case of a SI engine, by rotating the flywheel further in the clockwise direction, at a certain position, spark plug is activated by battery or magneto and spark ignition occurs. This angle is noted. In the case of the diesel engine, fuel injection starts at a given angle and stops at a later angle of the flywheel rotation. These are noted carefully.

(6) By further rotating the flywheel in the clockwise direction, the angles corresponding to the opening and closing of exhaust valves are noted with respect to TDC or BDC in the similar manner.

(7) If instead of angles, only the arc lengths are measured, the corresponding angles are calculated.

(8) Finally, the valve timing diagram is drawn for the given engine.

Port timing diagrams of two-stroke engines

Similar to the procedure followed in the measurement of valve timing diagram, a port timing diagram is drawn by manually operating the flywheel of a two-stroke engine. Since ports are involved, generally a cut-sectioned engine in a lab can be used for this study. Following steps are followed.

(1) Flywheel is rotated in the clockwise direction slowly. Angles corresponding to the TDC and BDC are marked when the piston reaches these locations.

(2) As the flywheel rotates and piston moves, the inlet port appears indicating the opening of the inlet port. This is recorded as the angle for inlet port opening. On further rotating the flywheel clockwise, when the piston completely covers the port, that angle is recorded as inlet valve closing.

(3) Similar procedure is followed to record the opening and closing of the transfer port and exhaust port.

(4) In the case of SI engine, the angle at which a spark is generated is noted. In the case of CI engine, the start and end angles of fuel injection are noted.

(5) These angles are indicated with respect to TDC and BDC in the port timing diagram.

There are several models for IC engines of different types through which the nature of the components used and working principle can be studied.

REFERENCES AND SUGGESTED READINGS

1. J. B. Heywood, Internal Combustion Engine Fundamentals, McGraw Hill Inc., 1988.
2. R. Stone, Introduction to Internal Combustion Engines, Macmillan Press Ltd., 1999.
3. H. N. Gupta, Fundamentals of Internal Combustion Engines, PHI Learning Pvt. Ltd., 2009.
4. N. Ganesan, IC Engines, Tata McGraw Hill Pvt. Ltd., 2012.

Dynamic QR Code for Further Reading

1. NPTEL course, IC Engines and Gas Turbines by Prof. Pranab K. Mondal, Department of Mechanical Engineering, IIT Guwahati.

Scan Me

2. A website showing IC engine components

Scan Me

3 I. C. Engine Systems

UNIT SPECIFICS

Through this unit, the following aspects are discussed:

- Fuel induction system for petrol engines - carburettors;
- Fuel injection systems for diesel engines - fuel injectors and pumps;
- Cooling system – air cooling and water cooling – thermosiphon and radiators;
- Ignition system – battery coil ignition and magneto ignition;
- Lubricating systems;
- Governing of IC engines – different methods;
- Concept of supercharging.

Important systems of IC engines are fuel injection system, ignition system, cooling system and lubricating system. This unit briefly presents the basics of these systems.

A mixture of petrol vapor and air is supplied to a petrol engine. The fuel system for petrol engine consists of a device that helps in thoroughly mixing the petrol vapor and air in proper proportions. This device is called carburettor. Different types of carburettors, which include simple and Zenith types, are briefly explained in this unit. A diesel engine has a fuel injection system that injects fuel droplets into hot turbulent air environment within the cylinder. The fuel injection system in a diesel engine therefore has a fuel pump and injectors called atomizers. A brief description of types of fuel pumps and injectors is discussed in this unit.

Due to material constraints, the components in an IC engine require continuous cooling. Based on the capacity of an engine, air or water may be used as cooling fluids. In general, small engines (low power) of two-wheelers employ air cooling and vehicles with multi-cylinder engines (high power) employ water cooling. Basics of air and water cooling are presented in this unit. Further, two types of water cooling systems are also briefly presented.

In SI engines, an ignition system is crucial. There are two types of ignition systems. One is the battery coil ignition system and the other is magneto ignition system. A brief discussion on both of these types is presented in this unit.

Lubricating system is another important system in all types of engines. A brief introduction of types of lubricating systems is reported in this unit.

Different types of governing mechanisms used in IC engines are presented subsequently. Finally, basics and objectives of supercharging are discussed.

RATIONALE

The third unit of this book helps the students to get an overall idea about the important systems in IC engines, namely, the fuel supply system, cooling system, ignition system and lubricating system. Students can understand the working of different types of carburettors used in petrol engines, and fuel injectors and pumps, used in diesel engines. This unit helps the students to understand the nature of air cooling system and two types of water cooling systems, namely, the thermosiphon and radiator based systems. Students will be able to describe battery coil and magneto ignition systems and explain their working principles. They can also draw the line diagrams of lubricating systems. This unit makes students to understand the concept of governing IC engines and methods used for this purpose. Students will also understand the concepts related to supercharging.

PRE-REQUISITES

Basic Mechanical Engineering (MEPC102)

UNIT OUTCOMES

List of outcomes of this unit is as follows:

U3-O1: Know fuel systems in petrol and diesel engines along with their working principles
U3-O2: Understand the types of cooling systems and compare them
U3-O3: Describe different types of ignition systems and outline their working principles
U3-O4: Know lubricating systems and draw line diagrams to describe them
U3-O5: Understand governing of engines and supercharging

Unit-3 Outcomes	EXPECTED MAPPING WITH COURSE OUTCOMES (1- Weak Correlation; 2- Medium Correlation; 3- Strong Correlation)				
	CO-1	CO-2	CO-3	CO-4	CO-5
U3-O1	-	3	-	-	-
U3-O2	-	3	-	-	-
U3-O3	-	3	-	-	-
U3-O4	-	3	-	-	-
U3-O5	-	3	-	-	-

3.1 FUEL SYSTEMS

In IC engines, a suitable fuel supply system is required to supply fuel (petrol or diesel) at an appropriate time instant and at a required rate based on the engine load and speed. In SI engines, a mixture of petrol vapor and air in appropriate proportions is supplied to the cylinder during the suction stroke. In CI engines, diesel is supplied through a pump to injectors (also known as atomizers) and small droplets of diesel are sprayed into the cylinder containing hot air towards the end of the compression stroke. Therefore, the fuel injection systems are quite different in these two engines. In this section, some fundamentals of fuel systems in SI and CI engines are discussed.

3.1.1 Fuel Systems for Petrol Engines

In petrol engines, a device called carburettor is used to mix petrol and air in the required proportions. A carburettor should be able to deliver a mixture of air and petrol vapor in required proportions based on the engine speed. Fig. 3.1 shows the typical fuel-air ratio as a function of throttle opening. A throttle valve is a device used to control the intake of the mixture. When it is fully closed, engine runs with a minimum speed and is said to be idling. When the throttle is fully open, engine runs at its maximum speed. There is a regime of operation called cruising, where engine operates with an almost constant value of fuel-air ratio. The actual fuel-air ratio may be quite different from the theoretical fuel-air ratio. The theoretical fuel-air ratio is the ratio of the amount of fuel (mass or volume) to the amount of air that is just sufficient to burn the given amount of fuel. The actual fuel-air ratio may be lean (having lesser fuel in the mixture than the theoretical) or rich (having more fuel in the mixture than the theoretical).

Idling range is indicated by the curve A-B in Fig. 3.1. When the engine has started and the throttle valve is almost fully closed, the engine requires a fuel-rich mixture, as indicated by point A in Fig. 3.1. As the throttle is opened from A to B, more air is added to the mixture getting into the engine and thus, the fuel-air ratio decreases. Generally, at point B, the mixture will be leaner. This condition provides a good fuel-economy. Further opening of the throttle valve from B to C provides cruising range. Carburettor should be able to provide a leaner mixture in this range at approximately same fuel-air ratio to provide a good fuel-economy. Further opening of the throttle beyond C, creates a condition that the engine operates at an almost fully opened throttle. Higher power is achieved with more fuel burnt. Fuel-air ratio increases to the rich condition at the maximum power condition, indicated by point D in Fig. 3.1. It is clear that the fuel system of the petrol engine should be capable of delivering a fuel-air mixture varying with engine operating condition that depends on the throttle opening.

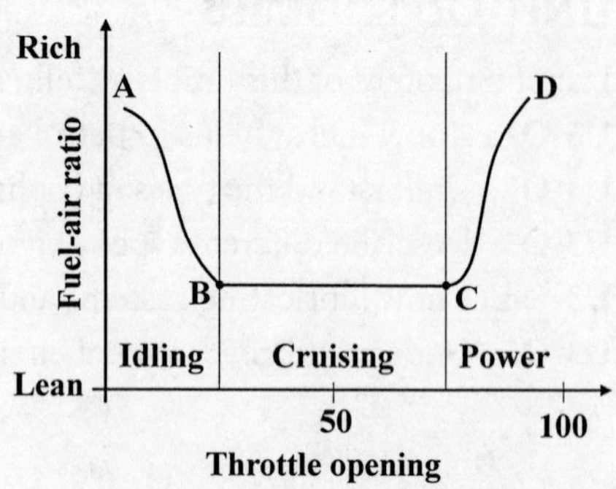

Fig. 3.1: Typical variation of fuel-air ratio as a function of throttle opening

Simple carburettor

If a fluid flows through a pipe with a constriction, such as a choke or an orifice or a venturi, the fluid accelerates and the pressure decreases. At the minimum area for the flow, usually called vena contracta, the velocity reaches a maximum value and the pressure reaches a minimum value. This pressure drop between the upstream section of the pipe and at vena contracta can be used to deliver another fluid into the pipe at the location where the area is minimum. This is called venturi effect. A simple carburettor works on the principle of the venturi effect. Fig. 3.2 presents a schematic of a simple carburettor.

A simple carburettor consists of a vertical carburettor pipe with a venturi and one end attached to an air filter, as shown in Fig. 3.2. It has a float chamber into which petrol is taken in from the main fuel tank. The float chamber has a float that maintains the level of the petrol inside it. When the level falls, the float drops down along with the needle valve, opening the fuel inlet port connected to the fuel tank and fuel flows in. When the fuel flows in, the liquid level increases in the chamber and the float gradually moves up due to buoyancy. When the required fuel level is reached, the port is closed by the needle valve. The float chamber has a small pipe projecting into the carburettor pipe, with a nozzle or an orifice fitted at its end. This is called the main jet. The exit of the main jet is located inside the venturi, where the cross-sectional area of the venturi is the minimum, called the throat. The liquid level in the small pipe is maintained just below the nozzle or orifice, at a small distance Z, as indicated in Fig. 3.2, such that the overflow of fuel is avoided. The float chamber has a vent hole that is exposed to a pressure (usually equal to the atmospheric pressure) that is higher than the pressure at the venturi throat section. The fuel surface in the float chamber is thus maintained at this vent pressure. The pressure at the throat of the venturi is lower and its value is dependent on the air flow rate through the carburettor tube. Based on the pressure difference between the float chamber fuel surface and venturi throat, petrol from the float tank flows into the carburettor pipe at a certain rate. The petrol vaporizes as it flows along with the air. Homogeneous air and fuel mixture exits the carburettor through a throttle valve, which is like a butterfly valve. Based on the engine speed, the throttle valve provides a certain opening area. Based on this, a certain amount of air flows into the carburettor. Pressure drop between the float chamber fuel surface and venturi throat varies with the air flow rate. Depending on this pressure drop, a given quantity of petrol is injected into the carburettor for the given throttle valve opening. When the throttle is fully open, the pressure drop is in the range of 35 mm to 50 mm of the mercury column. A simple calculation of mass flow rate of air can be carried out using Bernoulli's equation, assuming the flow to be incompressible. This is done considering one section just below the air filter (section 1) and another section (section 2) at the venturi throat. The theoretical mass flow rate of air in kg/s based on the pressure ratio between sections 2 and 1 (p_2/p_1) is expressed as,

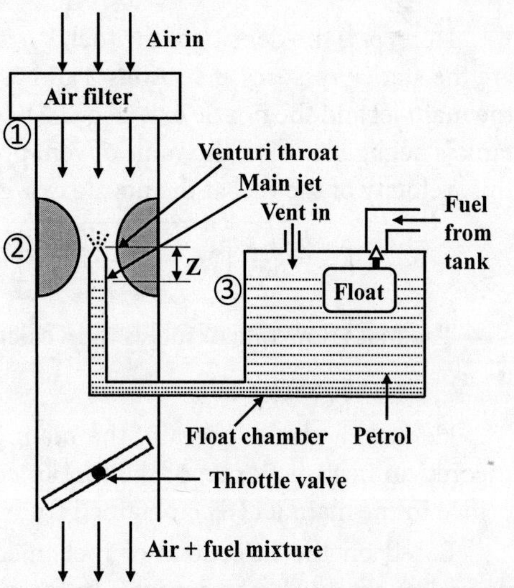

Fig. 3.2: Schematic of a simple carburettor [3]

$$\dot{m}_a = \frac{A_2 p_1}{R\sqrt{T_1}}\sqrt{2c_p\left[\left(\frac{p_2}{p_1}\right)^{\frac{2}{\gamma}} - \left(\frac{p_2}{p_1}\right)^{\frac{\gamma+1}{\gamma}}\right]} \tag{3.1}$$

Here, A is the area, T is the temperature in K, c_p is the specific heat at constant pressure, R is the specific gas constant and γ is the ratio of specific heats. Subscripts 1 and 2 indicate sections 1 and 2, respectively. For air, taking the values of R, c_p and γ as 287 J/kg-K, 1005 J/kg-K and 1.4, respectively, equation (3.1) is written as,

$$\dot{m}_a = 0.1562\frac{A_2 p_1}{\sqrt{T_1}}\sqrt{\left[\left(\frac{p_2}{p_1}\right)^{1.43} - \left(\frac{p_2}{p_1}\right)^{1.71}\right]} \qquad (3.2) \qquad (3.2)$$

The derivation of equation (3.1) is left as an exercise to the reader. It is clear that the mass flow rate of air depends on the throat area, pressure and temperature at section 1, and the ratio of pressure between sections 2 and 1. The actual mass flow rate of air is calculated by multiplying the theoretical mass flow rate in equation (3.2) with the value of coefficient of discharge (C_d). The value of C_d is usually obtained from experiments conducted using the given venturi. By measuring the static pressures at sections 1 and 2, and the temperature at section 1, the mass flow rate of the air can be calculated.

Similarly, to calculate the mass flow rate of the fuel, Bernoulli's equation is applied between the sections 2 and 3 (Fig. 3.2). It is written as,

$$\frac{p_3}{\rho_f} = \frac{p_2}{\rho_f} + \frac{V_{f2}^2}{2} + gZ \tag{3.3}$$

Here, ρ_f is the density of the fuel, V_{f2} is the velocity of the fuel at the nozzle or orifice exit, p_2 and p_3, are the static pressures at sections 2 and 3, respectively, and Z is the distance between the liquid level in the main jet and the nozzle exit (Fig. 3.2). It may be noted that the velocity of fuel at section 3, in the float tank is negligible. Also, the value of vent pressure p_3 is same as that of the atmospheric pressure p_1. Using this, velocity of the fuel at the nozzle exit is calculated as,

$$V_{f2} = \sqrt{\frac{2}{\rho_f}\left[(p_1 - p_2) - \rho_f gZ\right]} \tag{3.4}$$

The mass flow rate of fuel is then calculated using the continuity equation as,

$$\dot{m}_f = \rho_f V_{f2} A_j \tag{3.5}$$

Here, A_j is the exit area of the main jet. The actual fuel flow rate is calculated by multiplying the theoretical mass flow rate of the fuel in equation (3.5) by the coefficient of discharge of the nozzle or orifice in the main jet (C_{dj}), obtained from experimental measurements.

Based on the directions of fuel injection and air flow, carburettors are classified as updraught, downdraught and cross-draught. In the updraught type, air enters from the bottom and leaves at the top. The fuel injection takes place in the same direction as that of air flow. In the downdraught type, air flows from top to bottom (as shown in Figs. 3.2) and the fuel is injected in the opposite direction to that of air flow. The fuel flows freely due to gravity. In the cross-draught type, the carburettor tube is kept horizontally. The fuel is injected in upward direction, perpendicular to the air flow.

The simple carburettor depicted in Fig. 3.2 has been improved in several ways for several reasons. One such improved carburettor is called Zenith carburettor. It has a choke valve, secondary fuel supply pipe called the compensating jet, an additional (compensating) float chamber and an additional orifice connecting the two float chambers, apart from the components in the simple carburettor. Fig. 3.3 shows a schematic of an improved Zenith carburettor.

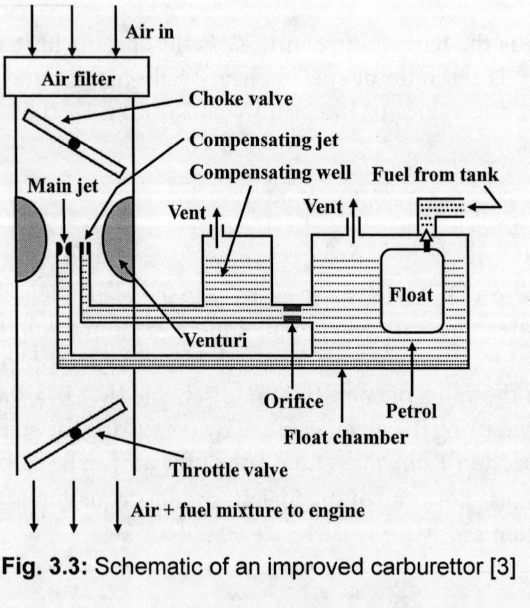

Fig. 3.3: Schematic of an improved carburettor [3]

The choke valve is a butterfly type of valve useful for cold start conditions. When a cold engine starts, especially at low atmospheric temperatures, the engine speed is quite low (~150 rpm). The manifold vacuum produced at this condition may not be enough to induct enough fuel into the carburettor. Thus, the resulting mixture will be very lean and it will be tough to ignite the mixture. Therefore, in cold start conditions, choke valve is kept partially closed to intake lesser amount of air, so that the resultant mixture is fuel rich and ignitable. When the engine warms up, the choke valve is fully opened and a proper lean and flammable mixture is formed. The compensating jet is attached to the additional float chamber called the compensating well. The compensating well is also vented to the atmosphere as the float chamber. The compensating jet is supplied with the fuel from the compensating well through an orifice. When the air flow rate increases, fuel supply through the main jet increases and through the compensating jet decreases. The total fuel supply rate from the main and compensating jets keeps the fuel-air ratio almost constant.

In modern carburettors, several auxiliary components are used. Some of them are air-bleed jet, emulsion tube, air valve and port. Similarly, there are several types of carburettors. Constant choke carburettors (Solex and Zenith carburettors), constant vacuum carburettor (S.U. and Carter carburettors), multiple venturi carburettor, multiple jet carburettor and so on. Details of different types of modern carburettors are available in standard textbooks on IC engines [1-4].

3.1.2 Fuel Systems for Diesel Engines

An important system responsible for proper working of a CI engine is the fuel injection system. A fuel injection system should meet the following requirements:

(1) Injection of the required quantity of fuel per cycle into the cylinder. Since this quantity is small, proper metering of the quantity is vital.
(2) Start and end of the injection should be accurate as per the set timing.
(3) The rate at which injection is done is also important.
(4) Injector should be able to atomize the fuel into small droplets for rapid vaporization.
(5) Proper injection over a given volume within the cylinder to ensure proper mixing.
(6) Ensure uniform distribution of fuel droplets.
(7) In the case of multiple cylinders, an equal quantity of fuel should be injected into each cylinder at appropriate timing.

The fuel injection systems are classified as air injection and solid (airless) injection systems. In the air injection system, an air compressor is used. Fuel is injected into the cylinder using compressed air. The advantage of an air injection system is that it provides better mixing of fuel and air and higher mean effective pressure. It can be used for injecting fuels with higher viscosity. Due to the requirement of compressed air, air injection systems are not used presently. Solid injection systems are also called airless mechanical injection systems. Here, a liquid fuel is directly injected into the cylinder.

Solid injection system comprises of a fuel tank, fuel feed pump to feed fuel from the main tank to the injection system, fuel filters, an injection pump to feed the fuel into the injector at high pressure, governor to control the amount of fuel injected based on the engine load and injector to inject the fuel at high pressure and atomize it. Fuel from the main fuel tank passes through a filter and a fuel feed pump and leaves at a slightly higher pressure. It passes through another filter, where fine impurities are removed. Subsequently, fuel enters the fuel injection pump, where it is pressurized in the range of around 200 - 1700 bar, based on the engine type and load. The fuel is then injected into the cylinder through an injector. There is an arrangement to take back the excess fuel supplied to the injector along with a pressure relief valve. A block diagram of a solid injection system is shown in Fig. 3.4.

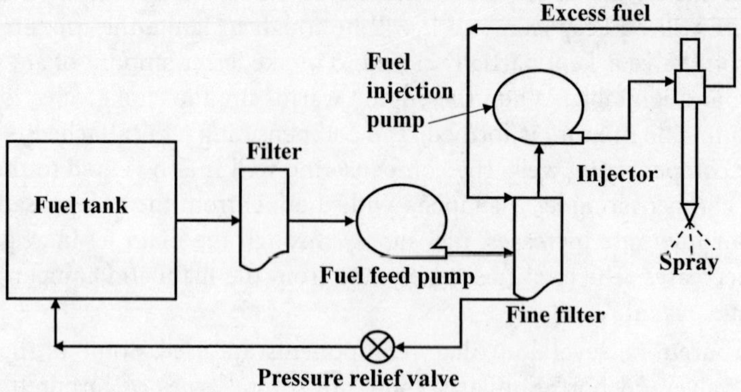

Fig. 3.4: Typical block diagram of a solid injection system

Solid injection systems are classified as (a) individual pump and nozzle system, (b) unit injector system, (c) common rail system and (d) distributor system. All these have the components shown in Fig. 3.4. However, they differ in the method of operation. Individual pump and nozzle systems, unit injector system and common rail systems are schematically shown in Fig. 3.5.

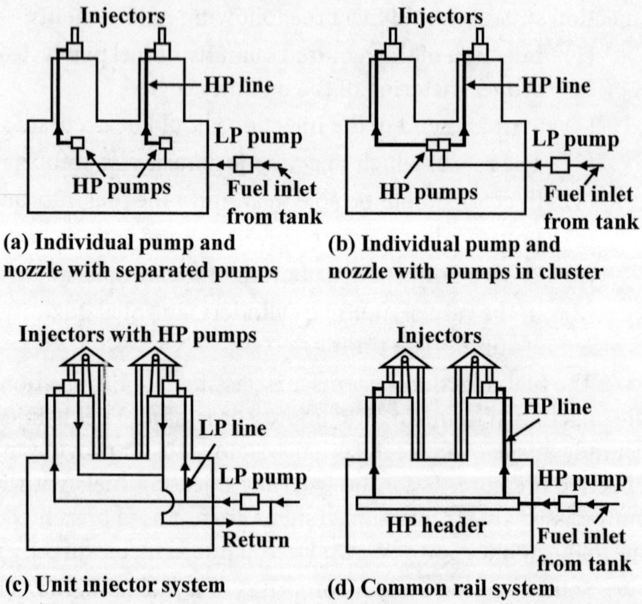

Fig. 3.5: Schematics of solid injection systems [4]

As the name suggests, each cylinder is provided with one pump and one injector in an individual pump and nozzle system. The pumps can be kept separated as shown in Fig. 3.5(a) or they can be in a cluster as shown in Fig. 3.5(b). Fuel is supplied to the high pressure (HP) pumps through a low pressure (LP) pump. The plunger of the high pressure pump is actuated by a cam, so that it produces the required fuel pressure at the correct time instant. The amount of fuel injected is controlled by the stroke of the plunger. In the unit injector system, the fuel pump and injector are combinedly kept in a single housing, called the unit, as shown in Fig. 3.5(c). Each cylinder has one such injector unit. Fuel is supplied up to the unit using a low pressure pump. At an appropriate instant of time, the plunger of the HP pump is activated and the injector sprays the fuel into the cylinder. The amount of fuel injected is controlled by the stroke of the plunger. The common rail system is shown in Fig. 3.5(d). Here, a HP pump supplies fuel under high pressure to a common high pressure header. From this, fuel is supplied to individual injectors through the high pressure lines. A mechanical system consisting of a push rod and rocker arm operates the appropriate valve to supply the fuel to a given cylinder through the dedicated injector. Here, the amount of fuel supplied to each cylinder is controlled by the push rod stroke.

A schematic of the distributor fuel injection system is shown in Fig. 3.6. In the distributor system, there is a rotating distributor, connected to multiple cylinders.

At a given time instant, fuel pump supplies the required quantity of fuel to the distributor, which then supplies it to a given cylinder. At the next appropriate time instant, the distributor receives the fuel from the fuel pump and supplies it to the next cylinder and so on. There is a metering system connected to the fuel pump that supplies the required amount of fuel to the rotating distributor. This aspect decreases the overall cost of the fuel system.

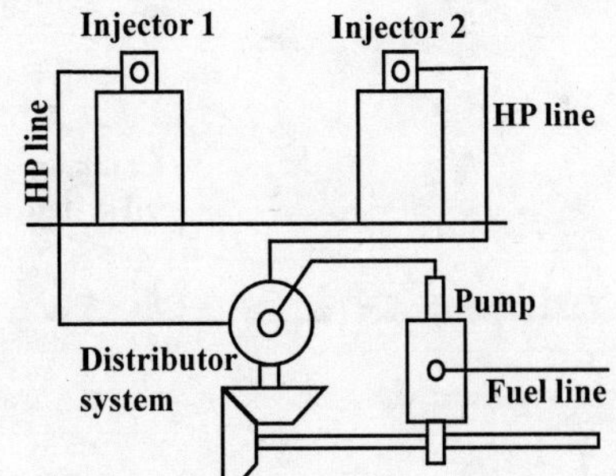

Fig. 3.6: Schematic of a distributor fuel injection system [4]

The fuel feed pump that supplies fuel from the main tank to the fuel injector pump is generally of spring loaded plunger type. The plunger is activated through a pushrod attached to a cam. When the cam is at its minimum height position, suction is created in the fuel feed pump and fuel is fed from the main fuel tank. When the cam reaches its maximum height, the fuel is pushed out of the feed pump to the fuel injector pump. Fuel injection pumps are designed to accurately measure and deliver the given quantity of fuel to the injector at high pressure (150 bar to 200 bar) at a given time instant. There are two types of fuel injection pumps. They are jerk type and distributor type.

An injector assembly comprises of needle valve, compression spring, a nozzle and an injector body. Fuel supplied from the fuel injection pump at high pressure works against the spring and lifts the nozzle valve and opens the injector orifice. As a result, the fuel is sprayed into the cylinder. When the required quantity of fuel is injected, the spring force acts on the nozzle valve and it moves down and closes the injector orifice. A small quantity of fuel leaks through the clearance between the nozzle valve and its guide path and drains back into the fuel tank. There is an adjustable screw that can be used to vary the spring tension and valve opening. A schematic of the fuel feed pump and injector is shown in Fig. 3.7.

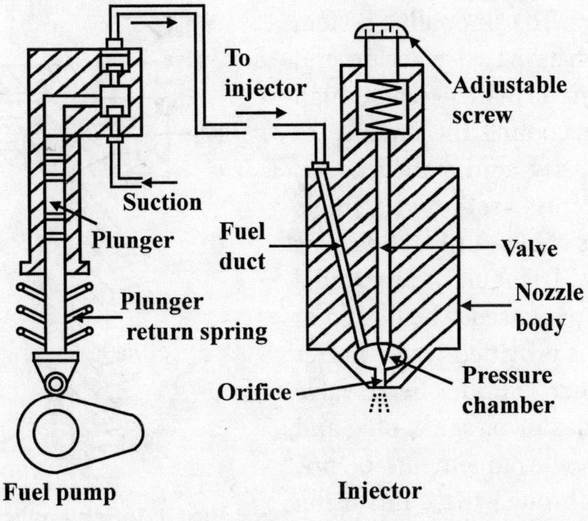

Fig. 3.7: Schematic of a fuel feed pump and injector [4]

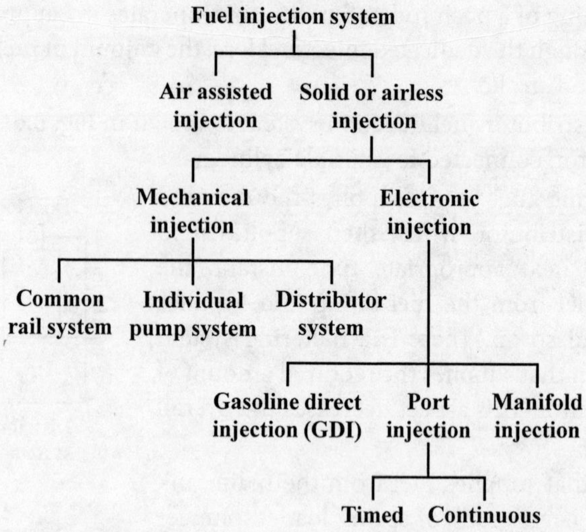

Fig. 3.8: Summary of different fuel injection systems

3.2 COOLING SYSTEMS

An engine requires a properly designed cooling system. Based on the capacity of the engine, air or liquid can be used as the cooling medium. Fundamentally, two types of cooling systems are used. They are liquid cooling system and air cooling system. A liquid cooling system is also called an indirect cooling system and the air cooling system is called the direct cooling system.

3.2.1 Air Cooling Systems

In an air cooling system, a stream of air flows around the cylinder periphery. The heat transfer rate is directly proportional to the temperature difference between the cylinder surface and the air. It is also directly proportional to the area of heat transfer. In order to increase the area of heat transfer, extended metallic surfaces or fins are provided to the periphery of the cylinder. The air cooling system is used in small engines such as in two-wheelers and small cars. It is also used in airplanes, where high velocity air is available for cooling the engine. To orient the air stream properly across the engine, baffles are used. A typical cross-section of a single cylinder engine with fins is shown in Fig. 3.9. Fins of different shapes, such as, triangular, trapezoidal and rectangular, are commonly used. The design of fins is such that more area is provided where hotter surfaces are present. Cylinder, cylinder head, valve ports, space around fuel injector or spark plug and so on are cooled by proper arrangements of fins and orienting the air flow through these fins using baffles.

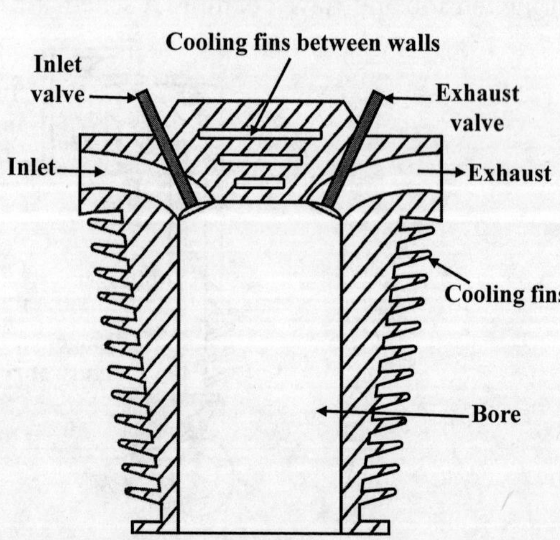

Fig. 3.9: Schematic of an engine cylinder with cooling fins [4]

3.2.2 Water Cooling Systems

In many liquid cooling systems, mainly water is used for cooling. In several modern vehicles, a mixture of water and anti-freeze chemicals such as ethylene glycol is used. Water or coolant is circulated through the jackets provided surrounding the outer surface of the engine cylinder, cylinder head, valve ports and so on. The water flows through the jacket exchanging heat from the hot parts of the engine. The hot water then flows through a radiator, where it is cooled by air. Radiator is a heat exchanger having several tubes through which the water flows and over the water tubes, air flows through passages having fins. Air is drawn through the radiator with the help of a fan as well as by the movement of the vehicle. The air stream exchanges heat with the hot water and cools the water to the required extent. The cool water is again sent through the jacket and this cycle continues. A thermostat is used to control the temperature of the water. The thermostat controls the flow of water through the radiator based on its temperature and prevents water circulation through the radiator if the water temperature is below a certain value. For example, during cold start-up, water is not circulated through the radiator until the engine warms up. In several automobiles, a water pump is used to circulate the water to the jacket through a tube fitted in the front end of the block. In a few cases, natural circulation of water caused by the thermosyphon effect is also used.

Fig. 3.10 shows the thermosyphon based water circulation. The water flows through the water jacket surrounding the cylinder of the engine (A) and is heated by the hot engine parts. Hot water has a relatively lower density. Thus, due to buoyancy, the hot water travels up and enters the top of the radiator (B). This hot water slowly cools down by exchanging heat with the air flowing past the radiator by convective heat transfer. Fan is used to increase the cooling rate by inducing forced convection. Relatively colder liquid moves down the radiator tubes causing recirculation in a natural manner. In order to ensure circulation and cooler water reaching back the engine, the water jackets in the engine are located at a lower height than the radiator. Even though this system has advantages in terms of simplicity, no pump requirement and natural water circulation, this system may not be able to take care of higher rate of water flow as required in high capacity engines.

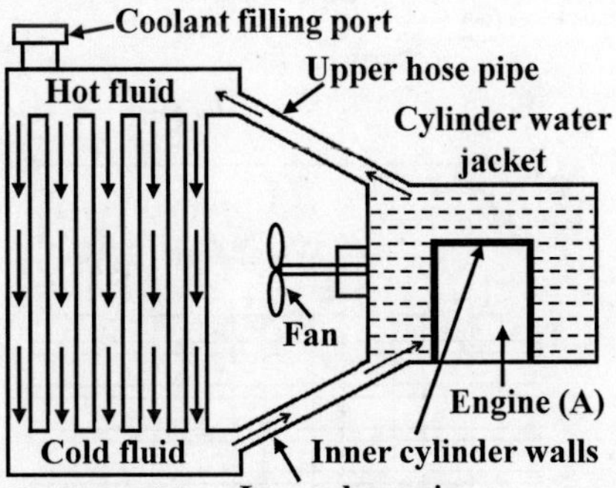

Fig. 3.10: Thermosyphon based water circulation system [4]

In several automobiles such as cars, busses and trucks, forced water circulation using a water pump is used. A block diagram of forced water cooling system, consisting of a water pump, thermostat, radiator and a pump, is shown in Fig. 3.11. Water is supplied to the engine jackets through a pump, which is usually a centrifugal pump. The bottom exit of the radiator tube, where colder water comes out, is connected to the suction side of the pump. The colder water at a required flow rate is supplied by the pump continuously. The water after exchanging heat with the engine parts flows through a thermostat. Based on the temperature of the water, thermostat allows the water to flow through the radiator. Or it is directly supplied to the pump. Bellow type and wax-element type thermostats are used in engine applications. The water flowing through the radiator tubes is cooled by the air flow. A fan draws the air through the spaces between the water tubes in the radiator. Air flow also occurs due to the forward movement of the vehicle.

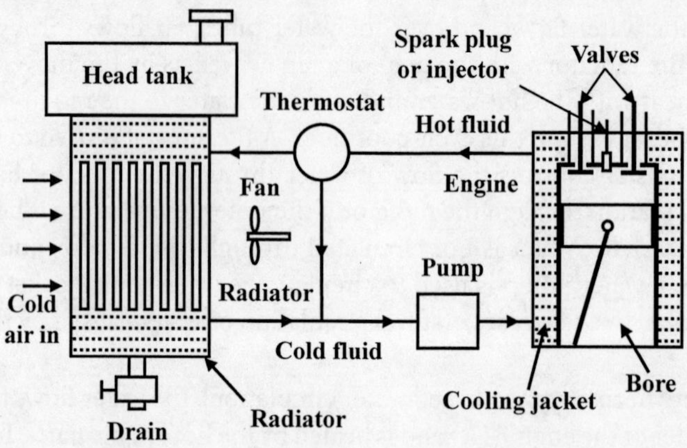

Fig. 3.11: Forced water cooling arrangement [4]

The radiator essentially has two tanks on the top and bottom. The inlet to the upper tanks has a filter system to filter out the dusts in the water. A tube bank (brass tubes with circular or elliptical cross-sections) embedded within several brass fins, constitute the core of the radiator. Water from the upper tank flows through the tube bank to the lower tank. During this, water is cooled by the air flow. A typical arrangement of a radiator is shown in Fig. 3.12 Honeycomb or cellular radiator core is also used in other designs.

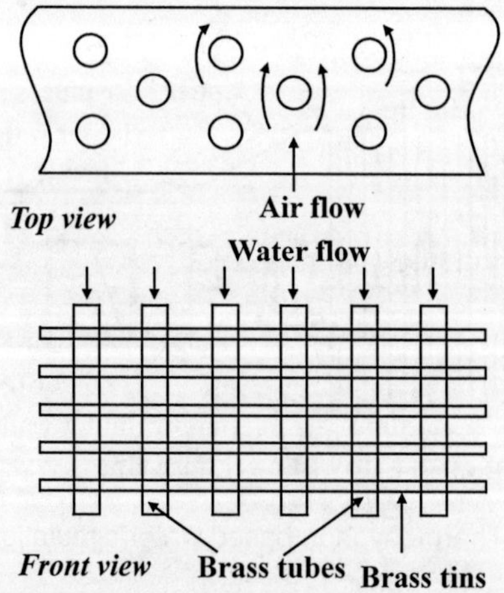

Fig. 3.12: Typical arrangement within a radiator with circular water pipes [4]

A comparison of air and water cooling systems are presented subsequently. Table 3.1 presents the advantages and limitations of water and air cooling systems.

Table 3.1: Comparison of air and water cooling systems

Water cooling system	Air cooling system
Advantages: (i) Due to higher rate of heat transfer, compact design is possible. (ii) Fuel consumption is relatively lower than that in air cooled engines. (iii) Cooling system can be conveniently located. (iv) More control is available in terms of water flow rate.	**Advantages:** (i) Design and installation of the engine without water jackets and with fins are simpler. (ii) Maintenance is cheaper, radiator and pumps are absent. (iii) Coolant liquid may freeze. Such a problem is not present here. (iv) Improved power-to-weight ratio.
Limitations: (i) Relatively complex cooling arrangement. (ii) Additional power for cooling affects power output of the engine. (iii) In the event of coolant leakage and failure, engine could be damaged severely. (iv) Cost and maintenance are high.	**Limitations:** (i) Can be used in small engines only. (ii) Cooling may not be uniform. (iii) High ambient temperature results in poor cooling. (iv) May produce more noise due to air flow through fins. (v) Results in higher operating temperature.

3.3 IGNITION SYSTEMS

In spark-ignition engines, an external energy source is required to ignite the fuel-air mixture. As the name suggests, the ignition energy source is provided by means of a spark generated between two electrodes of a spark plug towards the end of the compression stroke. A schematic of a typical spark plug is shown in Fig, 3.13. In an insulated housing, two electrodes are kept embedded in a shell. One is called the center electrode and another is the side electrode. A specific gap is maintained between these electrodes. The spark plug is connected to the cylinder head of an engine through the threaded portion. When the terminal nut is connected to electrical power, a high voltage exists between the two electrodes and a spark is produced in the spark gap. In burners (Bunsen burner or domestic cook stove), where the fuel-air mixture is continuously supplied, ignition is required only initially and the flame formed over the burner will ignite the incoming reactant mixture subsequently. However, in an SI engine, since the combustion occurs only during a given time period of a cycle and fresh (cooler) charge comes into the cylinder subsequently, the ignition system plays a vital role, and it should be triggered once in each cycle. This external energy source will just initiate the combustion process locally and will not influence the entire combustion phenomenon. Approximately, a spark energy of 1 milli-joule for a time period of a few micro-seconds will be sufficient to initiate the combustion process under ideal conditions. However, in practical conditions, spark energy of the order of about 40 milli-joules for a duration of around 0.5 milli-seconds will be required. The ignition system is classified based on the method of supply of the energy as battery ignition system (also called coil ignition system) and magneto ignition system. The Voltage required to produce a spark across the gap between the two electrodes of the spark plug is in the range of 10000 to 20000 volts.

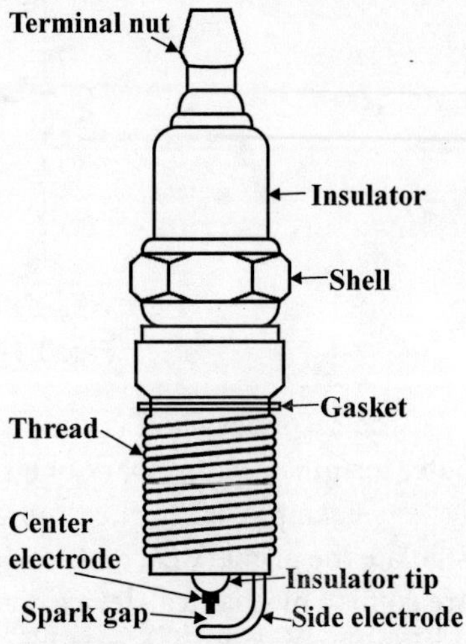

Fig. 3.13: Schematic of the spark plug

The battery or coil ignition system consists of a battery, an ignition coil, a condenser (or a capacitor), a ballast resistor (optional) a circuit (or contact) breaker, a distributor and spark plugs (one for each cylinder). A schematic of the coil ignition system is shown in Fig. 3.14. The ignition coil is used to step up the battery output of 6-12 volts to 10000 to 20000 volts required to produce a spark across the electrodes. The ignition coil has a primary winding and a secondary winding. The primary winding is made of 200 to 300 turns of thick wire (20 standard wire gauge) wound over a soft-iron core to produce a resistance of 1.15 ohms. The secondary winding is present inside the primary winding and it is formed by around 21000 turns of fine copper wire (40 standard wire gauge) wound on a soft-iron core. It is sufficiently insulated to withstand high voltage. One end of the primary coil is connected to the ballast resistor, ignition switch, ammeter and battery. The other end of the primary coil is connected to the condenser and the contact breaker.

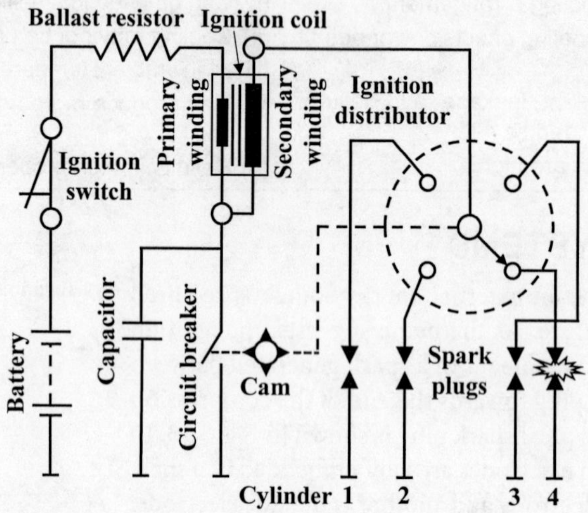

Fig. 3.14: Schematic of a battery or coil ignition system

The secondary coil is connected to the distributor with a central terminal of the spark plugs. The outer terminals of the spark plugs are earthed and connected to the body of the engine. The coil ignition system is employed in medium and heavy spark ignition engines. The ballast resistor is provided to regulate the primary current. An ignition switch is used to turn on or off the ignition system. The contact breaker is a mechanical device that is used for forming or breaking the ignition circuit connected through the ignition coil. It is operated by a cam. The ignition capacitor provides the same function as that of an electrical capacitor. The distributor distributes the electrical energy to individual spark plugs at correct time instant. Brush type and gap type distributors are generally used. A spark plug has a shell made up of steel, insulating material and two electrodes. The central electrode is connected to the secondary winding terminal that provides high tension (voltage) supply. The other electrode is attached to the steel shell by welding. The electrodes are well insulated with porcelain or other ceramic materials. The electrodes are usually made of high nickel alloy. Proper cooling is provided to the steel shell to dissipate the heat.

The magneto ignition system is a special type that has its own electric generator to provide the necessary energy for ignition. A magneto operates on the principle of a generator. A magneto can be a rotating armature type or rotating magnet type. In the rotating armature type, an armature consisting of primary and secondary windings rotate between the north and south poles of a stationary magnet.

In the rotating magnet type, a permanent magnet revolves inside the primary and secondary windings, which are kept stationary. A third type of magneto is called polar inductor type. It has an inductor apart from a magnet and an armature. Rotating magnet type magneto with an armature having primary and secondary windings is also called high tension magneto. It is commonly used in two-wheelers, mopeds, racing cars and reciprocating aircraft engines. A schematic of high tension magneto is shown in Fig. 3.15.

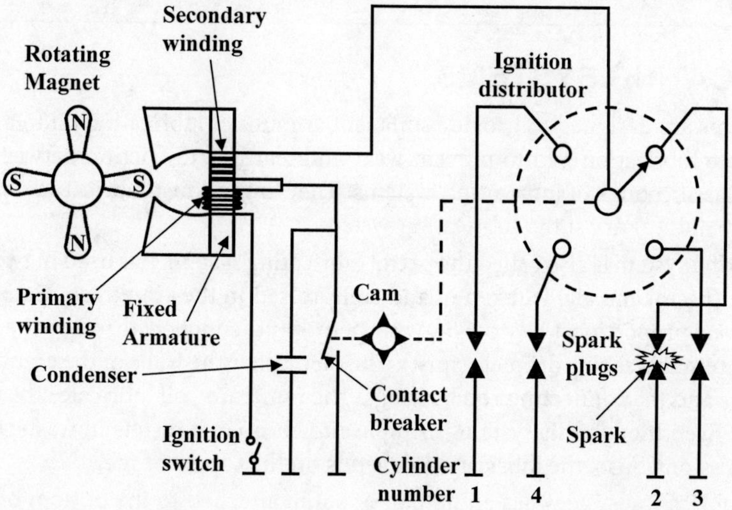

Fig. 3.15: Schematic of a rotating magnet type magneto ignition system

It has a fixed armature with primary and secondary windings, rotating system of magnets, contact breaker, capacitor, distributor, high tension cables and spark plugs. When the engine starts, the cam shaft rotates the magnet connected to it. As the magnet rotates, the magnetic flux changes and this induces an alternating current (AC) in the primary winding when the contact breaker is closed. This charges a capacitor (or condenser) connected to the circuit. The primary current also creates its own magnetic field around the primary and secondary windings. When the contact breaker is closed, the fully charged capacitor discharges. This creates a rapid change in the magnetic flux and as a result, a very high voltage is induced in the secondary winding. This high voltage is sufficient to trigger a spark in one of the spark plugs connected to the distributor through high tension cables. A magneto with no separate secondary winding is called a low tension magneto. Here, voltage step up occurs using an ignition coil. A magneto system is cheap, reliable and needs small maintenance. However, its performance is not up to the mark when the engine rotates at low speeds. It often requires a separate battery to start. The performance improves with increasing speed. A comparison between the coil and magneto ignition systems is reported in Table 3.2.

Table 3.2: Comparison of coil and magneto ignition systems

Battery (or Coil) ignition system	Magneto ignition system
Requires a battery	No battery is required
More maintenance cost	Lesser maintenance cost
Primary current is delivered by a battery	Primary current is generated by a magneto
Performance is very good at low speeds	Performance is poor at low speeds

Battery (or Coil) ignition system	Magneto ignition system
Slight decrease in efficiency with increasing speed	Efficiency improves with increasing speed
Occupies more space	Occupies less space
Used in cars and commercial vehicles	Used in two-wheelers, three-wheelers and racing cars

3.4 LUBRICATING SYSTEMS

Lubrication systems are designed to provide sufficient amount of lubricating oil to all the moving parts to impart adequate lubrication and to prevent wear and tear due to friction between the components. There are three classifications of lubricating systems. They are (a) mist lubricating system (b) wet sump lubricating system and (c) dry sump lubricating system.

Mist lubricating system is also called the petrol lubricating system. It is used in two-stroke SI engines, where the charge (petrol and air) is taken in and compressed in the crankcase. Here, the lubricating oil is mixed in a given proportion (3% to 6%) with petrol and supplied through the carburettor. Petrol vaporizes and oil remains as tiny droplets (mist). The oil reaches the walls of the crankcase and lubricates the main bearings and the connecting rod bearings. The remaining oil lubricates the piston, piston rings and the cylinder. Even though this system is simple and cheaper, it results in wastage of oil, production of smoke and emissions. Also, the lubrication depends on the supply of fuel.

Wet sump lubricating system has an oil pan or sump attached to the bottom of the crankcase that contains the oil. An oil pump is used to supply the oil from this sump to various parts of the engine. After flowing through the required parts of the engine, the oil returns back to the sump assisted by gravity. There are three types of wet sump lubricating systems. They are splash system, splash and pressure system, and pressure feed system. The typical components of wet sump lubricating system are a pump, strainer, filter, pressure regulator and breather. A line diagram of the wet sump lubrication system is shown in Fig. 3.16.

Oil is pumped using a gear pump or a rotor type pump. It passes through an oil strainer, which has a fine mesh screen to filter out particle impurities from the oil. A pressure relief valve is used to maintain a constant delivery pressure. When a certain set pressure is exceeded, this valve opens and some amount of the oil returns to the sump. A major portion of the oil is supplied to the main engine bearings to lubricate them. Some amount of oil passes through another filter, called cartridge filter, where solid particles in the oil are filtered out. This cartridge filter is also called a by-pass filter. Periodically all the oil will pass through this filter and get cleaned up. A clogged filter will not restrict the flow of oil to the engine components. Some fresh air enters the crankcase through the breather to cool the oil.

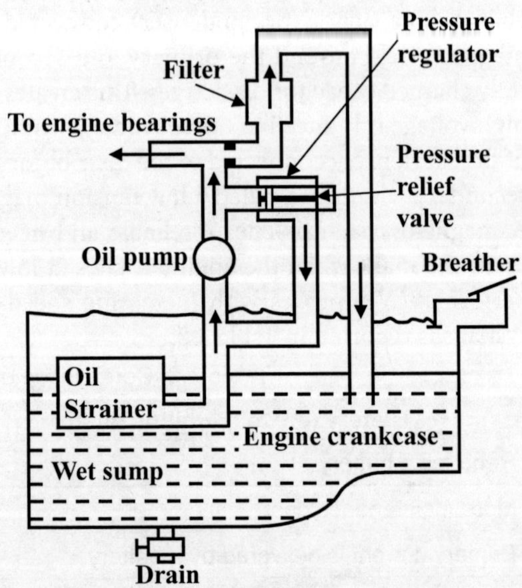

Fig. 3.16: Line diagram of a wet sump lubricating system

In the splash system, splash oil troughs are provided under the big ends of all the connecting rods as shown in Fig. 3.17. Oil from the crankcase is pumped from the sump to splash oil troughs through the strainer and a distributing pipe. A splasher, also called a dipper, is provided in each connecting rod. In each crankshaft revolution, the splasher dips into the oil in the trough and splashes it all over the interior of the crankcase, to the piston, cylinder walls and the bearing surface through holes drilled through the connecting rod. Splash system is commonly used in light motor vehicles.

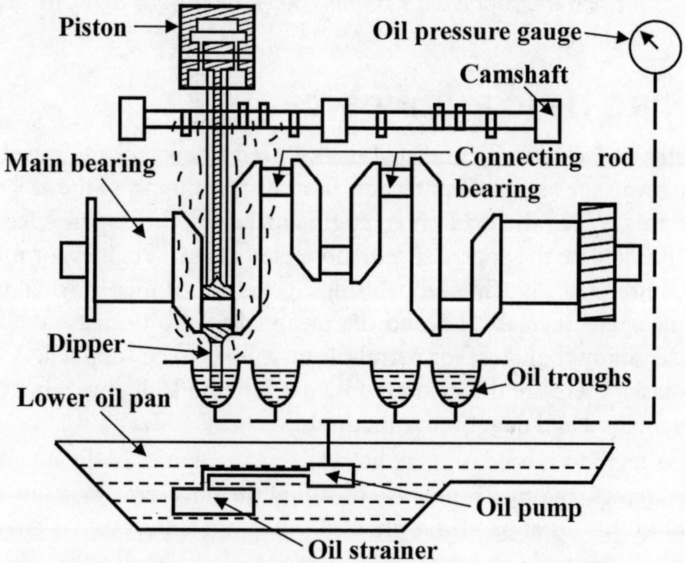

Fig. 3.17: Line diagram of a splash lubricating system

Fig. 3.18 presents the line diagram of a dry sump lubricating system. The dry sump lubricating system uses an external tank to store the oil.

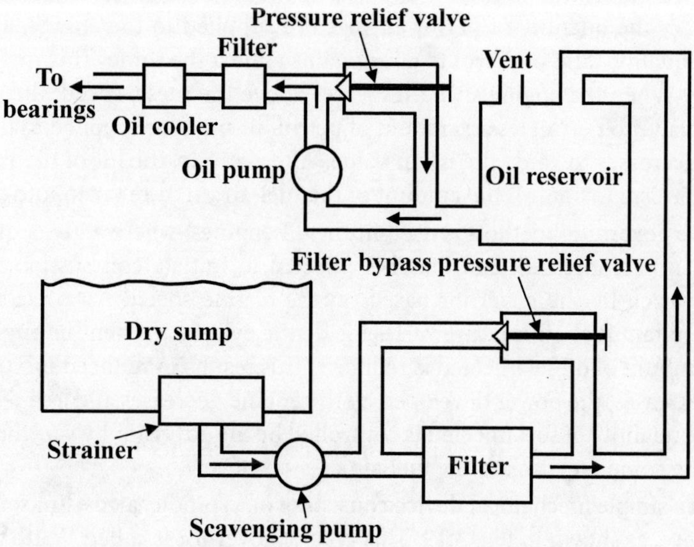

Fig. 3.18: Line diagram of a dry sump lubricating system

An oil pump takes the oil from this tank and circulates it to various bearings. In this manner, the dry sump lubricating system uses only the pressure feed method. The oil dripping from the cylinders and bearings into the crankcase passes through a strainer and is removed using a scavenging pump, which has a higher capacity than the oil pump. Oil from the scavenging pump passes through a filter and a bypass valve, and reaches the supply tank. In this manner, there will be no oil accumulated in the base of the engine crankcase. A pressure relief valve opens when the filter is clogged and enables the oil to by-pass the filter and reach the supply tank. Oil is cooled by using a dedicated oil cooler, where either water or air is used for cooling.

3.5 GOVERNING OF IC ENGINES

A governor is usually a mechanically operated device used to control the speed of the engine and to maintain a constant mean speed in different loads. Basically, the supply of the fuel or the fuel-air mixture is varied to achieve this. When the load on an engine increases, the engine speed decreases below the mean speed value. To increase the engine speed, more diesel (in CI engines) or more petrol-air mixture (in SI engines) is required. This is achieved by using a governor. Similarly, when the load on the engine decreases, the engine speed increases beyond the mean speed. To decrease the engine speed towards the mean value, lesser amount of diesel or petrol-air mixture is to be supplied. A governor is capable of accomplishing this task. There are three commonly used methods of governing. They are hit and miss method, qualitative method and quantitative methods.

The hit and miss method is used in small petrol and gas engines. In the hit and miss method, when the engine speed increases, the fuel supply is cut-off by the governor for a few cycles and the engine performs idle cycles in this duration. These are also called missed cycles. As a result, the engine speed decreases. This method is simple and governing is easier. However, this results in an uneven turning moment, abnormal noise and reduced efficiency. Another way followed in this method is to prevent the opening of the exhaust valve such that idle cycles with exhaust gases are performed by the engine in this duration.

The quantitative governing method is utilized in the SI engines. Here, the governor controls the throttle valve to vary the quantity of petrol-air mixture supplied to the engine, and thus, controls the engine speed. The quality, ratio of petrol to air, remains almost the same. This method is also called the throttle governing. When the engine speed increases above the mean speed, the governor mechanism closes the throttle valve to permit lesser amount of petrol-air mixture supplied to the engine. As a result, the engine speed decreases towards the mean value. Alternatively, the lift of the inlet valve is varied by the governor mechanism to control the amount of the fuel-air mixture taken into the cylinder.

The qualitative governing method is used in the CI engines, where a given quantity of air is taken into the cylinder and compressed, and diesel is injected to initiate combustion. Here, the amount of diesel injected is varied by the governor based on the engine speed. As a result, the quality (or the strength) of the resultant fuel-air mixture varies inside the cylinder. When the engine speed exceeds the mean speed, the amount of diesel injected is reduced. This results in reduced mixture quality. When the mixture quality decreases, the power developed by the engine decreases and as a result, the engine speed also decreases. The quantity of fuel injected is controlled by the governor by varying the stroke of the fuel pump or by-passing some fuel back to the fuel tank.

A governor is a simple mechanical device consisting of a spindle, arms, links, fly balls or fly weights, stoppers and a sleeve, as shown in Fig. 3.19. This type of governor is called Watt's governor. The bottom end of the spindle is connected to the crankshaft of the engine through a set of gears. As the spindle rotates, the fly balls connected to the arms move up due to centrifugal force. This lifts the sleeve connected to the links. There is a provision for connecting the sleeve and the throttle valve or the fuel valve, as shown in Fig. 3.19. As the sleeve moves up or down, the throttle valve or the fuel valve partially closes or opens. The stoppers are located at convenient locations to control the engine speed within a given range.

Improvements to the basic Watt's governor have been done to provide additional control to the governing process. When a central load is provided to the sleeve of a Watt's governor, a Porter governor is obtained. In the Porter governor, when fly balls are attached to extensions of lower links to modify the centrifugal force, a Proell governor is got. Hartnell governor consists of two bell crank levers instead of the links and a central compression spring. Rollers are provided at one end of the bell crank and fly balls are provided at the other end. Such spring loaded governors are used in heavy vehicles.

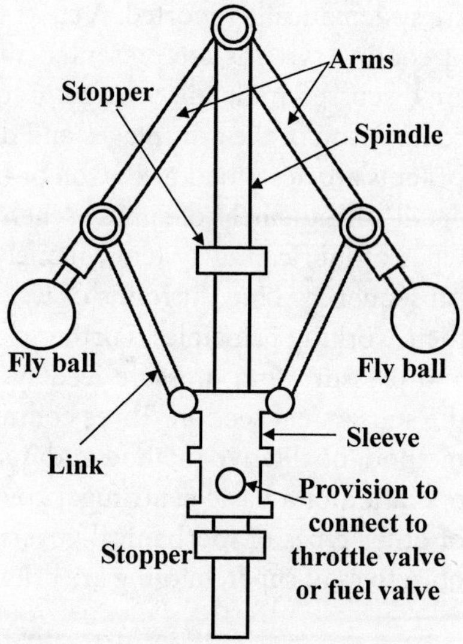

Fig. 3.19: Schematic of a basic Watt's governor

Apart from the mechanical governors, there are two other types of governors used. They are pneumatic and hydraulic governors. Pneumatic governors are used in small and medium-sized engines. Here, air circuit is used for the governing process. Accelerator pedal, connected to a suitable valve or diaphragm, does the governing. Hydraulic governors significantly reduce the high mechanical forces, bearing loads and possible torsional vibrations. The pressure difference across an orifice is used in the governing process. In the modern engines, electronically controlled governors are implemented.

3.6 OBJECTIVES OF SUPERCHARGING

Supercharging in an IC engine is employed to improve its power output. It is also called forced induction of the charge. Basically, the density of the air fed into the cylinders is increased in this process. Supercharging increases the oxygen availability for combustion when compared to conventional (naturally aspirated) charging. As a result, more air and fuel are inducted into the cylinder, which can be effectively burnt, and increase the power output of the engine. Here, a certain percent of engine power output is used for compressing the air. However, the net power output due to supercharging will be more than the power output of an engine with the same capacity using the naturally aspirated charge. Engine using supercharging should be sturdier to withstand additional forces. An additional pressure of the charge may lead to detonation (auto-ignition) in SI engines. Therefore, fuel with improved anti-knock properties should be used. Racing cars, marine engines and heavier automotive engines use supercharging. Supercharging is favourable for engines used in high altitudes, where the pressure drop effects will be compensated by supercharging. There are three types of superchargers used. They are centrifugal type, root's type and vane type. Further information on supercharging may be found in standard IC engine textbooks [1-4].

UNIT SUMMARY

This unit starts with the details of fuel systems used in petrol and diesel engines. The need for a carburettor and types of carburettors used are reported. The requirements of a diesel injector are then discussed. Types of fuel injection systems are reported. Details of solid injection system with the help of line diagrams are systematically reported. A chart to summarize different fuel injection systems is also included. Types of cooling systems are presented subsequently. Air cooling system and liquid (water) cooling system are discussed in detail. Schematics of natural and forced water circulations, and radiator are shown. A comparison of the advantages and disadvantages of air and water cooling systems is tabulated. Ignition systems are described next. Coil or battery ignition system and magnet ignition system are discussed in detail with the help of simple schematics. A comparison of these ignition systems are tabulated. Three types of lubricating systems, namely, mist, wet sump and dry sump lubricating systems are presented subsequently. Line diagrams of wet sump and dry sump lubricating systems are presented to describe their working principles. Further classifications in wet sump lubricating system, namely, splash, splash and pressure, and pressure feed system are briefly reported. Governing of IC engines is presented in the subsequent section. Three commonly used mechanical governing processes, which are hit and miss method, qualitative method and quantitative method, have been elaborated. With a simple sketch, the operation of a basic centrifugal governor, called Watt's governor, has been described. A brief mention of other types of mechanical governors, pneumatic and hydraulic governors is also made. Finally, the objectives of supercharging are briefly reported.

EXERCISES

Multiple Choice Questions

1. During idling conditions, with increasing throttle opening, the fuel-air ratio
(a) increases (b) remains almost constant
(c) decreases (d) none of these

2. When a fluid flows across an orifice, its velocity
(a) increases (b) decreases
(c) remains constant (d) none of these

3. Choke valve in a carburettor controls the flow of
(a) fuel (b) air
(c) fuel-air ratio (d) none of these

4. Fuel injector operates in the pressure range of
(a) 2 – 5 bar (b) 10 – 50 bar
(c) 1000 – 2000 bar (d) 150 – 200 bar

5. Gasoline direct injection system is
(a) an air assisted system (b) a solid injection system
(c) an electronic injection system (d) None of these

6. In a radiator,
   (a) water is used to cool the air
   (b) air is used to cool the water
   (c) air cools the engine
   (d) None of these
7. Thermostat in liquid cooling system is used to bypass
   (a) water from passing through the radiator
   (b) water from passing through the engine jackets
   (c) air from passing through the radiator
   (d) none of these
8. In a coil ignition system, wire of a primary winding is
   (a) thicker
   (b) thinner
   (c) same size as the wire used in the secondary winding
   (d) none of these
9. Lubricating system used in two-stroke engine is
   (a) a wet sump system
   (b) a mist lubricating system
   (c) dry sump lubricating system
   (d) none of these
10. Of the governing methods, the fuel supply is cut-off for a few cycles in
   (a) qualitative method
   (b) quantitative method
   (c) hit and miss method
   (d) none of these

Answers to Multiple Choice Questions									
1. (c)	2. (a)	3. (b)	4. (d)	5. (c)	6. (b)	7. (a)	8. (a)	9. (b)	10. (c)

Short and Long Answer Type Questions

1. What is the function of a carburettor?
2. What is venturi effect?
3. Describe the working principle of a simple carburettor with a schematic.
4. Describe the working principle of a zenith carburettor with a schematic.
5. List the requirements of a fuel injection system for diesel engines.
6. Explain the working principle of a solid injection system with a line diagram.
7. Draw the schematic of a common rail injection system.
8. Explain the working principle of a fuel feed pump.
9. What is the use of a fin?
10. Explain thermosyphon based water circulation system.
11. Draw a simple sketch of forced water cooling system and explain its working principle.
12. Tabulate the advantages and disadvantages of air and water cooling systems.
13. What is the typical energy supplied to produce a spark?
14. What is the range of voltage across the electrodes needed to produce a spark?
15. With a line diagram explain the working of a battery or a coil ignition system.

16. With a line diagram explain the working of a magneto ignition system.
17. Tabulate the differences between coil and magneto ignition systems.
18. What are the types of lubricating systems commonly used?
19. With a line diagram explain the working of a wet sump lubricating system.
20. What are the types of wet sump lubricating systems?
21. With a line diagram explain the working of a dry sump lubricating system.
22. What is meant by governing of IC engines?
23. What are the commonly used methods of IC engine governing? Explain them.
24. What are the types of mechanical governors?
25. What is supercharging? List its advantages.

REFERENCES AND SUGGESTED READINGS

1. J. B. Heywood, Internal Combustion Engine Fundamentals, McGraw Hill Inc., 1988.
2. R. Stone, Introduction to Internal Combustion Engines, Macmillan Press Ltd., 1999.
3. H. N. Gupta, Fundamentals of Internal Combustion Engines, PHI Learning Pvt. Ltd., 2009.
4. N. Ganesan, IC Engines, Tata McGraw Hill Pvt. Ltd., 2012.

Dynamic QR Code for Further Reading

1. Carburation, ignition and lubrication systems, fuel injection system modules in NPTEL Course on "IC Engines and Gas Turbines" by Prof. Pranav K. Mondal and Prof. Vinayak N. Kulkarni, IIT Guwahati.

Scan Me

2. NPTEL course on "Fundamentals of Automotive systems" by Prof. C. S. Shankar Ram, Department of Engineering Design, Indian Institute of Technology Madras.

Scan Me

4 Performance of I.C. Engines

UNIT SPECIFICS

Through this unit, the following aspects are discussed:

- Brake power, indicated power and friction power;
- Methods of determination of brake power, indicated power and friction power;
- Brake and indicated mean effective pressures;
- Brake and indicated thermal efficiencies;
- Mechanical efficiency and relative efficiency;
- Heat balance sheet;
- Numerical problems on I.C. engine performance.

Performance of IC engines can be understood through a series of tests and calculations. Engine power is evaluated using three quantities. They are brake power, indicated power and friction power. Brake power is calculated by measuring the forces at the engine crankshaft. Indicated power is calculated from the measurement of forces in the cylinder. The friction power is the difference of indicated power and the brake power. Methods of determining these powers have been discussed systematically in this unit.

Processes undergone by the engine can be represented in a p-V diagram. From this, the net work delivered by the engine can be determined. Using that the indicated mean effective pressure can be calculated. Similarly, brake mean effective pressure is calculated using brake power. These aspects are discussed in this unit.

Other performance metrics of an IC engine are its efficiencies. Theoretical efficiency of an engine is the air standard efficiency. From brake and indicated powers, brake and indicated thermal efficiencies, respectively, are calculated. An efficiency calculated based on the mechanical losses in an engine, such as frictional losses, is called mechanical efficiency. Relative efficiency is also called the efficiency ratio. It is the ratio of the actual efficiency to the air standard efficiency. Calculations of these efficiencies are illustrated in this unit.

Heat balance of an engine is an important parameter. Energy is supplied to an engine as fuel input. Apart from developing power, a significant part of this energy is carried away by the exhaust gases and cooling agents. A heat balance sheet or a diagram would provide an insight of the overall heat balance of the engine. This aspect is systematically discussed in this unit.

Illustrative numerical problems are provided to make the readers understand the calculation methodology for all these performance metrics.

RATIONALE

The fourth unit of this book helps the students to get an overall idea about the important performance metrics of IC engines, namely, brake power, indicated power, friction power, brake and indicated mean pressure, brake and indicated thermal efficiencies, mechanical and relative efficiencies. Students can understand the methods used to measure and calculate the brake, indicated and friction powers. This unit helps the students to understand the procedure followed to determine various other performance metrics. Students will be able to understand the energy flow in and out of an engine. They can also prepare the heat balance sheet based on the energy flow. This unit makes students to go through illustrative numerical problems demonstrating the calculation of performance metrics of an IC engine. Students will also be able to solve the numerical problems for various conditions.

PRE-REQUISITES

Basic Mechanical Engineering (MEPC102)

UNIT OUTCOMES

List of outcomes of this unit is as follows:

U4-O1: Know about the performance metrics of an IC engine

U4-O2: Understand power, mean pressure, efficiency and heat balance

U4-O3: Describe different methods used to arrive at the performance metrics

U4-O4: Understand the energy flow and prepare heat balance sheet

U4-O5: Solve numerical problems related to the performance of IC engines

Unit-4 Outcomes	EXPECTED MAPPING WITH COURSE OUTCOMES (1- Weak Correlation; 2- Medium Correlation; 3- Strong Correlation)				
	CO-1	CO-2	CO-3	CO-4	CO-5
U4-O1	-	-	3	-	-
U4-O2	-	-	3	-	-
U4-O3	-	-	3	-	-
U4-O4	-	-	3	-	-
U4-O5	-	-	3	-	-

4.1 ENGINE POWER

The fuel supplied to an engine contributes to the energy supply through the engine. This produced energy/power is distributed as three quantities, namely, brake power, indicated power and friction power. Brake power is basically the power available at the engine crankshaft (also called the drive-shaft). This is the power actually delivered by the engine and used to propel the vehicle. Therefore, the brake power is also called shaft power or delivered power. Indicated power is associated with the forces acting on the cylinder. It is the power developed by the working fluid (hot products of combustion of fuel and air), which exerts pressure on the piston inside the cylinder. Thus, it provides an indication of the extent of conversion of chemical energy of the fuel to heat. The indicated power is distributed as brake power and friction power. The friction power is used to overcome friction and pumping losses in an engine.

The pumping losses occur due to the movement of the piston against gas pressure inside the cylinder. The friction losses are contributed by the friction between piston rings and cylinder walls, between shaft and bearings, water pump and so on. The objective of an engine manufacturer should be to decrease the losses due to friction.

4.1.1 Methods of Determination of Engine Power

Brake power

Measurement of brake power of an engine is very important as it represents the actual power delivered by the engine. The torque and angular speed of the engine output shaft are measured to determine the brake power. A dynamometer is used for measuring the torque. Absorption-type and transmission-type are the two types of dynamometers, which are available in use. An absorption-type dynamometer is also called a brake dynamometer. This is because it measures the force required in attempting to stop the engine and uses that to calculate the power transmitted to the engine crankshaft. Prony brake, rope brake, hydraulic and eddy-current dynamometers are a few examples of brake dynamometers. Since the power absorbed by these dynamometers is dissipated as heat, a cooling system is required. In a transmission-type dynamometer, power transmitted to a load connected to the engine is measured using strain gauges or additional transmission arrangements. These are also called torquemeters. Torsion dynamometer, belt transmission dynamometer and epicyclic train dynamometer are the examples of transmission-type dynamometer.

A simple sketch of one of the absorption-type dynamometers, the Prony brake dynamometer, is shown in Fig. 4.1. It has a metal frame containing two blocks of brakes, made of wood. The wood blocks can press over a flywheel or a drum using an arrangement of springs, bolts and nuts. The pressure applied by the brakes on the flywheel or drum can be varied by adjusting the spring pressure using the bolts. The flywheel or the drum is connected to the crankshaft of the engine. The top part of the frame, called the load bar, extends up to a particular distance, r, from the centre of drum, and it is called the arm length. For cooling this dynamometer, water is passed on through the rim of the flywheel or the drum. An arrangement to hang masses is provided at the end of the load bar, as shown in Fig. 4.1. When the crankshaft rotates, the flywheel or the drum also rotates. The total weight of the masses, W (in N), is varied such that the load arm is kept horizontal. At this condition, the torque (T) is calculated as W × r (in N-m). If engine rotates as N revolutions per minute, the power absorbed by the brakes, which is the brake power, is calculated in kJ/cycle or kW, as,

$$BP = \frac{2\pi NT}{60} = \frac{2\pi NWr}{60} \quad (4.1)$$

In a rope-type dynamometer, multiple ropes are wounded over the rim of the flywheel or pulley maintaining uniform spacing between them. The schematic of the rope type dynamometer is shown in Fig. 4.2. The flywheel is coupled to the engine crankshaft. Bottom end of the ropes carry weights (W kg) and the other ends are connected to a spring balance indicating some reading (S kg). If d_f is the diameter of the flywheel and d_r is the diameter of the rope, then, the effective diameter, D, is calculated as $d_f + d_r$. The engine power is absorbed by the friction

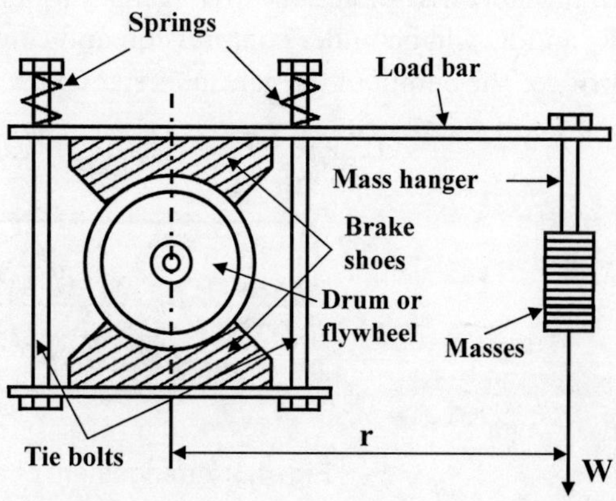

Fig. 4.1: Sketch of a Prony brake dynamometer

between the ropes and the rim of the flywheel. Brake torque is calculated as, (W – S) × g × (D/2) N-m. In a hydraulic dynamometer, the power is absorbed by a fluid, usually water, within which a rotor and a stator connected to the crankshaft rotate. The heat is carried away by the water flowing through the dynamometer. In an eddy current dynamometer, a stator having electromagnets is used. A rotor disc made of copper or steel, connected to the output shaft of the engine, rotates within the stator. As the rotor rotates in the magnetic field produced by the electromagnets, eddy current is produced in the stator, which oppose the rotor motion. The load is controlled by varying the current in the electromagnets. Here also, a moment arm measures the torque and cooling is required for the dissipation of generated heat. Readers may refer to standard textbooks on IC engines [1-4] to get more information in brake-type dynamometers.

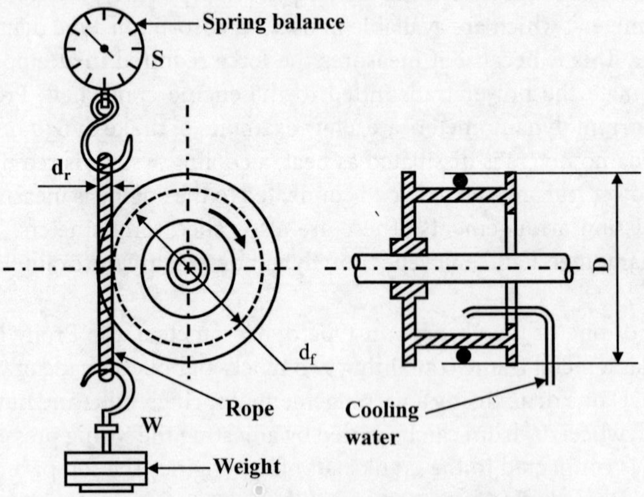

Fig. 4.2: Schematic of a Rope type dynamometer

A transmission-type dynamometer, also called the torque meter, has strain gauges connected to the rotating shaft. As the shaft rotates, angular deformation occurs and the strain gauges measure the strain. From this, the torque is calculated. The arrangement of strain gauges over the shaft is such that the torsion is recorded and axial or transverse load is not recorded. A schematic of the arrangement of strain gauges fixed to the rotating shaft for torque measurement is shown in Fig. 4.3. When the shaft rotates in the clockwise direction, strain gauges R_1 and R_4 will be under tension and elongate, and strain gages R_2 and R_4 will be under compression and contract. These strain gauges are connected to a Wheatstone bridge. The output of the galvanometer connected to it is proportional to the torque on the shaft.

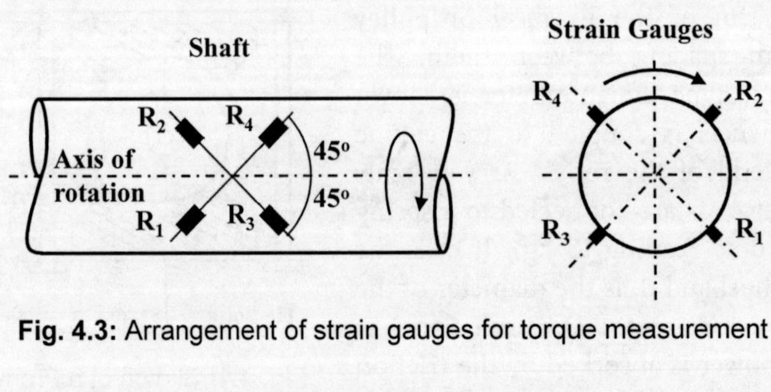

Fig. 4.3: Arrangement of strain gauges for torque measurement

Indicated power

The indicated power provides an indication of the conversion of chemical energy in the fuel to thermal energy inside the engine. It gives a measure of the potential energy output of the engine. The pressure inside the cylinder is measured as a function of the volume of the working fluid, or the crank angle, to determine the indicated power. For this, a mechanical indicator or an electronic indicator is used. An indicator consists of a pressure sensing device, a device for recording the piston displacement and/or angular position of the crankshaft over the complete cycle, and a recording or displaying device to draw pressure vs. volume or crank angle.

The mechanical indicator can be a piston-type indicator or a diaphragm-type indicator. In mechanical indicators, a small spring loaded piston works inside a small cylinder directly connected to the engine cylinder through a valve. Thus, the movement of the piston and the spring force can be suitably recorded. This indicator can exactly record the cycle by tracing the movement of the piston (to a reduced scale) and the gas pressure inside the engine cylinder. An arrangement is made to draw the pressure and piston position (volume) on a paper wrapped over an oscillating drum. The oscillation of the drum is coupled to the piston movement. The pressure variation as a function of volume is drawn on the paper using a stylus connected to the indicator. After the completion of the entire cycle, the paper is unwrapped from the drum to get the p-V diagram, called the indicator diagram. A typical indicated diagram obtained by a mechanical indicator is shown in Fig. 4.4. The clockwise loop of the indicator diagram is the power loop and the area bounded by this loop is the gross work done per cycle. The anti-clockwise loop is a negative loop that indicates the work done in charging and discharging (called the pumping loop). The indicated work done per cycle is the net work done by the engine per cycle. The gross work done per cycle contributes to the gross power GP and the pumping work done per cycle contributes to the pumping power. From these, the indicated power, IP, is calculated as,

$$IP = GP - PP$$

In mechanical indicators, a spring with a given spring constant (k_i in Pa/m) is used. The average height of the indicator diagram (h_i) is calculated as net area of the indicator diagram (A_{ni}) divided by the length of the indicator diagram, L_d. The indicated power estimated using a mechanical indicator is not much accurate due to the inertia of the moving parts, friction, backlash and so on.

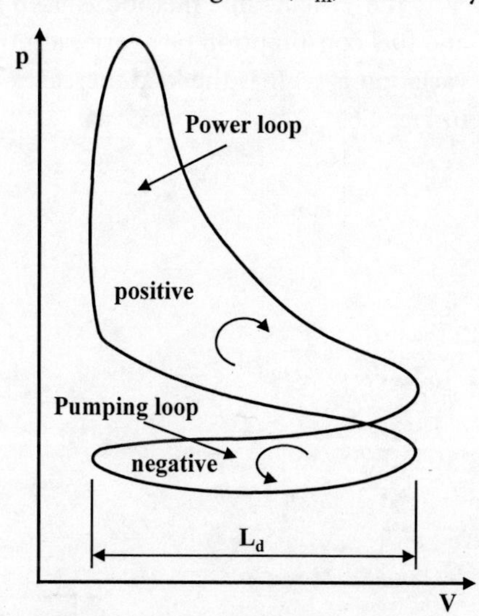

Fig. 4.4: Typical indicator diagram obtained using a mechanical indicator

An electronic indicator has four parts, namely, a pressure measuring device, a pre-amplifying device, a recording device and a display unit. The pressure measuring device is often called a pressure transducer. It is mounted in the cylinder head without projecting into the clearance volume, in a manner similar to a spark plug. It creates an electric signal based on the pressure is senses. Usually, a diaphragm senses the pressure inside the cylinder and transmits it to an element such as a piezoelectric crystal [3]. This element produces an electric signal, which is amplified by the pre-amplifier and displayed in an oscilloscope or recorded by the recorder. Various types of electronic indicators are currently used in engine tests and have replaced mechanical indicators. Typical pressure vs. crank angle (θ) diagram obtained from an electronic indicator from a CI engine is shown in Fig. 4.5. This p-θ diagram can be used to plot the indicator diagram in p-V coordinates. For this, the piston displacement, x, from the TDC position is calculated using the radius of the crank (r), length of the connecting rod (l) and the crank angle (θ).

This is written as,

$$x = l + r - r \times \cos\theta - \sqrt{l^2 - r^2 \sin^2\theta}$$

From the piston displacement, the corresponding volume (V) can be calculated and the p-V diagram can be drawn. From the area of the p-V diagram the net work done per cycle can be calculated, from which indicated power can be calculated.

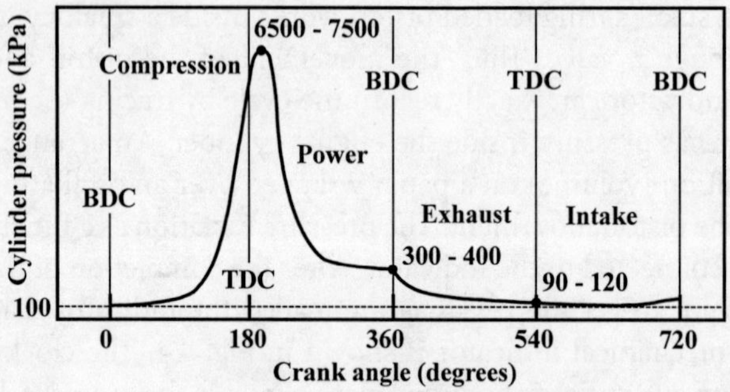

Fig. 4.5: A typical p-θ diagram

Friction power

Friction power is used to compensate for the internal losses in an engine. It is the difference between the indicated power and the brake power. Therefore, it can be calculated by measuring the indicated and brake powers. A few other methods of determining the friction power are Willan's line method, Morse test, motoring test and retardation test.

The Willan's line method is used in diesel engines. A graph between the brake power of an engine and fuel consumption rate varies almost linearly, especially at lower loads (lower torque) and non-linear variation is seen as the load increases. A typical plot of fuel consumption rate vs. brake power is shown in Fig. 4.6.

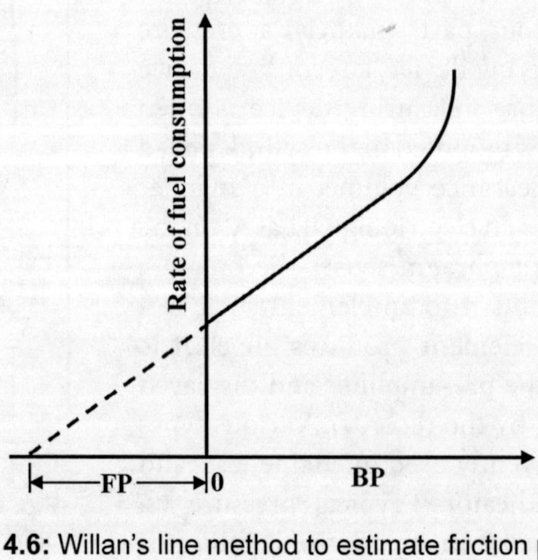

Fig. 4.6: Willan's line method to estimate friction power

It is apparent that even when the engine does not develop any power (BP = 0), some amount of the fuel is consumed. Basically, the energy from this fuel is spent on overcoming frictional losses. The magnitude of this energy can be determined by extrapolating the curve to the negative x-axis linearly to intercept at y = 0, indicating the point of zero fuel consumption. This is shown by a dashed line in Fig. 4.6. The magnitude of x-axis between the intercepted point and the origin is the friction power. This method requires many data points at lower loads to ascertain the linear variation of BP as a function of fuel consumption rate as BP approaches zero and to facilitate accurate linear extrapolation. This method cannot be used in petrol engines.

Morse Test

Morse test is used to calculate the indicated and friction powers of multi-cylinder engines. Here, the multi-cylinder engine is run at a given load and its speed and output are measured. This is kept as the baseline case. Then one cylinder is cut-off by disabling the spark plug for that cylinder if it is a petrol engine, or, by cutting off the fuel for that cylinder if it is a diesel engine. The cut-off cylinder will be motored by other cylinders. However, the engine speed and its power will reduce. The engine speed is increased to that of the baseline case by reducing the load. Now, the friction power will be the same as that in the baseline case, but its brake power will be lesser. If there are n cylinders in the engine, for the baseline case, the following relation can be written.

$$IP_1 + IP_2 + IP_3 + \ldots + IP_n = \sum_{i=1}^{n} BP_i + FP \tag{4.2}$$

Here, FP is the friction power of the engine, which will be present irrespective of the number of cylinders being active or inactive. If the first cylinder is cut-off, the relation for powers is written as,

$$IP_2 + IP_3 + \ldots + IP_n = \sum_{i=2}^{n} BP_i + FP \tag{4.3}$$

From equations (4.2) and 4.3), the indicated power of the first engine is determined as,

$$IP_1 = \sum_{i=1}^{n} BP_i - \sum_{i=2}^{n} BP_i$$

Similarly, the indicated power of other cylinders can be determined. The indicated power of the engine will be the sum of the indicated powers of all the cylinders.

$$IP = \sum_{i=1}^{n} IP_i$$

Then, the friction power is calculated as,

$$FP = IP - \sum_{i=1}^{n} BP_i \tag{4.4}$$

Motoring Test

In the motoring test, the engine is run with fuel (firing condition) at a given speed and load condition for a long time such that a steady state is reached, as indicated by the temperature of the engine components, lubricating oil and cooling water. A special dynamometer, called the swinging field type dynamometer is used to measure the engine brake power during this period. This dynamometer can run as a motor when its electric switching devices are activated. Now, the ignition or fuel supply is switched off and the dynamometer is run as a motor, so that the engine is motored at the same speed at which it was running previously. This process is carried out as quickly as possible. Now, the torque is measured, which will provide the value of the friction power. The sum of the brake power measured under the firing condition and the friction power measured under the motoring condition will provide the value of the indicated power. This method is not so accurate. This is because, during the changeover from firing to motoring, significant decrease in temperature of walls of the piston and cylinder can occur. Thus, the exact conditions during firing cannot be replicated during motoring. However, this method is useful for relative comparison of friction power between engines and when engine components such as piston rings, valve gear and so on are changed or tested.

Retardation Test

In the retardation test, an engine is retarded by cutting the fuel supply. First, the engine is run at a given speed at zero load. When it is running steadily, the fuel is cut-off. The speed is continuously recorded and the time taken for the speed to fall by a given value or percentage is noted. For example, it may take t_1 seconds for the engine speed to reduce by 1000 rpm from the original speed, under no load condition. This test is repeated by running the engine again at a given load (say 50 percent load) steadily and then retard it by cutting-off the fuel. Again, the time taken for the engine speed to reduce by a given value or percent is noted. Now, it may take t_2 seconds for the engine speed to reduce by 1000 rpm from the original speed, under the given load. From this information, the friction power can be calculated. The procedure for this is illustrated below.

The torque is calculated as a product of moment of inertia (I) and angular acceleration (α). Under no load condition, for the angular speed (rad/s) to drop from ω_1 to ω_2, the time taken is t_1 seconds. The torque under no load condition is only the frictional torque (T_f). Thus,

$$T_f = I\alpha_1 = I\frac{(\omega_1 - \omega_2)}{t_1}$$

Similarly, under a given load condition, for the angular speed to drop from ω_1 to ω_2, the time taken is t_2 seconds. The torque due to a given load condition is T_L. Thus, under a given load condition,

$$T_f + T_L = I\alpha_2 = I\frac{(\omega_1 - \omega_2)}{t_2}$$

From these, the frictional torque can be calculated as,

$$\frac{T_f}{T_f + T_L} = \frac{t_2}{t_1}$$

Or

$$T_f = \frac{T_L t_2}{t_1 - t_2}$$

Since, T_L can be measured at a given load and t_1 and t_2 are known from the retardation test, T_f can be determined. From T_f, the friction power, FP, can be determined as,

$$FP = \frac{2\pi N T_f}{60} \qquad (4.5)$$

Here, N is the average engine speed (in rpm) = $(2\pi/60) \times (\omega_1 + \omega_2)/2$.

More information on methods of determining engine power, fuel consumption rate, temperatures of the coolant and exhaust, and emissions can be found in standard test books on IC engines [1-4].

4.2 INDICATED AND BRAKE MEAN EFFECTIVE PRESSURES

The term Mean Effective Pressure (MEP) has been introduced in section 2.1.1 of Unit 2. MEP is defined as a mean (average) pressure that will produce the net work of the cycle and is written as,

$$W_{cycle} = MEP \times (V_{BDC} - V_{TDC})$$

In the analysis of air standard cycles, dealt in Unit 2, the net work is often expressed in J/kg of air. By multiplying the net specific work in J/kg with the mass flow rate of the air in kg/s, the net power output in W is obtained. In actual engines, the net work produced in a cylinder, called the indicated net work per cycle (ip), is obtained from the net area of the indicator diagram drawn in p-V coordinates. Using this, the indicated mean effective pressure (IMEP) can be defined as,

$$ip = IMEP \times (V_{BDC} - V_{TDC})$$

The indicated power is calculated as,

$$IP = ip \times cycles / s$$

$$IP = \frac{IMEP \times (V_{BDC} - V_{TDC}) \times n \times K}{1000 \times 60} = \frac{IMEP \times L \times A \times n \times K}{60000} kW \tag{4.6}$$

In equation (4.6), IMEP is indicated mean effective pressure in N/m² or Pa, n is number of power strokes per minute, K is number of cylinders in the engine, L is the length of the stroke in m, A is the area of cross-section of the piston in m². The value of n is N/2 for a four-stroke engine, where N is the number of revolutions per minute, and n = N for a two-stroke engine. The factor of 1000 in the denominator is for converting W to kW.

From the indicator diagram (Fig. 4.3), the average height of the indicator diagram (h_i) is calculated as net area of the indicator diagram (A_{ni}) divided by the length of the indicator diagram (L_d). If k_i is the spring constant of the mechanical indicator in Pa/m, then IMEP is calculated as $k_i \times h_i$.

Similar to IMEP, another useful quantity called the brake mean effective pressure, BMEP, can be defined using the brake power.

It is expressed as follows:

$$BP = \frac{BMEP \times L \times A \times n \times K}{60000} kW \tag{4.7}$$

IMEP contributes to BMEP and to Friction Mean Effective Pressure (FMEP). This can be written as,

$$IMEP = BMEP + FMEP$$

BMEP is useful for making relative comparison of engines with respect to their operating conditions.

4.3 ENGINE EFFICIENCIES

In general, efficiency is defined as the ratio of the net output generated by the engine to the heat supplied by the fuel. In unit-2, thermal efficiency for air-standard cycles (η_{th}) has been defined. This is also called thermodynamic efficiency. In the Otto cycle analysing the petrol engines, the thermal efficiency has been expressed in terms of the compression ratio. In the Diesel cycle analysing the diesel engines, the thermal efficiency has been defined in terms of compression and cut-off ratios.

In actual engines, based on the indicated and brake powers, indicated thermal efficiency and brake thermal efficiency, are respectively calculated. The indicated thermal efficiency is defined as,

$$\eta_{ith} = \frac{IP}{\dot{m}_f \times CV} \tag{4.8}$$

Here, η_{ith} is the indicated thermal efficiency, IP is the indicated power in kW, $\dot{m}_f$ is the mass flow rate of the fuel in kg/s and CV is the calorific value of the fuel in kJ/kg.

Similarly, the brake thermal efficiency is defined as,

$$\eta_{bth} = \frac{BP}{\dot{m}_f \times CV} \tag{4.9}$$

Here, η_{bth} is the brake thermal efficiency and BP is the indicated power in kW.

Another important parameter, called the mechanical efficiency, is defined as the ratio of power delivered by the engine (brake power) to the potential power produced in the engine (indicated power). It is written as,

$$\eta_m = \frac{BP}{IP} = \frac{BMEP}{IMEP} \tag{4.10}$$

To compare the actual efficiency of an engine to the theoretical efficiency of the cycle, relative efficiency or the efficiency ratio is defined as the ratio of brake thermal efficiency to the thermal efficiency of the air-standard cycle. It is written as,

$$\eta_{rel} = \frac{\eta_{bth}}{\eta_{th}}$$

To calculate the efficiency, the rate of fuel supply has to be measured. There are several types of metering devices used to measure the amount of fuel supplied to the engine accurately. Examples are the burette flow meter and orifice flow meter. Fuel supplied is often reported as specific fuel consumption. It is written as,

$$SFC = \frac{Rate\,of\ mass\ of\ fuel\ supplied}{Power}\left(\frac{kg}{kW-s}\right)$$

It is customary to report the specific fuel consumption as *grams per kW-hour* of power developed. Further, if the power in the denominator of equation (4.12) is indicated power, then SFC is called indicated-specific fuel consumption (ISFC). Based on brake power, brake-specific fuel consumption (BSFC) is obtained. It can be shown that BP × BSFC = IP × ISFC. Similarly, the air flow rate into the engine is also measured using air-box method and viscous-flow air meter.

A few other efficiencies are also used to analyse the performance of IC engines. Volumetric efficiency is used to analyse the performance of four-stroke engines. It is defined as the actual volume flow rate of air taken into the engine to the rate at which the piston displaces volume. For both CI and SI engines, only the volume flow rate of air is considered in this analysis. Scavenging efficiency is defined for two-stroke engines as the ratio of the remaining amount of the product mixture inside the engine at the beginning of the compression to the mass of the air that can be inducted. Combustion efficiency is defined as the ratio of the heat liberated by the engine to the calorific value of the fuel supplied to the engine. The emissions from the engine, such as the carbon monoxide (CO), carbon dioxide (CO_2), oxides of nitrogen (NO, NO_2 and N_2O, generally termed as NO_x), smoke and particulate matter (PM), also indicate the completeness of combustion, and therefore, the combustion efficiency. More information on these can be found in standard IC engines textbooks [1-4].

Indicated thermal efficiency varies in the range of 25% to 30% for SI engines and between 35% to 38% for CI engines. Mechanical efficiency can vary in the range of 65% to 85%, based on the losses. Relative efficiency varies 75% to 95% based on the amount of air supplied.

4.4 HEAT BALANCE OF AN ENGINE

Heat balance sheet of an IC engine is an important document required to assess the overall performance of the engine and to work on any possible improvements to increase the performance. The energy supplied to an engine is through the calorific value of the fuel supplied. The useful energy output from the engine is the brake power. The remaining part of the energy supplied flows with the exhaust gases and coolant. There may be some unaccounted energy that is lost from the engine. The heat balance is written as,

Rate of heat supply to the engine through fuel = brake power + rate of heat carried by the exhaust gases + rate of heat carried by the coolant + unaccounted energy flow out of the engine.

The rate of heat supply to the engine (kW) is calculated as the product of the mass flow rate of the fuel supplied to the engine, $\dot{m}_f$ (kg/s) and its calorific value, CV (kJ/kg). It is written as,

$$\dot{Q}_s = \dot{m}_f \times CV \tag{4.13}$$

The brake power (kW) is calculated using the measured torque delivered by the engine, as given in equation (4.1). The rate of heat lost by the cooling water is calculated as,

$$\dot{Q}_w = \dot{m}_w \times c_w \times (T_{wo} - T_{wi}) \tag{4.14}$$

Here, $\dot{Q}_w$ is the rate of heat carried by the cooling water in kW, $\dot{m}_w$ is the mass flow rate of cooling water in kg/s, c_w is the specific heat of the water in kJ/kg-K, T_{wo} is the temperature of the cooling water at the outlet in K and T_{wi} is the temperature of the cooling water at the inlet in K. Specific tests at different operating conditions are done to measure these quantities. The rate of heat carried away by the exhaust gases is usually measured by an instrument called exhaust gas calorimeter. Here, the exhaust gas mixture out of the engine is sent to a heat exchanger at an inlet temperature of T_{gi}. The mixture exchanges the heat with a stream of water and exits at a temperature of T_{go}. These temperatures are accurately measured. The mass flow rate of water ($\dot{m}_w$), its specific heat (c_w), and its inlet (T_{wi}) and outlet (T_{wo}) temperatures are accurately measured. The heat balance in the calorimeter is written as,

$$\dot{m}_g c_{pg} (T_{gi} - T_{go}) = \dot{m}_w c_w (T_{wo} - T_{wi}) \tag{4.15}$$

In equation (4.15), c_{pg} is the specific heat at constant pressure for the exhaust gas mixture and $\dot{m}_g$ is the mass flow rate of the exhaust gas mixture. The value of c_{pg} is calculated at the average temperature considering the composition of the mixture. Sometimes property of air is also used. From equation (4.15), the mass flow rate of the exhaust gas mixture is calculated. It can also be calculated if air-fuel ratio (AF) is given. Here, $\dot{m}_g = \dot{m}_f \times (1 + AF)$. Now, the rate of heat carried away by the exhaust gases ($\dot{Q}_g$) is calculated as,

$$\dot{Q}_g = \dot{m}_g \times c_{pg} \times (T_{go} - T_a) + \dot{m}_w c_w (T_{wo} - T_{wi}) \tag{4.16}$$

Here, T_a is the ambient temperature. Heat carried away by the exhaust gases may be split into heat carried by non-condensable (dry) gases and heat carried away by the water vapor if more information is made available. The unaccounted losses are calculated from the overall heat balance. A heat balance sheet, as shown in Table 4.1, is prepared for various operating conditions such as engine type, engine speed and load.

Table 4.1: Heat balance sheet (Engine type, speed and load)

Heat input rate	kW	%	Heat output rate	kW	%
Heat supplied by the fuel	S	100	(a) Brake power (b) Rate of heat carried by coolant (c) Rate of heat carried by exhaust gases (d) Rate of unaccounted heat losses	A B C D = S – (A+B+C)	a% b% c% d%
Total	**S**	**100**	**Total**	**S**	**100**

A plot of heat versus load is also drawn to understand the variation of each of the parameter in Table 4.1 with respect to the engine speed and load. In modern engines, technique such as turbo-compounding is used to reduce the heat losses from the exhaust gases to the ambient. A small turbine is used to extract energy from the exhaust gases and the turbine work is compounded to the engine work output.

4.5 ILLUSTRATIVE NUMERICAL PROBLEMS

4.1 A four-cylinder two-stroke SI engine has a bore of 100 mm and stroke of 175 mm. Through the indicator diagram, when the engine runs at 1600 rpm at full load, the mean effective pressure is calculated as 4 bar in the working (power) loop. During the pumping loop, the mean effective pressure is estimated as 0.5 bar. What is the indicator power of the engine?

Solution: IMEP = 4 – 0.5 = 3.5 bar = 3.5×10^5 Pa.

$$IP = \frac{IMEP \times L \times A \times n \times K}{60000}$$

Given: L = 175 mm = 0.175 m, d = 100 mm = 0.1 m, N = 1500 rpm and K = 4.

$A = \pi d^2/4 = 0.007854\ m^2$. The value of n = N, since it is a two-stroke engine.

$$IP = \frac{3.5 \times 10^5 \times 0.175 \times 0.007854 \times 1600 \times 4}{60000} = 51.313\,kW$$

4.2 A single cylinder SI engine develops a torque of 10 N-m, when running at 2000 rpm. The indicated power of the engine is calculated from the indicator diagram as 2.5 kW. Calculate the value of friction power as a percentage of the brake power. Also, calculate the value of mechanical efficiency.

Solution: Given: T = 10 N-m, N = 2000 rpm, IP = 2.5 kW.

$$BP = \frac{2\pi NT}{60} = \frac{2\pi \times 2000 \times 10}{60} = 2094.4\,W = 2.0944\,kW$$

The friction power is calculated as, FP = IP – BP = 2.5 – 2.0944 = 0.4056 kW.

Percentage friction power with respect to brake power = 100 × 0.4056/2.0944 = 19.36 %.

Mechanical efficiency, η_m = BP/IP = 0.83776 or 83.776 %.

4.3 An engine having four cylinders delivers 25 kW when it runs at 1500 rpm. The specific fuel consumption of engine is 375 grams of fuel kW-hour and the calorific value of the fuel is 44 MJ/kg. When one cylinder is non-operative, the output torque has been measured as 100 N-m. Determine the indicated thermal efficiency.

Solution: Given: BP (when four cylinders operate) = 25 kW, N = 1500 rpm, BSFC = 375 grams/kW-hour, CV = 44 MJ/kg, K = 4 and torque when one cylinder is cut-off is T = 100 N-m.

Average BP when three out of four cylinders are operative is: 2πNT/60000 = 15.708 kW.

Average IP per cylinder = BP (when four cylinders operate) – BP (when three cylinders operate)

= 25 – 15.708 = 9.292 kW.

Total IP = 4 × 9.292 = 37.168 kW.

In order to calculate the indicated thermal efficiency, indicated specific fuel consumption is calculated.

ISFC × IP = BSFC × BP ==> ISFC = 375 × 25/37.168 = 252.23 grams/kW-hour.

Fuel consumption rate based on indicated power is calculated as,

$$\dot{m}_f = \frac{ISFC \times IP}{3600 \times 1000} = 0.002605\, kg/s$$

It may be noted that the fuel consumption rate may also be straight away calculated using BSFC and BP. Now, indicated thermal efficiency is calculated as,

$$\eta_{ith} = \frac{IP}{\dot{m}_f \times CV} = \frac{37.168}{0.002605 \times 44000} \times 100 = 32.43\ \%.$$

4.4 A water-cooled single cylinder four-stroke diesel engine has a stroke and bore of 9 cm and 12 cm, respectively. The torque delivered by the engine is 25 N-m. Determine the brake mean effective pressure.

Solution: Given: d = 9 cm = 0.09 m, L = 12 cm = 0.12 m and T = 25 N-m.

$$BP = \frac{2\pi NT}{60} = \frac{BMEP \times L \times A \times n \times K}{60}$$

Here, n = N/2; since it is a four-stroke engine and K = 1. From this, BMEP is evaluated as,

$$BMEP = \frac{2\pi NT}{LAn} = \frac{2\pi NT}{L\frac{\pi d^2}{4}\left(\frac{N}{2}\right)} = \frac{16T}{d^2 L} = \frac{16 \times 25}{0.09 \times 0.09 \times 0.12} = 411522.63\, Pa = 4.1152\, bar.$$

4.5 A single cylinder four-stroke engine consumes 12 cubic centimetre (cc) of fuel in 24 seconds and 0.12 m^3 of air in 15 seconds. The engine is connected to a Prony brake. The total mass used for measurement of torque is 6 kg at the engine speed of 2500 rpm. The distance from the point where masses are hung to the centre of the drum is 0.5 m. Assume the density of air to be 1.2 kg/m^3 and the specific gravity of fuel to be 0.8. The calorific value of the fuel is 44 MJ/kg. Determine the air-fuel ratio and brake thermal efficiency.

Solution: Volume flow rate of air = 0.12/15 = 0.008 m^3/kg. Mass flow rate of air is density times the volume flow rate = 1.2 × 0.008 = 0.0096 kg/s.

Volume flow rate of fuel = 12 × 1 × 10^{-6}/24 = 5 × 10^{-7} m^3/s.

Density of the fuel = specific gravity × density of water = 0.8 × 1000 = 800 kg/m^3.

Mass flow rate of the fuel, $\dot{m}_f$ = 5 × 10^{-7} × 800 = 0.0004 kg/s.

Air-fuel ratio = mass flow rate of air/mass flow rate of fuel = 0.0096/0.0004 = 24.

Delivered power = BP = 2πNT/60. Torque, T = W × r.

W = m × g = 6 × 9.81 = 58.86 N and r = 0.5 m.

Thus, BP = 2π × 2500 × 58.86 × 0.5/60 = 7704.75 W = 7.7047 kW.

Brake thermal efficiency, η_{bth} = BP/($\dot{m}_f$ × CV) = 7.7047/(0.0004 × 44000) = 0.4377 or 43.77 %.

4.6 A four-stroke four cylinder SI engine has a bore of 80 mm and stroke of 120 mm. It consumes 6 grams of gasoline per second to develop a torque of 140 N-m at a speed of 3600 rpm. The CV of gasoline is 43 MJ/kg. Cylinder has a clearance volume is 75 cc. Determine BP, BMEP, brake thermal efficiency and relative efficiency. For air, c_p/c_v = 1.4.

Solution: Given: T = 140 N-m, N = 3600 rpm, d = 80 mm = 0.08 m, L = 120 mm = 0.12 m.

V_c = 75 cc = 75 × 10^{-6} m³. $\dot{m}_f$ = 6 g/s = 6.0 × 10^{-3} kg/s. CV = 43 MJ/kg = 43000 kJ/kg.

BP = 2πNT/60 = 2π × 3600 × 140/60 = 52778.75 W = 52.778 kW.

For four-stroke engine, n = N/2.

$$BMEP = \frac{2\pi NT}{LAnK} = \frac{2\pi NT}{L\frac{\pi d^2}{4}\left(\frac{N}{2}\right)K} = \frac{16T}{d^2LK}$$

$$= \frac{16\times 140}{0.08\times 0.08\times 0.12\times 4} = 729166.667\,Pa = 7.29167\,bar.$$

Brake thermal efficiency, η_{bth} = BP/($\dot{m}_f$ × CV) = 52.778/(6.0 × 10^{-3} × 43000) = 0.2045 = 20.45 %.

The displacement volume, V_s = πd²L/4 = 6.0318 × 10^{-4} m³. Maximum volume = $V_s + V_c$.

Compression ratio, r = $(V_s + V_c)/V_c$ = 9.042. Otto cycle efficiency, $\eta_{th} = 1 - 1/r^{(\gamma - 1)}$

= 1 – 1/9.042$^{0.4}$ = 0.5855 = 58.55 %.

Relative efficiency = $\eta_{rel} = \eta_{bth}/\eta_{th}$ = 20.45/58.55 = 0.3493 = 34.93 %.

4.7 A single cylinder four-stroke diesel engine has a bore of 30 cm and stroke of 45 cm. It been tested with a mechanical indicator for 60 minutes during which 8 litres of diesel (CV = 42000 kJ/kg, specific gravity = 0.8) has been supplied. The average net area of the indicator diagram has been 9 cm² and the length of the indicator diagram is 9 cm. The spring constant is 400 kPa/cm and the engine speed is 300 rpm. A rope dynamometer is used to measure the brake power. Effective brake wheel diameter is 1 m and the brake load is 200 kg. Spring balance connected to other end of the rope indicates 50 kg. Determine IP, BP, brake specific fuel consumption, mechanical efficiency and indicated thermal efficiency.

Solution: Given: d = 0.3 m, L = 0.45 m, CV = 42 MJ/kg, V_{fuel} = 8 litres = 0.008 m³, t = 60 minutes = 1 hour, specific gravity = 0.8, A_{ni} = 9 cm², L_d = 9 cm, k_i = 400 kPa/cm, N = 300 rpm.

In rope dynamometer: W = 200 kg, S = 50 kg, D = 1 m.

IMEP = average height of the indicator diagram (h_i) × spring constant (k_i).

Average height, $h_i = A_{ni}/L_d$ = 9 cm²/9 cm = 1 cm. Thus, IMEP = 1 cm × 400 kPa/cm = 400 kPa.

IP = IMEP × L × A × n/60 = 400 × 1000 × 0.45 × (π × 0.3 × 0.3 /4) × (300/2)/60; since n = N/2.

IP = 31808.6 W = 31.808 kW.

BP = 2π × N × T/60.

For rope dynameter, T = (W – S) × g × (D/2) = (200 – 50) × 9.81 × (1/2) = 735.75 N-m.

BP = $2\pi \times 300 \times 735.75/60 = 23114.3$ W = 23.114 kW.

Mass flow rate of fuel = $\dot{m}_f = (V_{fuel}/t) \times$ density of fuel = $(0.008/1) \times (0.8 \times 1000) = 6.4$ kg/h.

BSFC = $\dot{m}_f$/BP = 6.4/23.114 = 0.2768 kg/kW-h.

Mechanical efficiency, η_m = BP/IP = 23.114/31.808 = 0.7266 or 72.66 %.

Indicated thermal efficiency, η_{ith} = IP/($\dot{m}_f \times$ CV) = $31.808 \times 3600/(6.4 \times 42000) = 0.426$ or 42.6 %.

4.8 A four-stroke four cylinder engine has a bore of 0.05 m and stroke of 0.12 m. At a speed of 2800 rpm, it delivers a torque of 60 N-m. The clearance volume is 60 cc. Relative efficiency with respect to brake thermal efficiency is 0.6. CV of the fuel is 43000 kJ.kg. Determine the air standard efficiency, rate of heat supplied, fuel consumption rate and BMEP.

Solution: Given: d = 0.05 m, L = 0.12 m, N = 2800 rpm, K = 4, T = 60 N-m, $\eta_{rel} = \eta_{bth}/\eta_{th} = 0.6$, $V_c = 60$ cc = 60×10^{-6} m³. CV = 43000 kJ/kg.

Displacement volume of each cylinder, $V_s = \pi d^2 L/4 = \pi \times 0.05 \times 0.05 \times 0.12/4$ = 2.356×10^{-4} m³.

Compression ratio, r = $(V_s + V_c)/V_c = 4.926$.

Thermal efficiency, $\eta_{th} = 1 - 1/r^{(\gamma - 1)} = 1 - 1/4.926^{0.4} = 0.47155$ or 47.155 %.

Brake thermal efficiency, $\eta_{bth} = \eta_{rel} \times \eta_{th} = 0.6 \times 0.47155 = 0.283$ or 28.3 %.

BP = $2\pi \times N \times T/60 = 2\pi \times 2800 \times 60/60 = 17592.92$ W = 17.593 kW.

η_{bth} = BP/Rate of heat supplied ==> Rate of heat supplied = BP/η_{bth} = 17.593/0.283 = 62.166 kW.

Rate of heat supplied = $\dot{m}_f \times$ CV ==> $\dot{m}_f$ = Rate of heat supplied/CV = 62.166/43000 = 0.001446 kg/s.

$$BMEP = \frac{2\pi NT}{LAnK} = \frac{2\pi NT}{L\frac{\pi d^2}{4}\left(\frac{N}{2}\right)K} = \frac{16T}{d^2 LK} = \frac{16 \times 60}{0.05 \times 0.05 \times 0.12 \times 4} = 800000\,Pa = 8\,bar$$

4.9 A four cylinder SI engine produces a brake torque of 64 N-m when running at 2700 rpm. Morse test is carried out by cutting-off cylinder 1, 2, 3 and 4, individually, and corresponding brake torques of 46 N-m, 44 N-m, 45 N-m and 47 N-m, respectively, have been recorded. Calculate BP, IP and FP.

Solution: Given: $T_{1\text{-}4}$ = 64 N-m, when all cylinders operate, N = 2700 rpm, $T_{2\text{-}3\text{-}4}$ = 46 N-m, $T_{1\text{-}3\text{-}4}$ = 44 N-m, $T_{1\text{-}2\text{-}4}$ = 45 N-m and $T_{1\text{-}2\text{-}3}$ = 47 N-m.

When all cylinders operate, BP = $2\pi \times N \times T_{1\text{-}4}/60 = 2\pi \times 2700 \times 64/60 = 18095.57$ W = 18.096 kW.

When first cylinder is cut-off, $BP_1 = 2\pi N \times T_{2\text{-}3\text{-}4}/60 = 2\pi \times 2700 \times 46/60 = 13006.2$ W = 13.006 kW.

$IP_1 = BP - BP_1 = 18.096 - 13.006 = 5.09$ kW.

When second cylinder is cut-off, $BP_2 = 2\pi N \times T_{1\text{-}3\text{-}4}/60 = 2\pi \times 2700 \times 44/60 = 12440.7$ W = 12.44 kW.

$IP_2 = BP - BP_2 = 18.096 - 12.44 = 5.656$ kW.

When third cylinder is cut-off, $BP_3 = 2\pi N \times T_{1\text{-}2\text{-}4}/60 = 2\pi \times 2700 \times 45/60 = 12723.45$ W = 12.723 kW.

$IP_3 = BP - BP_3 = 18.096 - 12.723 = 5.373$ kW.

When fourth cylinder is cut-off, $BP_4 = 2\pi N\times T_{1\text{-}2\text{-}3}/60 = 2\pi\times 2700 \times 47/60 = 13288.94$ W = 13.289 kW.

$IP_4 = BP - BP_4 = 18.096 - 13.289 = 4.807$ kW.

$IP = IP_1 + IP_2 + IP_3 + IP_4 = 5.09 + 5.656 + 5.373 + 4.807 = 20.926$ kW

FP = IP – BP = 20.926 - 18.096 = 2.83 kW.

4.10 For a diesel engine, brake power is measured as 45 kW when fuel is supplied at a rate of 12 kg/h. CV of the fuel is 42 MJ/kg. To cool the engine water is circulated at a rate of 10 kg/minute and the difference in the temperature of water outlet and inlet is 50°C. The exhaust gases pass through a calorimeter, in which water is circulated at the rate of 10 kg/minute with a rise in its temperature of 35°. Exhaust gases leave the calorimeter at a temperature of 75°C to the ambient at 20°C. Specific heat of water can be taken as 4.2 kJ/kg-K and specific heat of exhaust gases can be taken as 1.1 kJ/kg-K. Air-fuel ratio is 20. Tabulate the heat balance for this engine.

Solution: Given: BP = 45 kW, $\dot{m}_f$ = 12 kg/h and CV = 42 MJ/kg, c_w = 4.2 kJ/kg-K, c_{pg} = 1.1 kJ/kg-K.

In radiator: $\dot{m}_{rw}$ = 10 kg/minutes, ΔT_{rw} = 50°C. In calorimeter: $\dot{m}_{cw}$ = 10 kg/minutes, ΔT_{cw} = 35°C.

Temperature of exhaust gas out of calorimeter, T_{go} = 75°C and ambient temperature, T_a = 20°C.

Heat supplied by the fuel, S = $\dot{m}_f \times$ CV = (12/3600) × 42000 = 140 kW.

Brake power, A = 45 kW.

Heat carried by coolant water, B = $\dot{m}_{rw}\times c_w \times (T_{wo} - T_{wi})$ = (10/60) × 4.2 × 50 = 35 kW.

Heat carried by exhaust gases, C = $\dot{m}_g \times c_{pg} \times (T_{go} - T_a) + \dot{m}_{cw} c_w (T_{wo} - T_{wi})$.

Air-fuel ratio (AF) is given as 20. That is, the ratio of mass flow rate of air to the mass flow rate of the fuel is 20. Mass flow rate of exhaust gases will be the sum of mass flow rates of fuel and air.

Mass flow rate of exhaust gases, $\dot{m}_g = \dot{m}_f + \dot{m}_f \times AF$ = (12/3600) + (12/3600) × 20 = 0.07 kg/s.

C = 0.07 × 1.1 × (75 – 20) + (10/60) × 4.2 × 35 = 28.735 kW

Unaccounted heat loss rate = D = S – (A + B + C) = 140 – (45 + 35 + 28.735) = 31.265 kW.

Table 4.2 presents the heat balance sheet.

Table 4.2: Heat balance sheet (example 4.10)

Heat input rate	kW	%	Heat output rate	kW	%
Heat supplied by the fuel	140	100	(a) Brake power	45	32.14%
			(b) Rate of heat carried by coolant	35	25%
			(c) Rate of heat carried by exhaust gases	28.3735	20.53%
			(d) Rate of unaccounted heat losses	31.265	22.33%
Total	**140**	**100**	**Total**	**140**	**100**

UNIT SUMMARY

This unit starts with the classification of engine power. Brake power, indicated power and friction power are defined. The methods used to measure the brake power, such as absorption and transmission methods are discussed. Prony brake dynamometer and strain gauge based transmission dynamometer are explained. Methods of determining the indicated power using an indicator diagram obtained by mechanical and electronic indicators are explained. Willan's line method, Morse test, motoring test and retardation test for determining friction power are systematically discussed. Subsequently, the indicated and mean effective pressures are mathematically defined. Following this, the engine efficiencies such as air-standard thermal efficiency, brake thermal efficiency, indicated thermal efficiency, mechanical and relative efficiencies are defined and discussed. A note on measuring fuel and air flow rates is included. Heat balance of an engine is systematically illustrated. Finally, illustrative examples are provided to understand the performance of engines, based on the theoretical aspects covered in this chapter.

EXERCISES

Multiple Choice Questions

1. Power developed by the working fluid inside the cylinder is
   (a) indicated power (b) friction power
   (c) brake power (d) none of these
2. Power delivered by the engine is
   (a) indicated power (b) friction power
   (c) brake power (d) none of these
3. Rope dynamometer is used to measure
   (a) friction power (b) brake power
   (c) indicated power (d) none of these
4. Strain gauge transmission dynamometer measures
   (a) torque (b) speed
   (c) tensile force (d) compression force
5. Positive loop of an indicator diagram is called
   (a) pumping loop (b) power loop
   (c) net power (d) none of these
6. Willan's line method is used to estimate
   (a) indicated power (b) brake power
   (c) friction power (d) none of these
7. Mechanical efficiency is a ratio of
   (a) indicated power to brake power (b) indicated power to friction power
   (c) brake power to indicated power (d) brake power to friction power

8. Specific fuel consumption is the ratio of the rate of mass of fuel supplied to
   (a) mass of air supplied
   (b) power of the engine
   (c) mass of exhaust gas leaving the engine
   (d) none of these
9. Heat supplied to an engine is the product of
   (a) mass flow rate of fuel and its calorific value
   (b) mass flow rate of fuel-air mixture and calorific value of the fuel
   (c) mass flow rate of fuel and heat carried by of exhaust gases
   (d) none of these
10. Heat carried by the exhaust gas is measured by
   (a) gas calorimeter
   (b) Junker's calorimeter
   (c) bomb calorimeter
   (d) none of these

Answers to Multiple Choice Questions									
1. (a)	2. (c)	3. (b)	4. (a)	5. (b)	6. (c)	7. (8)	8. (b)	9. (a)	10. (a)

Short and Long Answer Type Questions

1. Explain the term indicated power.
2. What is the principle of operation of an absorption dynamometer?
3. Explain the working of a Prony brake dynamometer with a simple sketch.
4. Write the expressions for calculating torque in a rope type dynamometer.
5. With a simple sketch, show the arrangement of strain gauges fixed on a shaft to measure torque.
6. Draw a typical indicator diagram and show the power and pumping loops clearly.
7. Write an expression for calculating the position of the piston with respect to the crank angle using the radius of the crank and the length of the connecting rod.
8. Explain Willan's line method.
9. Write expressions for calculating indicated powers of individual cylinders in a multiple cylinder engine using Morse test.
10. How is friction power estimated using motoring test?
11. Explain with equations on how friction power is calculated in retardation test.
12. How is indicated mean effective pressure calculated from an indicator diagram data?
13. Write an expression connecting brake power and brake mean effective pressure.
14. Write expressions for indicated and brake thermal efficiencies.
15. What is specific fuel consumption? How is it calculated?
16. Define mechanical efficiency and relative efficiency using appropriate expressions.
17. Define volumetric efficiency.
18. Write a statement for the overall heat balance of an engine.
19. How is heat supplied to an engine calculated?
20. Write an expression to evaluate the heat carried by the coolant gas.
21. What is the working principle of exhaust gas calorimeter?

22. Write the energy balance in an exhaust gas calorimeter.
23. List the entries in a typical heat balance sheet of an IC engine.

Numerical Problems

1. A single cylinder SI engine develops a torque of 15 N-m, when running at 2500 rpm. The mechanical efficiency of the engine is 78.54%. Calculate the values of indicated power and friction power.
2. A water-cooled single cylinder four-stroke diesel engine has a bore of 10 cm and it is a square engine (square engine has stroke equal to its bore). The torque delivered by the engine is 30 N-m. Determine the brake mean effective pressure.
3. A six cylinder two-stroke SI engine has a bore of 125 mm and a stroke of 175 mm. When the engine runs at 1500 rpm at full load, the mean effective pressure is calculated as 5 bar in the power loop and as 1 bar in the pumping loop. What is the indicator power of the engine?
4. An engine having four cylinders delivers 35 kW when it runs at 1800 rpm. The specific fuel consumption of engine is 400 grams of fuel kW-hour and the calorific value of the fuel is 42 MJ/kg. When one cylinder is cut-off, the output torque is measured as 120 N-m. Determine the indicated thermal efficiency.
5. A four-stroke four cylinder SI engine has a bore and stroke of 100 mm. It consumes 8 grams of gasoline per second to develop a torque of 150 N-m at a speed of 3600 rpm. The CV of gasoline is 42 MJ/kg. Cylinder has a clearance volume is 80 cc. Determine BP, BMEP, brake thermal efficiency and relative efficiency. For air, $c_p/c_v = 1.4$.
6. A four-stroke engine consumes 16 cubic centimetre (cc) of fuel in 32 seconds and 0.15 m^3 of air in 18.75 seconds. The engine is connected to a Prony brake. The total mass used for measurement of torque is 5 kg at the engine speed of 2500 rpm. The load arm length is 0.6 m. Assume the density of air to be 1.2 kg/m^3 and the specific gravity of fuel to be 0.8. The calorific value of the fuel is 43 MJ/kg. Determine the air-fuel ratio and brake thermal efficiency.
7. A four cylinder engine produces a brake torque of 80 N-m when running at 3000 rpm. Morse test is carried out by cutting-off cylinder 1, 2, 3 and 4, individually, and corresponding brake torques of 59 N-m, 56 N-m, 58 N-m and 57 N-m, respectively, have been recorded. Calculate BP, IP and FP.
8. A six cylinder four-stroke engine has a bore of 60 mm and stroke of 100 mm. At a speed of 3000 rpm, it delivers a torque of 50 N-m. The clearance volume is 50 cc. Relative efficiency with respect to brake thermal efficiency is 0.55. CV of the fuel is 42000 kJ.kg. Determine the air standard efficiency, rate of heat supplied, fuel consumption rate and BMEP.
9. A single cylinder four-stroke diesel engine has a bore of 0.3 m and stroke of 0.5 m. It been tested with a mechanical indicator for 45 minutes during which 6 litres of diesel (CV = 42000 kJ/kg, specific gravity = 0.8) has been supplied. The average net area of the indicator diagram is 10 cm^2 and the length of the indicator diagram is 10 cm. The spring constant is 400 kPa/cm and the engine speed is 300 rpm. A rope dynamometer is used to measure the brake power. The diameter of the flywheel is 1 m and the diameter of the rope is 0.2 m. The total brake load used is 225 kg. Spring balance showed a reading of 80 kg. Determine IP, BP, brake specific fuel consumption, mechanical efficiency and indicated thermal efficiency.

10. For a gasoline engine, the brake power is measured as 55 kW and the rate of fuel supply is measured as 5 cm^3/s. The CV of the fuel is 43 MJ/kg and its specific gravity is 0.75. To cool the engine water is circulated at a rate of 9 kg/minute in the radiator. The water came into the radiator at 20°C and left at 75°C. The exhaust gases pass through a gas calorimeter, in which water is circulated at the rate of 12 kg/minute The water came into the calorimeter at 20°C and left at 50°C. Exhaust gases leave the calorimeter at a temperature of 70°C to the ambient at 20°C. Specific heat of water can be taken as 4.2 kJ/kg-K and specific heat of exhaust gases can be taken as 1.0 kJ/kg-K. Air-fuel ratio is 15. Tabulate the heat balance for this engine.

REFERENCES AND SUGGESTED READINGS

1. J. B. Heywood, Internal Combustion Engine Fundamentals, McGraw Hill Inc., 1988.
2. R. Stone, Introduction to Internal Combustion Engines, Macmillan Press Ltd., 1999.
3. H. N. Gupta, Fundamentals of Internal Combustion Engines, PHI Learning Pvt. Ltd., 2009.
4. N. Ganesan, IC Engines, Tata McGraw Hill Pvt. Ltd., 2012.

Dynamic QR Code for Further Reading

1. L25 on the "Performance parameters of IC engines" and L27 on "Tutorial: IC engines" in NPTEL course on "Introduction to aerospace propulsion" by Prof. Bhaskar Roy and Prof. A. M. Pradeep, Department of Aerospace Engineering, Indian Institute of Technology Bombay.

2. NPTEL course on "Fundamentals of Automotive systems" by Prof. C. S. Shankar Ram, Department of Engineering Design, Indian Institute of Technology Madras.

5 Air Compressors, Refrigeration & Air Conditioning

UNIT SPECIFICS

Through this unit, the following aspects are discussed:

- Uses of air compressor;
- Types of air compressors – reciprocating and rotary air compressors;
- Single-stage and multistage reciprocating air compressors;
- Centrifugal, axial flow and vane type air compressors;
- Refrigerant and refrigeration systems;
- Air compression and vapor compression refrigeration systems;
- Air-conditioning systems.

Compressed air is used in several applications. Two types of compressors, namely reciprocating and rotary compressors, are used depending on the application. Based on the pressure requirement, either a single-stage compressor or a multistage compressor is employed. These aspects are discussed in this unit.

Subsequently, the construction and working principles of the single-stage reciprocating air compressor are presented along with a line diagram. Its thermodynamic analysis has been illustrated using p-v diagram. The working principle of multistage reciprocating air compressors are presented after this. Advantages of multistage air compressors over single-stage compressors have also been discussed in this unit.

Working principles of various rotary air compressors such as centrifugal, axial flow and vane type compressors have also been presented in this unit.

Refrigerators are cooling devices, which find significant applications in various food processing and pharma industries, as well as in households. A refrigerator uses a special working fluid called refrigerant. Working principle and performance of refrigerators are discussed in this unit. Brief discussions on the components, working principles and applications of air refrigeration system and vapor compression refrigeration system have also been presented in this unit.

Finally, the principle of air-conditioning and types of air-conditioning systems are presented. The necessity of air conditioning, season based performance requirements for home comfort and in industries are discussed in this unit. Working principle of the window air-conditioner is also reported in this unit.

RATIONALE

The fifth unit of this book helps the students to get an overall idea about three important devices namely, air compressor, refrigerator and air-conditioner, along with their types and applications. Students will be able to understand the working principles of single-stage and multistage reciprocating air compressors.

This unit helps the students to understand the working of rotary air compressor of different types – centrifugal, axial and vane type. Students will be able to understand the concept of refrigeration and its applications. They can also know about the components and working of air refrigeration system and vapor compression refrigeration system. This unit makes students to understand the principle of air-conditioning, working of air-conditioning systems and defining comfort levels for various seasons. Students will also be able to understand the working of a window air-conditioner.

PRE-REQUISITES

Basic Mechanical Engineering (MEPC102)

UNIT OUTCOMES

List of outcomes of this unit is as follows:

U5-O1: Know about air compressors and their applications

U5-O2: Understand the working of single-stage and multistage reciprocating air compressors

U5-O3: Understand the working of rotary air compressors

U5-O4: Know about refrigeration systems, their performance and applications

U5-O5: Understand air-conditioning systems, comfort level and seasonal air-conditioning

Unit-5 Outcomes	EXPECTED MAPPING WITH COURSE OUTCOMES (1- Weak Correlation; 2- Medium Correlation; 3- Strong Correlation)				
	CO-1	CO-2	CO-3	CO-4	CO-5
U5-O1	-	-	-	3	-
U5-O2	-	-	-	3	-
U5-O3	-	-	-	3	-
U5-O4	-	-	-	-	3
U5-O5	-	-	-	-	3

5.1 AIR COMPRESSORS

Air compressors are used to increase the pressure of air or any gas or a gas mixture or vapor to a desirable pressure ratio by consuming energy from the surrounding. The energy is usually supplied in the form of electrical work. Compressed air is used in several applications. These include pneumatic tools used in manufacturing, air brakes in automobiles, pneumatic conveyors used for solid particle transport, inflating tubes and tyres of vehicles, spray painting, and so on.

Thermodynamic analysis of an air compressor is carried out by considering a control volume (CV) as shown in Fig. 5.1. Here, air at a mass flow rate of $\dot{m}_1$ kg/s enters the control volume with p_1, T_1, v_1 and h_1, as the corresponding pressure, temperature, specific volume and specific enthalpy, respectively. Similarly, air at a mass flow rate of $\dot{m}_2$ kg/s exits the control volume with p_2, T_2, v_2 and h_2, as the corresponding pressure, temperature, specific volume and specific enthalpy, respectively. The rate of heat and work interactions are $\dot{Q}$ and $\dot{W}_c$, respectively.

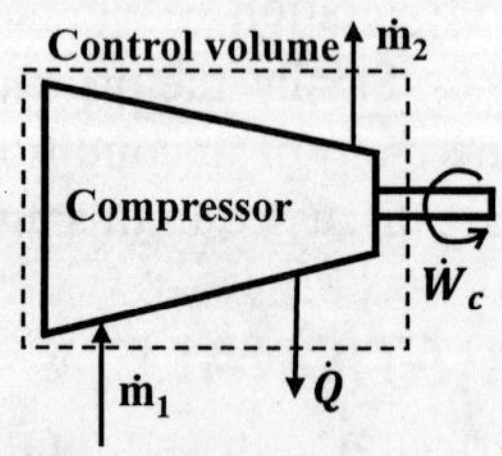

Fig. 5.1: Thermodynamic analysis of an air compressor.

Neglecting the changes in potential and kinetic energies, the mass and energy conservation equations can be written as,

$$\frac{dm_{cv}}{dt} = \dot{m}_1 - \dot{m}_2 \tag{5.1}$$

$$\dot{Q} - \dot{W}_c = \frac{dU_{cv}}{dt} + \dot{m}_2 h_2 - \dot{m}_1 h_1 \tag{5.2}$$

Most of the time, compressor operates under steady conditions. The time derivative in equations (5.1 and 5.2) can therefore be removed and $\dot{m}_1 = \dot{m}_2 = \dot{m}$. The working fluid, air, is considered as an ideal gas, obeying the equation of state given as pv = RT, where p is the pressure in Pa, v is the specific volume in m^3/kg, T is the temperature in K and R is the specific gas constant in J/kg-K (for air, R = 287 J/kg-K and $\gamma = c_p/c_v = 1.4$). If the heat interaction can be neglected ($\dot{Q} = 0$), then expressing Δh as $c_p\Delta T$, the work supplied to the compressor is written as,

$$\dot{W}_c = \dot{m}c_p\left(T_1 - T_2\right) = \dot{m}\left(\frac{\gamma R}{\gamma - 1}\right)T_1\left(1 - \frac{T_2}{T_1}\right) = \dot{m}\left(\frac{\gamma}{\gamma - 1}\right)p_1 v_1\left(1 - \frac{T_2}{T_1}\right) \quad 5.3 \tag{5.3}$$

In equation (5.3), the compressor power is negative, indicating that this power has to be supplied to the compressor from the surroundings. The ratio of exit to inlet temperature (T_2/T_1) can be written in terms of pressure ratio (p_2/p_1) considering a reversible adiabatic process that obeys the equation, pv^γ = constant. The specific work in W per kg/s flow rate of air ($\dot{W}_c/\dot{m}$) required for the adiabatic compression process (absolute value) is then written as,

$$w_c = \left(\frac{\gamma}{\gamma - 1}\right)p_1 v_1\left(\left(\frac{p_2}{p_1}\right)^{\frac{\gamma-1}{\gamma}} - 1\right) \tag{5.4}$$

The compression process is shown in p-v and T-S diagrams in Fig. 5.2. The reversible adiabatic (isentropic) process is shown as 1-2″. If the compression process is not a reversible adiabatic process, but it is a reversible polytropic process ($\dot{Q} < 0$) that obeys the equation, pv^n = constant, then the specific work required for the compression process is calculated by replacing γ in equation (5.4) by the polytropic index n. It is written as,

$$w_c = \left(\frac{n}{n - 1}\right)p_1 v_1\left(\left(\frac{p_2}{p_1}\right)^{\frac{n-1}{n}} - 1\right) \tag{5.5}$$

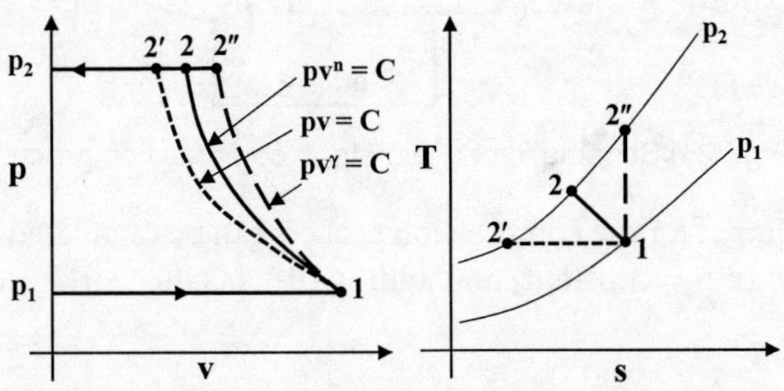

Fig. 5.2: Schematics of p-v and T-s diagram showing the compression processes.

The polytropic process is shown as 1-2 in both p-v and T-S diagrams in Fig. 5.2. The heat transfer can be determined from the first law. It may be noted that the work supplied to the compressor during a reversible polytropic process (1-2) is lesser than the work supplied in the reversible adiabatic process (1-2″), when n is less than γ. This is enabled by cooling the compressor by using fins for air cooling or an external water jacket for water cooling. If the compressor is cooled such that the temperature of the gas remains constant, then such a process can be depicted in p-v and T-s diagrams as shown by 1-2′ in Fig. 5.2. As seen from Fig. 5.2, the reversible isothermal process requires the minimum work among the three cases. The specific work supplied during reversible isothermal compression is expressed as,

$$w_c = p_1 v_1 \ln\left(\frac{p_2}{p_1}\right) \tag{5.6}$$

There are two important performance metrics for evaluating compressors. They are isentropic efficiency and isothermal efficiency. Isentropic efficiency is the ratio of the work supplied to the compressor in an isentropic process (1-2" in Fig. 5.2) to the actual work supplied, when the process is irreversible. Similarly, the isothermal efficiency is the ratio of the work supplied to the compressor in an isothermal process (1-2' in Fig. 5.2) to the actual work supplied.

However, practically cooling is generally not very effective. Therefore, multi-stage compression process is used to reduce the work input to the compressor. In this case one-stage air is compressed from low pressure to an intermediate pressure. The air then passes through an intercooler, which is a heat exchanger. Air is cooled at almost constant pressure and flows through the next stage of the compressor, where it is compressed from the intermediate pressure to the next high pressure and so on. Multi-stage compression reduces the overall work supplied for the compression process and also results in a lower exit temperature of the air after compression. A schematic of a two-stage compression process is shown in Fig. 5.3. Here, the air is steadily compressed in the first stage compressor from p_1 to p_c. Then, air passes through a heat exchanger, called an intercooler, where it is cooled before entering the second stage compressor. It exits the intercooler at a lower temperature (generally equal to the inlet temperature of the first stage) and at a pressure of p_d. The heat is removed by another fluid like water. In the second stage compressor, the air is again steadily compressed from p_d to p_2. The required pressure ratio is p_2/p_1. Multi-stage compressors with more than two stages can also be used based on the value of the required pressure ratio (final pressure/initial inlet pressure).

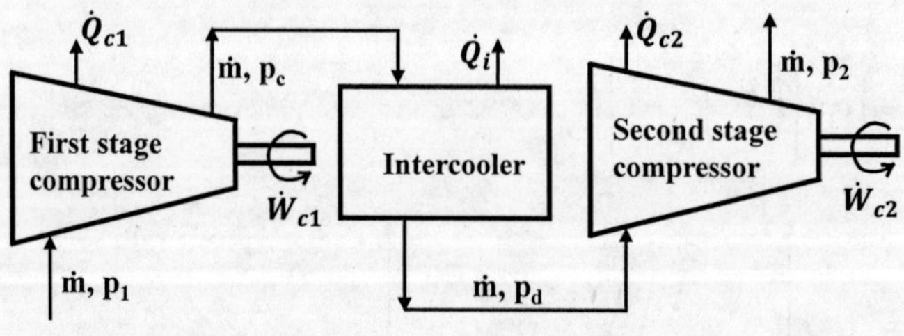

Fig. 5.3: Schematic of a two-stage compression process

The specific work required for the compression process can be calculated by considering the process to be reversible polytropic (pv^n = constant) and adding the specific works required for two stages. This is expressed as,

$$w_c = \left(\frac{n}{n-1}\right) p_1 v_1 \left(\left(\frac{p_c}{p_1}\right)^{\frac{n-1}{n}} - 1\right) + \left(\frac{n}{n-1}\right) p_d v_d \left(\left(\frac{p_2}{p_d}\right)^{\frac{n-1}{n}} - 1\right) \tag{5.7}$$

Generally, the pressure drop across the intercooler may be negligible so that p_d will be almost same as that of the intermediate pressure, p_c. The optimal value of the intermediate pressure, p_c, which results in the minimum specific work supplied for a two-stage compression process, can be shown to be equal to p_c (= p_d) = $(p_1 \times p_2)^{0.5}$. In the intercooler, if the temperature drops to the inlet value of the first stage (ideal intercooler), then $T_d = T_1$. It may be noted that this leads to the pressure ratio in each stage being the same; $p_c/p_1 = p_2/p_c$. Using the above and the equation of state (pv = RT), the minimum specific work required for two-stage compression process, in terms of the pressure ratio of each stage, can be written as,

$$w_c = 2\left(\frac{n}{n-1}\right)RT_1\left(\left(\frac{p_c}{p_1}\right)^{\frac{n-1}{n}} - 1\right) \tag{5.8}$$

The two-stage compression process is depicted in p-v and T-s diagrams as shown in Fig. 5.4. The process in each stage is considered as a polytropic process (pv^n = constant). From the p-v diagram, it is clear that the two-stage compression process (1-c-d-2) consumes lesser work than the single-stage compression process (1-2′). The work reduction is indicated by the shaded area in Fig. 5.4.

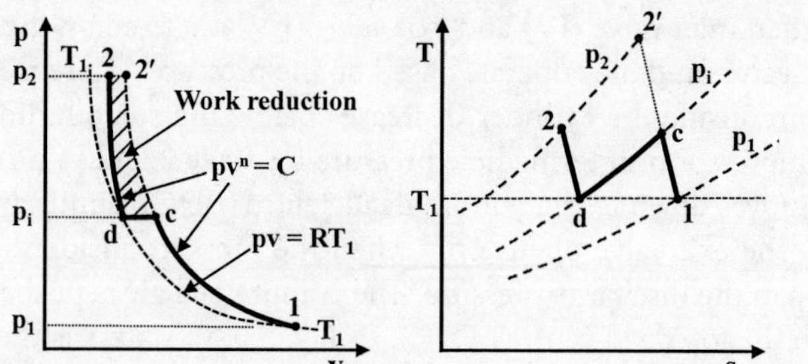

Fig. 5.4: Schematics of p-v and T-s diagrams for two-stage compression process

From the T-s diagram, it is apparent that the temperature of the air after being compressed to p_2 is much lower as shown in state 2 for the two-stage compression process when compared to the state 2′ attained in the single-stage compression process. The minimum specific work required for M-stage compression process, in terms of the overall pressure ratio (p_2/p_1), can be written as,

$$w_c = M\left(\frac{n}{n-1}\right)RT_1\left(\left(\frac{p_2}{p_1}\right)^{\frac{n-1}{Mn}} - 1\right) \tag{5.9}$$

There are several advantages in employing multistage compressors over single-stage compressors. These are (1) moderate pressure ratio in each stage, (2) controlled temperature rise of air, (3) lesser work requirement for the given pressure ratio and (4) smaller size and lesser weight of compressor. Multi-stage compressors are used in several applications owing to these advantages.

5.1.1 Types of Air Compressors

Air compressors, which can be either single-stage or multistage, are generally classified based on the type of operation as reciprocating and rotary air compressors. Reciprocating compressor uses piston-cylinder arrangement and is called positive displacement type compressor. It takes a certain quantity of air into the cylinder, compresses it to the required pressure by the action of the piston movement and discharges it to a high pressure tank or a system. Reciprocating compressors can produce high pressures, but the flow rates are quite low. For example, pressure as high as 2000 bar at a flow rate of approximately 2.5 m^3/s can be achieved with a two-stage reciprocating compressor. On the other hand, much higher flow rate ($\approx$150 m^3/s) with a relatively lower pressure ratio can be achieved by using rotary compressor. Centrifugal, axial-flow and vane type compressors are examples of rotary air compressors. In these, centrifugal compressor and axial flow compressor are of dynamic type, where the flow of air is continuous through the compressor. Compression is accomplished as the air passes through a set of stator and rotor vanes. Vane type rotary compressor is a positive displacement type compressor, where the air is compressed by the vane movement that creates a variable volume. There are other types of rotary compressors such as screw compressor, scroll and lobe type compressors used in select applications. A different class called ejector type compressor is also used in specific applications. Some features of reciprocating and rotary type air compressors are discussed in the following sections.

5.1.2 Reciprocating air compressors

A schematic of a single cylinder reciprocating air compressor is shown in Fig. 5.5. It consists of a piston working within a cylinder. Inlet valve (IV) and exit valve (EV) are fixed on the cylinder head. These are basically spring loaded valves and they operate based on the pressure difference. For instance, inlet valve opens when the pressure inside the cylinder decreases below the surrounding pressure (atmospheric pressure for stage 1 compressor or intermediate pressure for stage 2 and so on) and air is taken into the cylinder as the piston moves down to the bottom dead centre (BDC). Similarly, as the piston moves up, the air is compressed. The exit valve opens only when the pressure inside the cylinder increases to a value slightly greater than the discharge pressure. The compressed air is pushed out of the exit value as the piston moves up to the top dead centre (TDC). In Fig. 5.5(a), state 1 is the instant when the piston is in BDC and air has entered the cylinder. At this state, based on the stage of this compressor, the pressure (p_1) is equal to either the atmospheric pressure or the intermediate pressure. Process 1-2 is the compression process. In Fig. 5.5(b), the position of the piston at state 2 is shown. Here, the pressure of the air (p_2) is slightly more than the discharge pressure and the exit valve opens. Ideally, p_2 is taken to be equal to the discharge pressure for calculations.

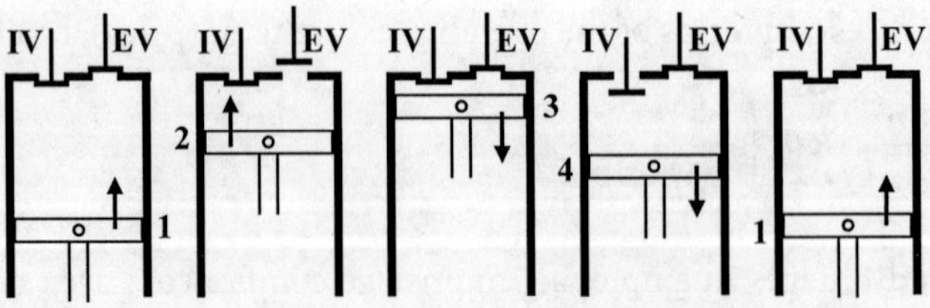

Fig. 5.5: Schematic of a reciprocating air compressor

As the piston moves up from state 2 to the TDC, the compressed air is discharged out of the cylinder, leaving a small quantity of air in the clearance volume. At state 3, shown in Fig. 5.5(c), the discharge valve closes. Ideally, 2-3 is a constant pressure process ($p_3 = p_2$). When the piston moves down from TDC, the air in the clearance volume expands and the pressure decreases. When the pressure of the air decreases from p_3 to a value slightly less than the inlet pressure, the inlet valve opens. This is shown as state 4 in Fig 5.5(d). Ideally, p_4 is taken to be equal to the inlet pressure (p_1) for calculations. Air enters into the cylinder as the piston moves down to BDC and the cycle completes. Ideally, 4-1 is a constant pressure process. State 1 is reached as shown in Fig. 5.5(e).

The processes undergone by the air in the reciprocating compressor are shown in p-v diagram in Fig. 5.6. The ideal cycle, where the valves are assumed to open and close instantaneously, is shown in Fig. 5.6(a). As discussed, intake and discharge processes, 4-1 and 2-3, respectively, occur at constant pressure. Compression and expansion processes, 1-2 and 3-4, are generally reversible polytropic processes, obeying pv^n = constant. In the actual cycle shown in Fig. 5.6(b), it may be noted that the pressure continuously varies and some lag is present when valves open and close.

In reciprocating compressor, as the piston reaches TDC, there is a small volume of air present above the piston surface trapped in the clearance volume (V_3). This state is shown in Fig. 5.5(c). Due to the expansion of the air in the clearance volume, the volume of the air taken in during the intake process is reduced. Since air in the clearance volume expands from V_3 to V_4, the volume intake of fresh air is effectively reduced to $V_1 - V_4$. The displacement volume is $V_1 - V_3$.

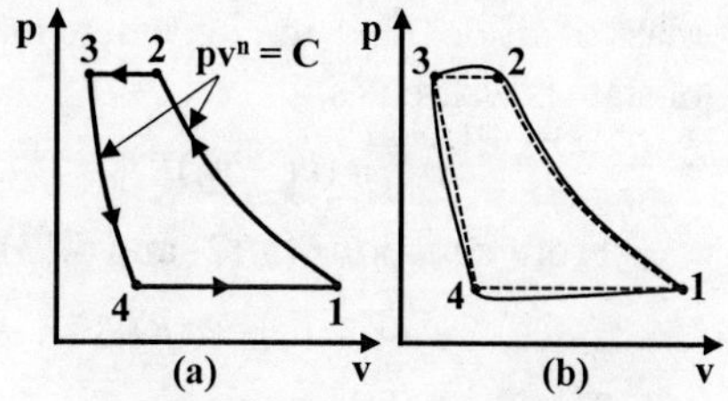

Fig. 5.6: Processes of reciprocating compressor in p-v coordinates – (a) ideal cycle and (b) actual cycle

The ratio of the effective intake volume to the displacement volume is called volumetric efficiency. The effectiveness of the reciprocating compressor is also measured by the volumetric efficiency, which is defined as,

$$\eta_{vol} = \frac{V_1 - V_4}{V_1 - V_3} \tag{5.10a}$$

Clearance ratio (CR), defined as the clearance volume to the displacement volume; CR = $V_3/(V_1 - V_3)$, is also used for analysis. CR is also called Clearance Factor (CF). For a polytropic expansion (pv^n = C), the volumetric efficiency can be written in terms of CR and pressure ratio (p_2/p_1) as,

$$\eta_{vol} = 1 + CR\left[1 - \left(\frac{p_2}{p_1}\right)^{\frac{1}{n}}\right] \tag{5.10b}$$

The volumetric efficiency decreases with an increase in pressure ratio (p_2/p_1) and clearance volume. It increases with an increase in the index of the polytropic compression, n. However, increasing n would result in an increase in the work supplied for compression. By using multi-stage compression, the pressure ratio of each stage can be kept under a limit and thus, the volumetric efficiency can be improved.

In section 5.1, using steady state steady flow energy equation, the specific work done on the air has been expressed in equation (5.5), considering the compression to obey a polytropic process. There is no clearance volume used to obtain equation (5.5). The work supplied for compression in a reciprocating compressor can be calculated from the area enclosed by the indicator diagram (Fig. 5.6). For thermodynamic analysis, the ideal cycle shown in Fig. 5.6(a) can be considered. The work for the cycle (magnitude) is calculated from the work interaction in each of the four processes. It is expressed as,

$$-W_{cycle} = \frac{p_1V_1 - p_2V_2}{n-1} + p_2\left(V_3 - V_2\right) + \frac{p_3V_3 - p_4V_4}{n-1} + p_1\left(V_1 - V_4\right) \tag{5.11a}$$

$$W_{cycle} = -\frac{n}{n-1}\left(p_1V_1 - p_2V_2 + p_3V_3 - p_4V_4\right) \tag{5.11b}$$

It may be noted that the second and fourth terms in equation (5.11a) represent the flow work during discharge and intake, respectively. Also, $p_4 = p_1$ and $p_3 = p_2$. At the state 3 (after discharge) and state 4 (before intake), same amount of air is present in the clearance volume. Let the mass of the air in the clearance volume be m_c kg. Temperature at state 4 will be equal to T_1, which is same as the temperature of the air being taken in during intake process. Here, the equation of state is written as,

$$p_1V_4 = m_cRT_1 \tag{5.12}$$

The volume of air taken in per cycle from 4 to 1 at a temperature of T_1 and pressure of p_1 is equal to $(V_1 - V_4)$ m³. As the intake process occurs, mass of the air increases with volume. At state 1, let the mass of air be $(m_c + m_i)$ kg, where m_i is the mass of air inducted into the compressor. Here, the equation of state is written as,

$$p_1V_1 = (m_c + m_i)RT_1 \tag{5.13}$$

From equations (5.12) and 5.13), it can be shown that,

$$p_1(V_1 - V_4) = m_iRT_1 \tag{5.14}$$

The mass of the air compressed during 1-2 is $(m_c + m_i)$. The temperature and pressure at state 2 are T_2 and p_2, respectively. The equation of state at state 2 is written as,

$$p_2V_2 = (m_c + m_i)RT_2 \tag{5.15}$$

During 2-3, the air is discharged at a pressure of p_2 and temperature of T_2, leaving some mass of air in the clearance volume, equal to m_c. The volume discharged is equal to $(V_2 - V_3)$ m³. At state 3, the equation of state is written as,

$$p_2V_3 = m_cRT_2 \tag{5.16}$$

From equations (5.15) and 5.16), it can be shown that,

$$p_2(V_2 - V_3) = m_iRT_2 \tag{5.17}$$

Using equations (5.14) and (5.17), equation (5.11) is written as

$$W_{cycle} = -\frac{n}{n-1}\left[p_1(V_1 - V_4) - p_2(V_2 - V_3)\right] = -\frac{n}{n-1}m_iR(T_1 - T_2) \tag{5.18}$$

The specific work for the cycle is calculated by dividing the work by the mass of air discharged. It is expressed as,

$$w_{cycle} = \frac{W_{cycle}}{m_i} = -\frac{n}{n-1}RT_1\left(1 - \frac{T_2}{T_1}\right) = -\frac{n}{n-1}RT_1\left[1 - \left(\frac{p_2}{p_1}\right)^{\frac{n-1}{n}}\right] \tag{5.19}$$

Noting that $p_1v_1 = RT_1$, the specific work required for the cycle is written as,

$$w_{cycle} = \left(\frac{n}{n-1}\right)p_1v_1\left(\left(\frac{p_2}{p_1}\right)^{\frac{n-1}{n}} - 1\right) \tag{5.20}$$

Equation (5.20) is same as equation (5.5), showing that the clearance volume has no effect on the specific work done for compression. However, it has a significant effect on the mass of the air being compressed and delivered. With clearance volume, the mass inducted and delivered is equal to $m_g = (m_1 - m_4)$ and without clearance volume, it is equal to m_1.

When the pressure ratio (p_2/p_1) is in the range of 3 to 5, single stage compressor is employed. When the pressure ratio exceeds this, multi-stage compressor is used. Advantages in using multistage reciprocating air compressors are: (1) Improved overall volumetric efficiency. (2) Smaller cylinders in each stage. (3) More uniform torque and better mechanical balance from multi-cylinders. (4) Lesser lubrication difficulties due to reduced maximum temperature as a result of intercooling. (5) Reduced leakage losses due to limited pressure ratio.

5.1.3 Rotary Air Compressors

Rotary compressors are used when the mass flow rate of compressed air is large. However, the pressure ratio is relatively lower when compared to reciprocating compressors, where the mass handled is lower. Rotary compressors are further classified as positive displacement compressors and dynamic or steady flow compressors. In positive displacement compressors, in one cycle, a solid surface moves through a given volume, so that an exact amount of air is trapped in the given volume. The air is compressed by the reduction in the volume encountered by the rotating surfaces. Roots blower and vane-type compressors are examples of this category. In dynamic or steady flow compressors, kinetic energy of the rotor, which rotates with respect to a stator, causes the compression. Centrifugal and axial-flow compressors are examples for this category.

Vane-type rotary compressor

A vane-type rotary compressor consists of a rotor carrying several movable spring loaded vanes made of special cast alloys or synthetic fiber materials. The rotor shaft is fixed eccentrically on a stator housing such that the passage volume between the rotor and stator decreases from the air inlet port to the discharge port. The spring loaded vanes, which are free to move, are always kept pressed against the stator wall by the centrifugal force due to rotor rotation. The inlet and the discharge ports do not cover the entire width of the rotor or the vanes and the outer edges of the vanes are always in contact with the stator surface. A certain amount of air from the inlet port is trapped between two set of vanes and is compressed when passing through the reducing volume towards the discharge port before it is discharged. The main disadvantage of this type of compressor is the leakage of air back from high pressure to low pressure side. This limits the pressure ratio. Fig. 5.7 presents the schematic of a vane-type rotary compressor.

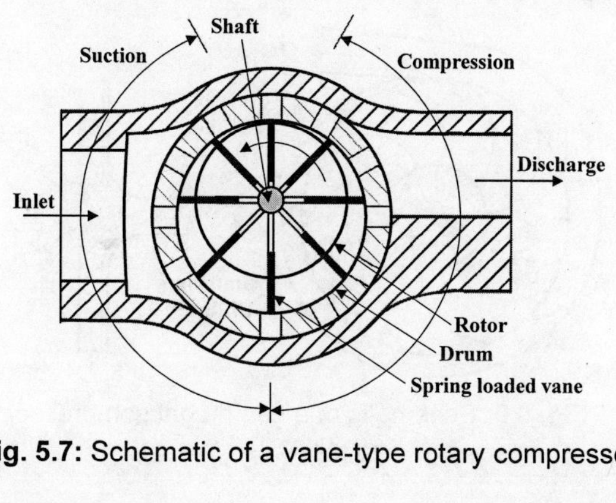

Fig. 5.7: Schematic of a vane-type rotary compressor

Roots compressor

A Roots compressor (also called Roots blower) can operate at low to moderate pressure ratios. A schematic of a typical Roots compressor with two lobes is shown in Fig. 5.8. It consists of two lobes rotating within a casing in opposite directions. The clearance between the outer edges of lobes and casing wall is kept as small as possible. Lobes can be of involute or cycloidal shapes. One of the lobe is driven directly by the motor shaft and the second lobe is driven by a gear connected to the first lobe. As the rotor (lobes) rotates, air is trapped between the casing and outer surfaces of the lobes. This amount of air is displaced to the delivery side with the further rotation of the rotor. Compression is accomplished due to back flow of high pressure air from the receiver and rotor doing the work of pushing the given amount of air against this discharge pressure to the receiver. Two lobe design results in pulsation of delivery pressure and this is reduced by using a three lobe design.

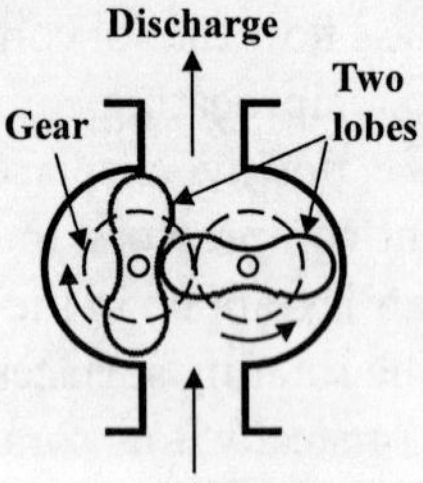

Fig. 5.8: Schematic of a Roots compressor with two lobes

Centrifugal compressor

A schematic of a centrifugal compressor is shown in Fig. 5.9. It has an impeller (rotor) with a set of vanes. The impeller is connected to the drive shaft and it rotates within a casing. The casing also has a set of vanes, called diffuser guide vanes. Low pressure air enters in axial direction and is discharged in radial direction through the diffuser vanes. Compression is accomplished as the air passed through the rotating vanes in the rotor and diffuser vanes in the casing. The kinetic energy of the rotating impeller is responsible for the compression process. The velocity decreases and the static pressure increases in the stationery diffuser. The vane design is carefully done to accomplish proper compression. Radial, backward-curved and forward-curved vanes are commonly used. In multi-stage centrifugal compressors, the air leaving the diffuser from the first (earlier) stage is ducted towards the centre of rotation to make it enter the impeller of the next stage. A pressure ratio of 10 can be accomplished with multi-stage compression.

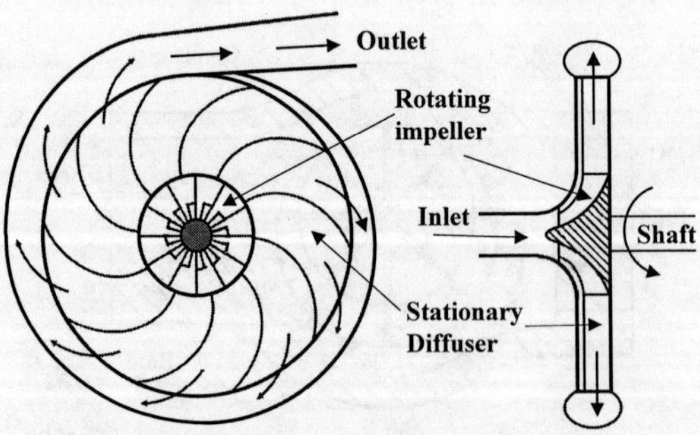

Fig. 5.9: Schematic of a centrifugal compressor

Axial-flow compressor

A schematic of an axial-flow compressor is shown in Fig. 5.10. This is similar to a steam turbine or a reaction turbine. It has a rotor disc with a set of blades at its edges. The rotor disc rotates within the casing that has a set of fixed blades. Air flows in the axial direction and its velocity changes as it passes through the set of blades. Pressure rise occurs as the air passes through the passages of both moving and fixed blades. One set of moving and fixed blades constitutes one stage of the compressor. Usually, the pressure rise in one stage is limited to around 1.5. Multi-stage compression is used to increase the pressure ratio.

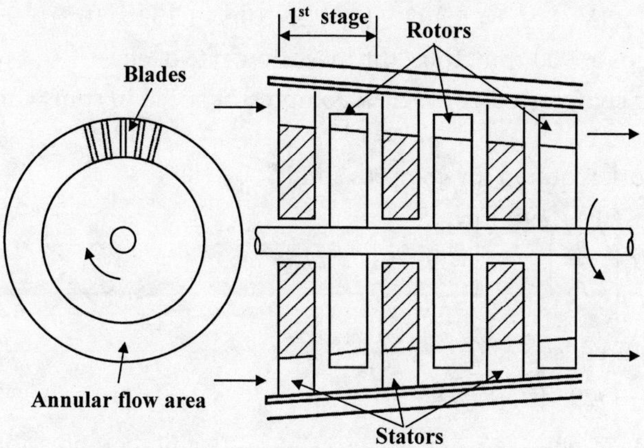

Fig. 5.10: Schematic of an axial-flow compressor

5.1.4 Illustrative Problems on Compressors

5.1 A single-stage adiabatic reciprocating compressor delivers 30 kg/minute of air at a pressure of 1200 kPa by receiving air at 100 kPa and 25˚C from the ambient. Its isentropic efficiency is 90%. Take c_p of air as 1005 J/kg-K and $\gamma = 1.4$. What is the power required for compression.

Solution: Given: $p_1 = 100$ kPa, $p_2 = 1200$ kPa, $p_1 = 25°C = 298$ K, $\dot{m} = 30$ kg/minute = 0.5 kg/s and $\eta_{isen} = 0.9$. Consider an isentropic process between p_1 and p_2. Then,

$$\frac{T_{2s}}{T_1} = \left(\frac{p_2}{p_1}\right)^{\frac{\gamma-1}{\gamma}} \Rightarrow T_{2s} = 298\left(\frac{1200}{100}\right)^{\frac{1.4-1}{1.4}} = 606.1K$$

Using the definition of isentropic efficiency,

$$\eta_{isen} = \frac{Isentropic\,work\,supplied}{actual\,work\,supplied} = 0.9 = \frac{c_p(T_{2s} - T_1)}{c_p(T_2 - T_1)} \Rightarrow T_2 = 640.3\,K$$

The actual temperature at the end of compression is T_2 = 640.3 K. Power required for compression is:

$$\dot{W}_c = mc_p(T_2 - T_1) = 0.5 \times 1005 \times (640.3 - 298) = 172005.75W$$

5.2 A single stage reciprocating compressor has a bore of 100 mm and stroke of 110 mm. Its clearance ratio is 0.05. It takes ambient air at 20°C and at a pressure of 100 kPa. The pressure ratio of compression is 3.5. If the expansion process is polytropic with an index of 1.3, Calculate the volumetric efficiency, mass flow rate if the compressor runs at 900 rpm and power required for compression. Take R of air as 287 J/kg-K.

Solution: Given: d = 100 mm = 0.1 m, L = 110 mm = 0.11 m, CR = 0.05, $T_1 = 20°C = 293$ K, n = 1.3, N = 900 rpm, $p_1 = 100$ kPa and $p_2/p_1 = 3.5 = p_3/p_4$ (referring Fig. 5.6a)

Referring Fig. 5.6(a), the swept volume $V_s = V_1 - V_3 = \pi d^2L/4 = 8.64 \times 10^{-4}$ m³.

CR = 0.05 = $V_3/(V_1 - V_3)$. Thus, clearance volume, $V_3 = 4.32 \times 10^{-5}$ m³.

$V_1 = V_3 + V_s = 9.072 \times 10^{-4}$ m^3. For process 3-4, $p_3(V_3)^n = p_4(V_4)^n$ ==> $V_4 = 1.132 \times 10^{-4}$ m^3.
Volumetric efficiency, $\eta_{vol} = (V_1 - V_4)/V_1 - V_3) = 0.9189 = 92\%$.
Mass of the air taken in per cycle = density of air taken in × volume of air taken in
$m = [p_1/(RT_1)] \times (V_1 - V_4) = 1.189 \times (9.072 \times 10^{-4} - 1.132 \times 10^{-4}) = 9.44 \times 10^{-4}$ kg.
Compressor runs at 900 rpm, thus, the mass flow rate of air,
$\dot{m}$ = mass of air compressed per cycle × compressor speed in rpm = m × N = 0.8496 kg/minute = 0.01416 kg/s.
The specific work required for compression is:

$$w_c = \frac{n}{n-1} RT_1 \left[\left(\frac{p_2}{p_1}\right)^{\frac{n-1}{n}} - 1\right] = 122153.76 J/kg$$

The power required is:

$$\dot{W}_c = w_c \times \dot{m} = 1729.7W$$

5.3 If one more stage with same pressure ratio and same compression index is added to the compressor in the problem 5.2, calculate the overall pressure ratio and the overall specific work required for compression. Take R of air as 287 J/kg-K.
Solution: Given: second stage pressure ratio = 3.5, n = 1.3. If second stage with same pressure ratio is added, overall pressure ratio is $p_3/p_1 = (p_2/p_1) \times (p_3/p_2) = 3.5 \times 3.5 = 12.25$. The specific work required for compression is:

$$w_c = 2\left(\frac{n}{n-1}\right) RT_1 \left(\left(\frac{p_3}{p_1}\right)^{\frac{n-1}{2n}} - 1\right) = 244307.5 J/kg$$

5.4 A two-stage air compressor with ideal intercooling works with an overall pressure ratio of 9. Air at 300 K and 100 kPa is taken from ambient in the first stage. Polytropic compression with an index of 1.35 occurs at both stages. Take R of air as 287 J/kg-K and γ = 1.4. Calculate the specific work required for the compressor and heat transfer in the intercooler.
Solution: Given: T_1 = 300 K, p_1 = 100 kPa, n = 1.35 and $p_2/p_1 = 9$. Referring Fig. 5.4, the states at intercooler entry and exit are c and d, respectively. The specific work required for the compression is:

$$w_c = 2\left(\frac{n}{n-1}\right) RT_1 \left(\left(\frac{p_2}{p_1}\right)^{\frac{n-1}{2n}} - 1\right) = 218873.75 J/kg$$

Referring Fig. 5.4, the intermediate pressure is p_c (= p_d). Then for minimum compression work, the pressure ratios are $p_c/p_1 = p_2/p_c = (9)^{0.5} = 3$. Thus, p_c = 300 kPa.
Temperature at the entry of intercooler is calculated from: $T_c/T_1 = (p_c/p_1)^{(n-1)/n}$
==> T_c = 398.85 K.
Temperature at the exit of the intercooler for perfect or ideal intercooling is same as T_1; T_d = 300 K.
Heat rejected per kg of air is $q = c_p \times (T_c - T_d) = \gamma R/(\gamma-1) \times (398.85 - 300) = 99294.825$ J/kg.

5.5 Consider a two-stage centrifugal compressor with pressure ratio of 2.5 in each stage. The compressor handles 4 kg/s of air flow rate from an ambient at 20°C and 1 bar pressure. Isentropic efficiency of both stages of compressor is 0.85. Intercooler cools the air from the first stage to 320 K. Take c_p of air as 1005 J/kg-K and $\gamma = 1.4$. Determine the overall compressor power and heat rejected in the intercooler.

Solution: Let 1-2 be the compression process of the first stage, 2-3 be the process in the intercooler and 3-4 be the compression process in the second stage.

Given: $p_2/p_1 = 2.5 = p_4/p_3$, $\dot{m} = 4$ kg/s, $T_1 = 20°C = 293$ K, $p_1 = 1$ bar, $\eta_{isen} = 0.85$ and $T_3 = 320$ K.

Consider an isentropic compression process 1-2s between p_1 and p_2. The temperature at the end of isentropic compression is T_{2s}. Then,

$$\frac{T_{2s}}{T_1} = \left(\frac{p_2}{p_1}\right)^{\frac{\gamma-1}{\gamma}} \Rightarrow T_{2s} = 293(2.5)^{\frac{1.4-1}{1.4}} = 380.7\,K$$

Temperature at state 2 after the actual compression process, T_2, is calculated using isentropic efficiency.

$$\eta_{isen} = 0.85 = \frac{c_p(T_{2s} - T_1)}{c_p(T_2 - T_1)} \Rightarrow T_2 = 396.2\,K$$

Similarly, consider an isentropic compression process 3-4s between p_3 and p_4. The temperature at the end of isentropic compression is T_{4s}. Then,

$$\frac{T_{4s}}{T_3} = \left(\frac{p_4}{p_3}\right)^{\frac{\gamma-1}{\gamma}} \Rightarrow T_{4s} = 320(2.5)^{\frac{1.4-1}{1.4}} = 415.8\,K$$

Temperature at state 4 after the actual compression process, T_4, is calculated using isentropic efficiency.

$$\eta_{isen} = 0.85 = \frac{c_p(T_{4s} - T_3)}{c_p(T_4 - T_3)} \Rightarrow T_4 = 432.7\,K$$

The compressor power is calculated as follows:

$$\dot{W}_c = \dot{m} \times c_p \times \left[(T_2 - T_1) + (T_4 - T_3)\right] = 4 \times 1005 \times \left[(396.2 - 293) + (432.7 - 320)\right]$$

$$\dot{W}_c = 867918\,W = 867.92\,kW$$

The heat transfer in the intercooler is got as follows:

$$\dot{Q} = \dot{m} \times c_p \times (T_3 - T_2) = 4 \times 1005 \times (320 - 396.2) = -306324\,W$$

The heat lost in the intercooler is 306.32 kW.

5.2 REFRIGERATION

The term refrigeration means keeping a space or objects in cool condition. This is accomplished by transferring heat from the space or object at a low temperature to a region (surroundings) at a high temperature. It may be noted that this is not a spontaneous heat transfer process and would require aid in the form of work from the surroundings. Any refrigeration system should obey the Clausius statement: "It is impossible for a system working in a thermodynamic cycle to transfer heat from a low temperature region to a high temperature region without the aid of work transfer from the surroundings". The objective of a refrigerator is to keep a given space at a low temperature than the hotter surroundings. On the other hand, in cold regions, ambient will be at a low temperature and a room or space has to be kept hotter for human comfort. Here, a heat pump is used to pump heat from the cold ambient to the room to keep it at a higher temperature. The objective of a heat pump is to keep the room hotter than the cold surroundings. As opposed to a heat engine, in a refrigerator or a heat pump, heat is transferred from the cold temperature region to the hot temperature region, and work is supplied to the system from the surroundings. Hence, refrigerator or heat pump is called a reverse heat engine. Fig. 5.11 presents the schematic of a refrigeration system. Refrigerator has several components. When all the components are considered together, it is analysed as a system and it operates in a thermodynamic cycle.

The temperature of the space that is cooled is T_C. In order to keep this space at T_C, heat transfer amounting to Q_C per cycle is transferred from this space to one of the components of the refrigerator (schematically shown as R). One of the components of the refrigerator receives an energy in the form of work (W per cycle) from the surroundings. One of the components in the refrigerator rejects heat amounting to Q_H per cycle to a source at a temperature of T_H (usually the ambient). First law for the refrigerator system working in a thermodynamic cycle is written as, $Q_C + W = Q_H$.

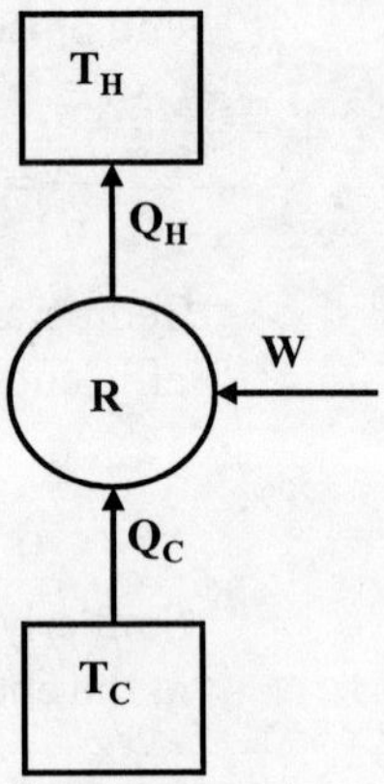

Fig. 5.11: Schematic of energy transfers in a refrigeration system

The performance metric of a refrigerator is estimated by evaluating the ratio of objective energy transfer to the energy transfer that costs. Here, in order to maintain the space at T_C, heat by an amount, Q_C is taken in by the refrigerator. This is the objective energy transfer. The energy that costs is the work energy (usually electrical energy) supplied to the refrigerator from the surroundings. The performance metric of the refrigerator is called Coefficient of Performance (COP) and is expressed as,

$$COP = \frac{Q_C}{W} = \frac{Q_C}{Q_H - Q_C} \tag{5.21}$$

The unit of Q_C is W. In commercial terms, one ton of refrigeration is equivalent to $Q_C = 3.5167$ kW. For a heat pump, the objective energy transfer is Q_H, since this heat has to be supplied to the space to keep it at T_H, and the energy that costs is W. So, for a heat pump, COP = Q_H/W.

Refrigerants

Working fluid in refrigerator is called refrigerant. They go through a cycle and carry heat through various devices in the system. For example, in vapor compression refrigeration system, the refrigerant flows through an evaporator (a heat exchanger) at low pressure to receive heat from the space to be cooled and is completely vaporized. The pressure in the evaporator is slightly lower than its saturation pressure at the lowest temperature. The vapor is compressed in a gas compressor to high pressure, which is slightly more than its saturation pressure at ambient temperature. Then, it flows at high pressure through another heat exchanger called condenser. Here, it rejects the heat to the ambient and condenses to liquid. Finally, the refrigerant liquid flows through a throttle valve, where its pressure decreases to that of the evaporator. Therefore, there are various properties, which qualify the fluid to be a refrigerant. They are, boiling point, freezing point, critical temperature, latent heat of vaporization, specific heat, density, viscosity and so on. A refrigerant should have low boiling and freezing points. It should have high critical temperature (well above the maximum condensing temperature). It should have high latent heat of vaporization. The specific heat, vapor density and viscosity should be low. Further, some chemical aspects are also used to qualify a refrigerant. The refrigerant should be non-toxic, non-corrosive, non-flammable, and should not react with moisture and lubricating oil.

Ammonia and sulphur dioxide have been used as refrigerants in the past. However, ammonia is flammable and sulphur dioxide produce irritation to human. Then, organic refrigerants such as hydrocarbon (HC), fluorocarbon (FC). Hydrofluorocarbon (HFC), hydrochlorofluorocarbons (HCFC) and chlorofluorocarbons (CFC) have been used. Freons, which are fluorocarbons of methane and ethane, have been commonly used. They contain one or more halogens such as chlorine, bromine and fluorine. Although they possess all the required properties of a refrigerant, they are not quite environmentally friendly, because they produce a few compounds that affect the ozone layer. Presently, mixtures having the desirable properties for refrigerants, as well as which do not produce compounds affecting ozone are being researched.

5.2.1 Air Refrigeration System

Air refrigeration system uses air as the working substance and its thermodynamic cycle is basically same as the reversed Brayton cycle, which is a gas turbine power plant cycle. It is also called Joule cycle or Bell-Coleman cycle. The components of an air refrigeration system are schematically shown in Fig. 5.12. It consists of an air compressor usually run by an electric motor, where air is compressed from low pressure p_L to a high pressure p_H, a heat exchanger that facilitates heat removal from the compressed air to a high temperature region, an air turbine in which the air expands and its pressure reduces to p_L, and another heat exchanger that takes in heat from the low temperature region.

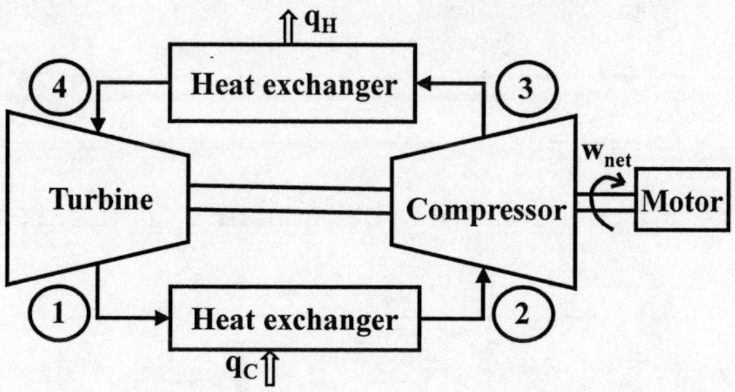

Fig. 5.12: Schematic of an air refrigeration system

The compression (2-3) and expansion (4-1) processes are isentropic in an ideal cycle. In actual cycle these processes will have isentropic efficiencies less than unity. The work produced during the expansion in the turbine is supplied to the compressor. The motor supplies the balance (net) work required for the compressor. The processes in the heat exchangers (3-4 and 1-2) occur at constant pressures of p_H and p_L, respectively. The thermodynamic cycle in a T-S diagram is shown in Fig. 5.13. The process 1-2 occurs at constant pressure, p_L ($p_1 = p_2 = p_L$). Here, heat is added to the air, amounting to q_C J per kg/s of air flow, and its temperature increases from T_1 to T_2. Air is then compressed in an isentropic process (ideally) from p_L to p_H, as shown by 2-3 in Fig. 5.13. Temperature increases from T_2 to T_3. Then, heat is rejected from the air in the heat exchanger during 3-4, where p remains at p_H ($p_3 = p_4 = p_H$). In the heat exchanger, a coolant (either atmospheric air or water) is used to exchange heat from the air. The value of T_3 should be higher than the incoming water or air temperature in the heat exchanger for the heat transfer to occur. Therefore, the value of p_H should be such that T_3 is higher than the temperature of coolant entering the heat exchanger for the cycle to be practically feasible. Larger the difference between T_3 and incoming coolant temperature to the heat exchanger, smaller will be the mass flow rate of air required for attaining the given cooling capacity. Incoming coolant temperature will be closer to T_4. For this, a higher pressure ratio is required. Process 4-1 represents the isentropic (ideal) expansion process. For air to receive heat from the colder space, the temperature T_1 should be less than the temperature of cold space, which is close to T_2. If T_1 is as low as possible, mass flow rate of air required for a given capacity will be smaller.

For ideal cycle, 2-3 and 4-1 are isentropic processes. These obey,

$$\frac{T_3}{T_2} = \left(\frac{p_H}{p_L}\right)^{\frac{\gamma-1}{\gamma}} = \frac{T_4}{T_1} \Rightarrow \frac{T_2}{T_1} = \frac{T_3}{T_4} \quad (5.22)$$

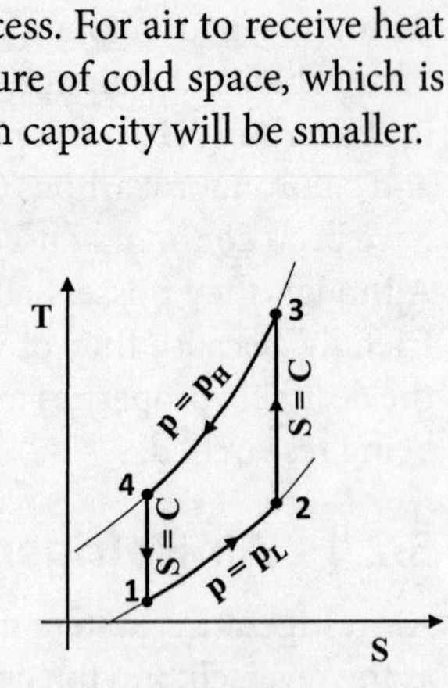

Fig. 5.13: Basic reversed Brayton cycle in a T-S diagram

Considering steady-state operation and neglecting the changes in kinetic and potential energies, the specific work interactions (absolute values) during compression and expansion are:

$$w_c = h_3 - h_2 = c_p(T_3 - T_2); w_e = h_4 - h_1 = c_p(T_4 - T_1) \quad (5.23)$$

The specific heat interactions (absolute values) are written as,

$$q_C = h_2 - h_1 = c_p(T_2 - T_1); q_H = h_3 - h_4 = c_p(T_3 - T_4) \quad (5.24)$$

The net specific work per kg/s flow of air required is $w_c - w_e$. The COP of the refrigerator is evaluated as,

$$COP = \frac{q_C}{w_c - w_e} = \frac{(T_2 - T_1)}{(T_3 - T_2) - (T_4 - T_1)}$$

$$= \frac{(T_2 - T_1)}{(T_3 - T_4) - (T_2 - T_1)} = \frac{1}{\left(\frac{T_3 - T_4}{T_2 - T_1} - 1\right)} \quad (5.25)$$

The ratio $(T_3 - T_4)/(T_2 - T_1)$ can be shown to be equal to T_4/T_1 using equation (5.22). Thus,

$$COP = \frac{1}{\left(\frac{T_4}{T_1} - 1\right)} = \frac{1}{\left(\left(\frac{p_H}{p_L}\right)^{\frac{\gamma-1}{\gamma}} - 1\right)} = \frac{1}{\left(r^{\frac{\gamma-1}{\gamma}} - 1\right)} \quad (5.26)$$

In equation (5.26), r is the pressure ratio (p_H/p_L). This expression is derived using isentropic process. For r = 1, COP is infinite. As the value of r increases, the COP value decreases. In the actual cycle, there are deviations from the isentropic processes during compression and expansion. Similarly, there will be some pressure drop as the air flows through compressor, turbine and heat exchanger. However, in thermodynamic analysis, pressure drop is usually neglected. The isentropic efficiencies ($\eta_{isen,c}$ and $\eta_{isen,e}$) are used for the analysis of compression and expansion processes. These are defined as,

$$\eta_{isen,c} = \frac{h_2 - h_{3s}}{h_2 - h_3} \text{ and } \eta_{isen,e} = \frac{h_4 - h_1}{h_4 - h_{1s}} \quad (5.27)$$

Here, the subscript 's' denotes the state reached through an isentropic process and that without the subscripts are states attained through the actual process.

Illustrative example

5.6 Consider an air refrigeration system working on Joule cycle. Temperature at the entry of compressor is 260 K and that at the inlet of the turbine is 310 K. The pressure ratio is 3.5. If the refrigeration capacity of 1.5 tonnes is required, evaluate the mass flow rate of air and COP of the system. The isentropic efficiency of compressor and that of the turbine are 0.9. Take for air, c_p = 1.005 kJ/kg-K and γ = 1.4.

Solution: Refer Fig. 5.13. Given: T_2 = 260 K, T_4 = 310 K, $p_H/p_L = p_3/p_2 = p_4/p_1$ = 3.5 and refrigeration capacity = 1.5 tonnes.

Considering isentropic processes, the following expression holds good: 1.43036

$$\frac{T_{3s}}{T_2} = \left(\frac{p_H}{p_L}\right)^{\frac{\gamma-1}{\gamma}} = \frac{T_4}{T_{1s}}$$

From this, T_{3s} and T_{1s} are calculated as 371.9 K and 216.7 K, respectively. Applying isentropic efficiency, the actual temperatures of states 3 and 1 are determined.

$$\eta_{isen,c} = 0.9 = \frac{h_2 - h_{3s}}{h_2 - h_3} = \frac{T_2 - T_{3s}}{T_2 - T_3} \Rightarrow T_3 = 384.3\,K$$

$$\eta_{isen,e} = 0.9 = \frac{h_4 - h_1}{h_4 - h_{1s}} = \frac{T_4 - T_1}{T_4 - T_{1s}} \Rightarrow T_1 = 226\,K$$

The specific heat transfer (absolute) from cold space is,

$$q_C = h_2 - h_1 = c_p\left(T_2 - T_1\right) = 34.17\,kJ/kg$$

The net specific work per kg/s flow of air required is $w_c - w_e$. This is written as,

$$w_c - w_e = c_p\left[\left(T_3 - T_2\right) - \left(T_4 - T_1\right)\right] = 40.5\,kJ/kg$$

COP of the cycle is q_C/w_{net} = 0.843.

For isentropic compression and expansion processes, COP_{isen} depends only on pressure ratio and can be calculated from equation (5.26) as 2.3236. The reduction in the COP of the actual cycle is due to associated irreversibility. The capacity of refrigeration is 1.5 tonnes. This is expressed as,

$$\dot{Q}_c = 1.5 \times 3.5167 = 5.27505\,kW$$

The mass flow rate of air required for this capacity is determined as,

$$\dot{Q}_c = \dot{m} \times q_c = \dot{m} \times 34.17 = 5.27505\,kW \Rightarrow \dot{m} = 0.1544\frac{kg}{s}.$$

The main application of the air refrigeration system is that of cooling an aircraft cabin. A schematic of aircraft cabin cooling system is shown in Fig. 5.14. An aircraft engine works on a gas turbine cycle. It takes air from the atmosphere, compresses it in an air compressor, uses the high pressure air to burn the fuel in a combustor and the hot products expand through a turbine to propel the aircraft. In Fig. 5.14, only the cooling cycle is shown. The air entering the compressor (point 1) from the atmosphere is very cold due to the high altitude and enters with a high velocity due to the inlet passage design. This is called ramming effect. Some amount of the cold air (point 2) and compressed air (which will be warmer) are passed through a heat exchanger (point 3). The warmer air from the heat exchanger is sent to the cabin of the aircraft (point 4) after expanding in an air turbine (point 5). It may be noted that this is an open cycle, where air is taken from the atmosphere. It is let back to atmosphere after cooling the cabin or as hot products of combustion. The thermodynamic analysis of aircraft cabin cooling system is not included in this textbook. Readers can refer to standard textbooks [1-4] for knowing more about this analysis.

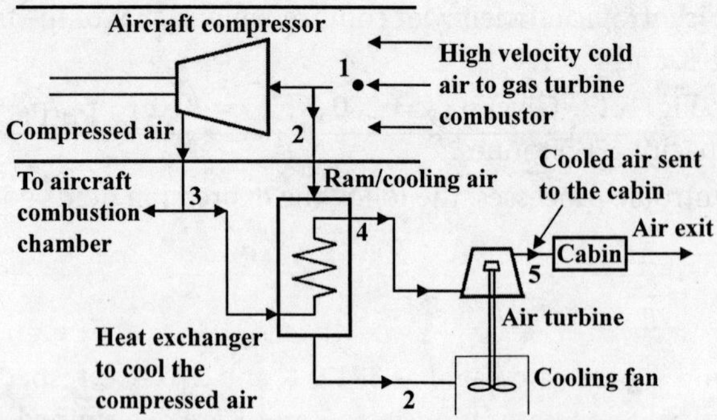

Fig. 5.14: Schematic of an aircraft cabin cooling system

5.2.2 Vapor Compression Refrigeration System

Most commonly used refrigeration system is the vapor compression refrigeration system. A schematic view of the devices in a vapor compression refrigeration system is shown in Fig. 5.15.

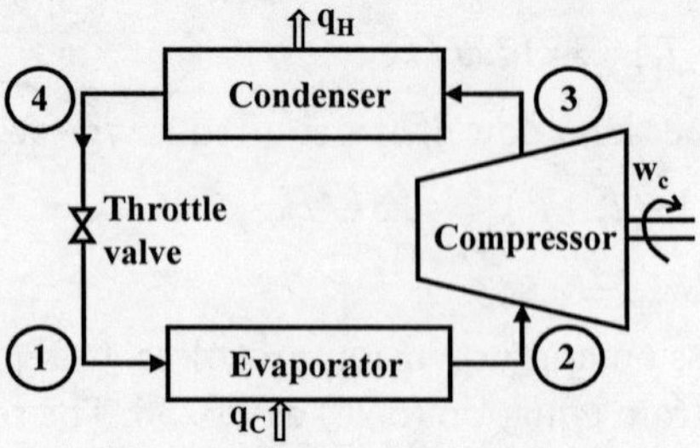

Fig. 5.15: Schematic of a vapor compression refrigeration cycle

The main components in a vapor compression refrigeration cycle are compressor, condenser, throttle valve and evaporator. Unlike the air refrigeration system, the fluid used in this system is a refrigerant, and while flowing through these devices in a cycle, the phase of the refrigerant changes. Therefore, tables (exactly like steam tables) or correlations have to be used to fix the properties of the refrigerant in this cycle at each state [2]. Evaporator is a heat exchanger that receives heat (q_C per kg of refrigerant per cycle) from the space to be cooled. The refrigerant enters the evaporator as a mixture of liquid and vapor and leaves as a vapor (generally saturated vapor, sometimes superheated vapor) due to the heat transfer. Ideally, the evaporator operates at a constant pressure. The vapor is then compressed in the compressor, which receives work from the surroundings (w_c per kg of refrigerant per cycle). The refrigerant becomes superheated vapor. Temperature at the exit of the compressor is higher than the saturation temperature at the compressor exit pressure. Then, the superheated vapor is cooled in condenser during a constant pressure process. At the exit of the condenser, the refrigerant is in a saturated liquid state (sometimes it is at a sub-cooled liquid state also). The pressure of the liquid refrigerant is reduced by allowing it to pass through an adiabatic throttle valve (sudden expansion device), which is an irreversible process. Ideally, there is no work or heat transfer and the enthalpy remains a constant. Due to sudden expansion, some vapor is formed at the exit of the throttle valve. The mixture of liquid and vapor enters the evaporator and the cycle continues.

The basic vapor compression refrigeration cycle is shown in a T-S diagram in Fig. 5.16. In this diagram, saturation lines corresponding to saturated liquid and saturated vapor states are included.

Temperature at 1 and 2 are the same and equal to the saturation temperature at p_L, which is called the evaporator pressure. State 1 is fixed by two properties, namely, the pressure, p_L, or the temperature, T_1, and the specific enthalpy of the fluid. Since process 4-1 is an adiabatic throttling process, heat and work interactions, as well as the changes in the potential and kinetic energies are zero. Thus, by energy conservation, enthalpy is conserved; $h_1 = h_4$. In the basic cycle, state 2 is considered as a saturated vapor state at p_L. In the actual cycle, this state may be a superheated state at p_L. Isentropic compression is shown by the process 2-3s and the actual compression is shown by 2-3. For isentropic compression, the state 3s is fixed by pressure, p_H, and the specific entropy, s_{3s}, which is equal to the entropy at state 2 (s_2). Finally, the state 4 is considered as a saturated liquid state at p_H. The value of h_4 is obtained as the saturated liquid enthalpy, h_f, from saturated pressure table corresponding to a pressure of p_H and is equal to h_1. The process 1-2 in the evaporator is a heat addition process. Phase change occurs at constant pressure, p_L, as the refrigerant exchanges heat from the space to be cooled, and the temperature is equal to the saturation temperature at p_L. The pressure, p_L, should be such that the saturation temperature is slightly lower than the temperature in the space to be cooled, so that the heat transfer occurs. During the compression process, 2-3, pressure increases to p_H and refrigerant becomes a superheated vapor. For actual compression (shown as dashed line in Fig. 5.16), the value of the isentropic efficiency of the compressor is specified.

In the condenser, heat is lost to the ambient. Pressure, p_H, should be such that the saturation temperature of the refrigerant is slightly higher than the ambient temperature for the heat transfer to occur. Finally, the saturated liquid at p_H expands to p_L in the adiabatic throttle valve. Since this is an irreversible process, it is shown as a dashed line in Fig. 5.16.

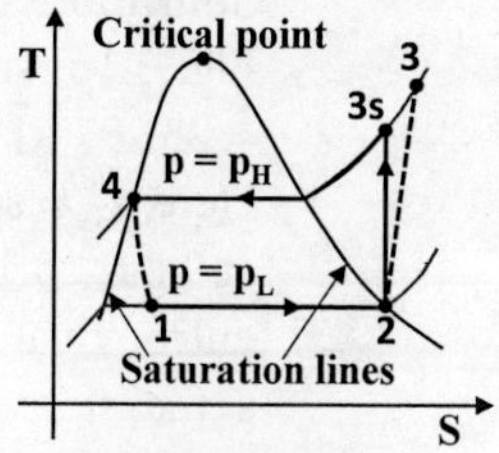

Fig. 5.16: Basic refrigeration cycle in a T-S diagram

The heat added to the system in the evaporator per unit flow rate of refrigerant is calculated as,

$$q_c = h_2 - h_1 \tag{5.28}$$

Here, h_1 is equal to h_4, which is h_f @ p_H, and $h_2 = h_g$ @ p_L or T_{sat} @ p_L. These are got from saturation tables based on pressure or temperature. The specific work required for the compressor (absolute value) is evaluated as,

$$w_c = h_3 - h_2 \tag{5.29}$$

The value of h_3 is got after evaluating the value of h_{3s} for isentropic compression between 2 and 3. From superheated tables of the refrigerant, corresponding to the pressure p_H, h_{3s} is retrieved using the value of entropy at the isentropic exit state: $s_{3s} = s_2$. The value of s_2 is equal to s_g @ p_L or T_2. Once h_{3s} is evaluated, h_3 is calculated using the isentropic efficiency as,

$$\eta_{isen,c} = \frac{h_2 - h_{3s}}{h_2 - h_3}$$

The heat transfer in the condenser (absolute value) is calculated as,

$$q_H = h_4 - h_3 \tag{5.30}$$

The COP of the cycle is evaluated as COP = q_c/w_c.

Illustrative example

5.7 Consider a vapor compression refrigeration cycle operating at steady state with R134a as the working fluid. Saturated vapor enters the compressor at 1.6 bar and saturated liquid leaves the condenser at 9 bar. The mass flow rate of the refrigerant is 5 kg/min. Assuming no pressure losses in the condenser or the evaporator, determine (a) the compressor power in kW for an isentropic efficiency of 67% (b) the refrigeration capacity in tons and (c) the coefficient of performance. The properties of R134a at different states can be taken from the following tables.

Properties of Saturated R134a: Saturation table

T (°C)	Saturation pressure (bar)	h_f (kJ/kg)	h_g (kJ/kg)	s_f (kJ/kg-K)	s_g (kJ/kg K)
-15.62	1.6	29.78	237.97	0.1211	0.9295
35.53	9	99.56	266.18	0.3656	0.9054

Properties of Saturated R134a: Superheated table at 9 bar

T (°C)	h (kJ/kg)	s (kJ/kg-K)
40	271.25	0.9217
50	282.34	0.9566
60	293.21	0.9897

Solution: Considering basic vapor compression refrigeration cycle and referring to Fig. 5.16, state 2 is saturated vapor at 1.6 bar. From saturation table, for 1.6 bar, $h_2 = h_g = 237.97$ kJ/kg. State 3 is evaluated after finding state 3s considering isentropic compression. Here, $s_{3s} = s_2 = s_g$ @ 1.6 bar = 0.9295 kJ/kg-K. Enthalpy at state 3s is got from superheated table at 9 bar corresponding to entropy value of s_{3s}. By interpolating the superheated table between entropy values of 0.9217 and 0.9566, h_{3s} is obtained as 273.73 kJ/kg. To find the enthalpy at actual state 3, isentropic efficiency is used as follows:

$$\eta_{isen,c} = 0.67 = \frac{h_2 - h_{3s}}{h_2 - h_3} \Rightarrow h_3 = 237.97 - \left(\frac{237.97 - 273.73}{0.67}\right) = 291.34\frac{kJ}{kg}.$$

The value of enthalpy at state 4 is h_f @ 9 bar = 99.56 kJ/kg as taken from saturation table. The enthalpy at state 1 is equal to that of state 4 (adiabatic throttling process); $h_1 = 99.56$ kJ/kg.

(a) Compressor power (absolute value) = $\dot{m} \times (h_3 - h_2) = (5/60) \times (291.34 - 237.97) = 4.45$ kW.

(b) Refrigeration capacity in tons = $(\dot{m} \times q_C)/3.5167 = (5/60)\times(237.97 - 99.56)/3.5167 = 3.28$ tonnes.

(c) COP = $q_C/w_C = (237.97 - 99.56)/(291.34 - 237.97) = 2.59$.

5.3 AIR-CONDITIONING

The technique of controlling the temperature and water vapor present in air inside rooms and confined spaces, as per the human comfort level, is called air-conditioning. Atmospheric air contains oxygen and nitrogen in major proportions, along with small amounts of water vapor, argon, carbon dioxide and so on. In these, water vapor (also called moisture) is the only condensable element under atmospheric conditions. Atmospheric air with moisture and other gases is called moist air, or in simple terms, just "air". The moist air excluding the moisture is specifically called "dry air" (which has elements those will not condense under normal conditions). Therefore, for air-conditioning calculations, the air is considered as a mixture of dry air and water vapor. Humidity indicates the amount of water vapor present in the atmospheric air. If air occupies a pressure, p, (say 1 bar, for example), then the sum of partial pressures of dry air, p_a, and water vapor, p_v, will be equal to p ($p = p_a + p_v = 1$ bar). Liquid water in contact with atmospheric air evaporates depending on the temperature of the air. For example, at an air temperature of 35°C, liquid water coming in contact can evaporate and the maximum partial pressure of water vapor in the air will be around 0.05627 bar at this temperature. This data can be taken from steam tables. For this case, p = 1 bar (atmospheric pressure), p_v = 0.05627 bar and p_a = 0.94373 bar. The maximum partial pressure of water vapor present in air at a given temperature (T) is equal to its saturation pressure (p_{sat} or p_g at the given T) and this air is called "saturated air". The value of p_{sat} or p_g can be obtained from a steam table for a given temperature. No more water can be added to the saturated air at the same temperature. However, not necessarily the maximum amount of moisture should always be present in air at a given temperature. That is, its partial pressure, p_v can be less than its saturation pressure, p_{sat} at the given air temperature. Humidity is specified as relative humidity and specific humidity. Relative humidity (φ) is the ratio of p_v and p_{sat} at a given air temperature ($\varphi = p_v/p_{sat}$). For saturated air, the relative humidity is 1 or 100% (since, $p_v = p_{sat}$, for saturated air). The specific humidity (ω) is also called the humidity ratio. It is defined as the ratio of the mass of the water vapor to the mass of the dry air. It is expressed in terms of partial pressures of water vapor and air as,

$$\omega = 0.622\left(\frac{p_v}{p_a}\right) = 0.622\left(\frac{p_v}{p - p_v}\right) \tag{5.31}$$

If the air in a room has no moisture, then it creates a "dry" condition, irrespective of the temperature of the air, and creates irritation in nasal passages, eyes and so on. For human comfort, some amount of moisture is required in the air. Similarly, if too much moisture is present in air (say like in saturated air), this also creates discomfort like sweating. Relative humidity in the range of 40% to 60% is considered to be comfortable for human beings. Similarly, for human comfort, air in the room should have a temperature within a given range, which is usually between 18°C to 26°C.

There are several processes used for air-conditioning. They are sensible heating, sensible cooling, humidification, dehumidification, evaporative cooling and a certain combination of these. Sensible heating is used to heat the air from a low to a high temperature. In winter season, the ambient will be cooler and the ambient air has to be heated to a certain level and circulated in the room. Sensible cooling is used during summer, where the temperature of air is reduced to the required level and circulated within a given space. If the moisture content in air is lower than the desired level, humidification process is used to increase the relative humidity of the air. Here, water is sprayed into a stream of air flow. Dehumidification is the process of removal of moisture from the air to reduce the relative humidity. Cold surfaces are used to accomplish this. Evaporative cooling is a process used to cool the air as well as to humidify the air. When hot air with very little or no moisture content (almost dry air) passes through a porous structure saturated with water, the water evaporates by taking the heat from air. The temperature of the air reduces as well as its moisture content increases. Since several of these processes are involved, an air-conditioning system is in general called HVAC (Heating, Ventilation and Air-Conditioning) system.

5.3.1 Classification of Air-Conditioning Systems

The air-conditioning system is classified based on the arrangement of the air-conditioner as central air-conditioning system, unitary air-conditioning system, window air-conditioner and split air-conditioner. In general, these systems use vapor compression refrigeration concept for cooling. The capacity of the air-conditioner is decided by the cooling load in a given space and the required temperature to be maintained.

Central and unitary air-conditioning systems

In the central air-conditioning system, various components such as compressor, evaporator, condenser, pumps and so on are installed in a central place. Air is processed in Air Handling Units (AHU) and supplied to various rooms through ducts with required controls. The air exiting the rooms after circulating reach AHU through a duct and it is mixed with more fresh air and processed again. Central air-conditioning systems are of huge capacity (100 to 300 tonnes). In unitary air-conditioning system, well assembled packaged units are installed for serving conditioned air to larger spaces. In commercial buildings, these systems may be installed in the ground floor or on rooftop. The system can serve the whole or part of the building space, based on the required capacity. These unitary systems are not as large as central air-conditioning system and can have a capacity in the range of 5 to 10 tonnes.

Window air-conditioner

These are individual small units having capacity in the range of 1 to 2 tonnes. They are installed by creating a slot of required size in the windows of the room. A schematic of a window air-conditioner is shown in Fig. 5.17.

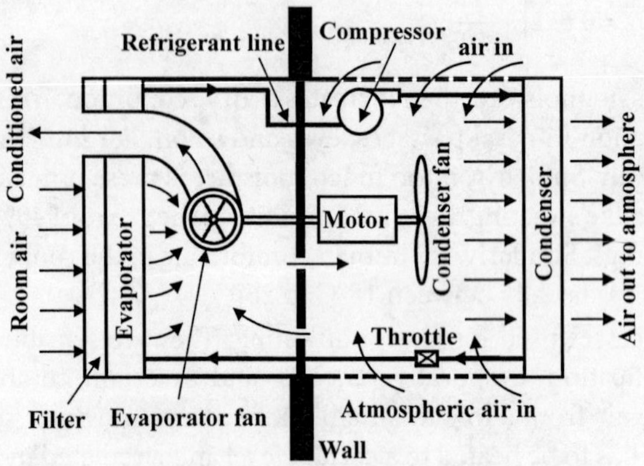

Fig. 5.17: Schematic of a window air-conditioner

Compressor, heat exchangers and fans are part of the single unit that is divided by a partition. The evaporator is installed facing the room inside the inner partition. Compressor and condenser are installed in the outer partition. Heat is rejected to the ambient from the condenser, through which atmospheric air is circulated by an axial pump. The air in the room is sucked by a centrifugal fan. The air flows over the evaporator, where it is cooled and dehumidified. It is recirculated in the room. Some amount of fresh air is also allowed to flow into the room through an adjustable vent. Advantages of the window air-conditioner are compact size, easy installation and suitable for small spaces. A few disadvantages are lesser COP than central systems, no humidification process, no proper control of relative humidity and higher noise.

Split air-conditioner

Since fans and compressor in window air-conditioner are in the same unit, the noise generated in the window air-conditioner is quite high. Instead of mounting the compressor and condenser in the same unit, they are kept in a separate unit outside the building. This unit is named as condensing unit. Since most of the noise comes from this unit, by keeping this unit outside the room, the noise level is significantly reduced. The centrifugal fan and evaporator are kept inside the room as a separate unit. This is called cooling unit. The condensing and cooling units can be kept up to 10 meters apart. These are also individual small units having capacity in the range of 1.5 to 4 tonnes. The main advantages of the split air-conditioner is there is no need for making a slot in the window and the noise level inside the room is significantly reduced. However, there are disadvantages such as increased pressure drop, lower COP and no fresh air injection to the room.

An air-conditioner system is also classified as comfort air-conditioning system and industrial air-conditioning system based on its functionality. Air-conditioners in shopping complexes, hospitals, schools, offices and so on, focus on human comfort and are categorized as comfort air-conditioning systems. Air-conditioners installed in industries for specific purposes are classified under the industrial air-conditioning systems. More details of various air-conditioning units can be found in standard textbooks [1-4].

5.3.2 Seasonal Air-Conditioning

Specific processes are required to condition the air based on the season. In summer, the atmospheric air will be hot and it may have some amount of moisture based on the water bodies available in a given location. Cooling and dehumidification are the main processes in summer air-conditioning. In dry locations, a humidifier is also installed. In winter, the air will be cold and may have adequate moisture as well. Heating and humidifying are the main processes in winter air-conditioning. A re-heater is also used to control the air temperature. Therefore, an air-conditioning system should be installed with devices to carry out the required air-conditioning processes and to deliver the conditioned air to the required space.

Summer air-conditioning

A schematic of a summer air-conditioning system is shown in Fig. 5.18. Outdoor air is taken in and blended with recirculating air. It passes through a filter, and a cooling and dehumidifying unit, where its temperature decreases. Some amount of water condenses and its specific humidity decreases. Based upon the moisture content in the air, some amount of water is sprayed in humidifier to increase the humidity to the comfortable level as required. This process may be required only in dry regions. In the humidifier, the temperature of the air could decrease and a re-heater is used to adjust the temperature to the required level. A blower is used to circulate the air in the required space. The air coming out is partly recirculated and the remaining is exhausted.

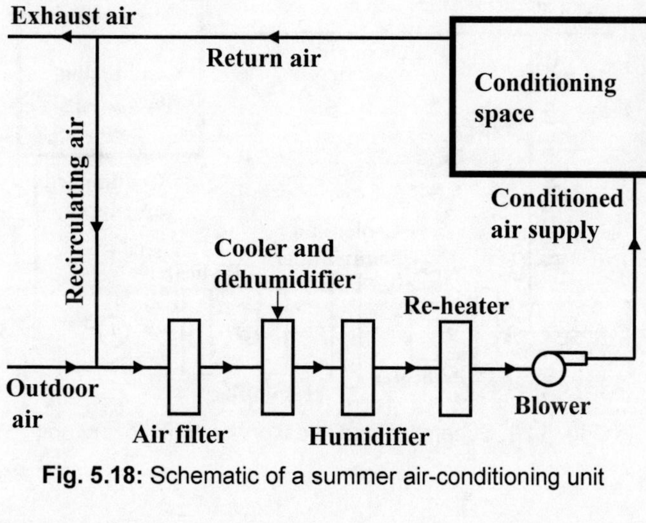

Fig. 5.18: Schematic of a summer air-conditioning unit

Winter air-conditioning

A schematic of a winter air-conditioning system is shown in Fig. 5.19. Outside air that is cold and with some humidity is taken and blended with the recirculating air. It passes through an air filter and a preheater. The temperature of the air is sufficiently raised in the preheater. To maintain a sufficient amount of moisture in the conditioned air, a humidifier is used, where the specific humidity of air is increased. Finally, a re-heater is used to adjust the temperature of the air to the required level. A blower is used to circulate the air to the required space. The return air coming out is partly recirculated and remaining is exhausted.

All-season air-conditioning

A combination of summer and winter air-conditioning systems with more controls constitutes the all-season air-conditioning system. A schematic of all-season air-conditioning system is shown in Fig. 5.20. During summer, the preheater is kept inactive and the humidifier and re-heater are used as required. During winter, the cooler and dehumidifier remain inactive. Appropriate controls are used to operate these devices as required and to supply air to rooms with required properties.

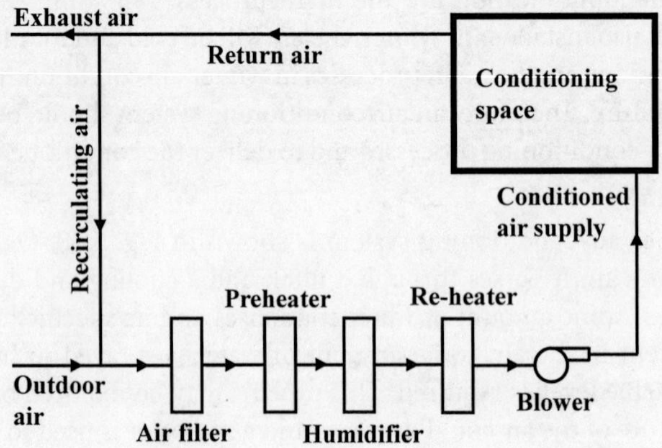

Fig. 5.19: Schematic of a winter air-conditioning unit

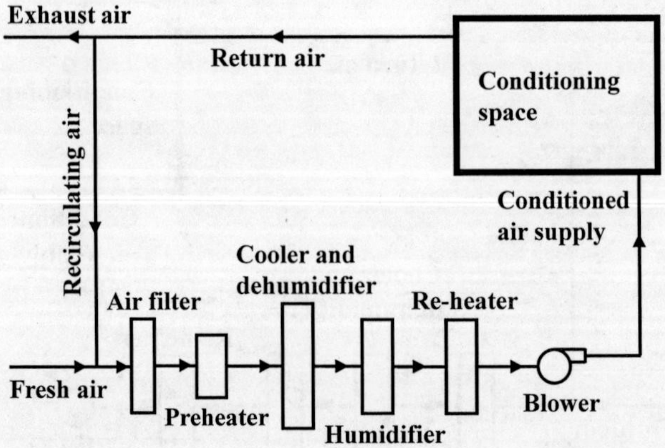

Fig. 5.20: Schematic of all-season air-conditioning unit

UNIT SUMMARY

This unit starts with discussions on air compressor, its uses and thermodynamic analysis. Adiabatic, polytropic and isothermal compression processes are discussed. The need for multistage compression and the minimum work required for a multistage compression process are reported. Types of compressors are then explained. The characteristics of reciprocating and rotary compressors are revealed. Working principle of a single-stage reciprocating compressor is explained along with its thermodynamic analysis for determining the work required. Volumetric efficiency, important for reciprocating compressors, is defined mathematically. Four types of rotary compressors are explained with simple sketches. Illustrative examples are included for compressor calculations. Subsequently, refrigeration is discussed. Properties of refrigerants, air refrigeration cycle and vapor compression refrigeration cycles are explained. Numerical examples for air and vapor compression refrigeration cycles are included. Aircraft cabin cooling is schematically explained. Finally, topics on air-conditioning are reported. Definition of relative and specific humidity, comfort level, classifications of air-conditioning systems and seasonal air-conditioning have been discussed.

EXERCISES

Multiple Choice Questions

1. During the compression process, the temperature of air
(a) increases (b) decreases
(c) remains constant (d) none of these

2. In polytropic compression process, the following relationship is obeyed for air:
(a) $pv = C$ (b) $pv^{\gamma} = C$
(c) $pv^{n} = C$ (d) none of these

3. Isothermal compression requires
(a) maximum work (b) minimum work
(c) zero work (d) none of these

4. Reciprocating air compressor delivers
(a) higher pressure at low flow rate (b) lower pressure at high flow rate
(c) lower pressure at low flow rate (d) higher pressure at high flow rate

5. Rotary compressor delivers
(a) higher pressure at low flow rate (b) lower pressure at high flow rate
(c) lower pressure at low flow rate (d) none of these

6. Clearance factor is a ratio of
(a) displacement volume to clearance volume
(b) displacement volume to maximum volume
(c) clearance volume to displacement volume
(d) none of these

7. COP of a refrigerator is a ratio of
   (a) heat supplied to heat rejected
   (b) heat rejected to work supplied
   (c) heat supplied to work supplied
   (d) work supplied to heat supplied.
8. In an adiabatic throttling process,
   (a) internal energy remains constant
   (b) enthalpy remains constant
   (c) entropy remains constant
   (d) none of these
9. Relative humidity of air is a ratio of
   (a) vapor pressure of moisture to its saturation pressure
   (b) vapor pressure of moisture to the air pressure
   (c) saturation pressure of moisture to the air pressure
   (d) none of these
10. Evaporating cooling accomplishes
   (a) cooling and humidification
   (b) cooling and dehumidification
   (c) cooling alone
   (d) none of these

Answers to Multiple Choice Questions									
1. (a)	2. (c)	3. (b)	4. (a)	5. (b)	6. (c)	7. (a)	8. (b)	9. (a)	10. (a)

Short and Long Answer Type Questions

1. Write mass and energy conservation equations for a control volume around a compressor.
2. With neat sketches of p-V and T-S diagrams, explain isothermal, adiabatic and polytropic compression processes.
3. Write expressions of specific work supplied during adiabatic, polytropic and isothermal compression processes.
4. Write an expression for work supplied during two-stage compression process.
5. Draw two-stage compression process in p-V and T-S diagrams.
6. Explain the working of a single-stage reciprocating compressor using a simple sketch.
7. Derive the expression for specific work required for a single stage reciprocating compressor using a p-V diagram.
8. With a simple sketch explain the working of a vane-type rotary compressor.
9. With a simple sketch explain the working of a Roots compressor.
10. With a simple sketch explain the working of a centrifugal compressor.
11. With a simple sketch explain the working of an axial-flow compressor.
12. Write the Clausius statement.
13. Write the expressions for COP of a refrigerator and a heat pump.
14. List important properties of refrigerants.
15. Write briefly about the types of refrigerants.
16. Draw a schematic of a Bell-Coleman cycle and derive the expression for COP in terms of pressure ratio.

17. Explain the working principle of a vapor compression refrigeration system.
18. Draw the basic vapor compression refrigeration cycle in a T-S diagram.
19. Write expressions for isentropic efficiencies of compressor and turbine.
20. Write expressions for relative humidity and specific humidity.
21. What are the types of air-conditioners – briefly explain.
22. With a simple sketch, explain the working of a window air-conditioner.
23. With a schematic explain how summer air-conditioning is done.
24. With a schematic explain how winter air-conditioning is done.
25. With a schematic explain how all-season air-conditioning is done.

Numerical Problems

1. A single-stage adiabatic reciprocating compressor delivers 20 kg/minute of air at a pressure of 1300 kPa by receiving air at 100 kPa and 20°C **from the ambient. Its isentropic efficiency is** 85%. Take c_p of air as 1005 J/kg-K and $\gamma = 1.4$. What is the power required for compression.
2. A single stage reciprocating compressor has a bore of 90 mm and stroke of 100 mm. Its clearance ratio is 0.06. It takes ambient air at 25°C and pressure of 100 kPa. The pressure ratio of compression is 4. If the expansion process is polytropic with an index of 1.35, Calculate the volumetric efficiency, mass flow rate if the compressor runs at 900 rpm and power required for compression. Take R of air as 287 J/kg-K.
3. A two-stage air compressor with ideal intercooling works with an overall pressure ratio of 16. Air at 298 K and 100 kPa is taken from ambient in the first stage. Polytropic compression with an index of 1.3 occurs at both stages. Take R of air as 287 J/kg-K and $\gamma = 1.4$. Calculate the specific work required for the compressor and heat transfer in the intercooler.
4. Consider a two-stage centrifugal compressor with pressure ratio of 3 in each stage. The compressor handles 3 kg/s of air flow rate from an ambient at 293 K and 1 bar pressure. Isentropic efficiency of both stages of compressor is 0.9. Intercooler cools the air from the first stage to 300 K. Take c_p of air as 1005 J/kg-K and $\gamma = 1.4$. Determine the overall compressor power and heat rejected in the intercooler.
5. Consider an air refrigeration system working on Bell-Coleman cycle. Temperature at the entry of compressor is 270 K and that at the inlet of the turbine is 320 K. The pressure ratio is 4. If the refrigeration capacity of 2 tonnes is required, evaluate the mass flow rate of air and COP of the system. The isentropic efficiency of compressor is 0.85 and that of the turbine are 0.9. Take for air, $c_p = 1.005$ kJ/kg-K and $\gamma = 1.4$.
6. Refrigerant R134a enters the compressor of a refrigerator as saturated vapor at 150 kPa at a rate of 0.3 m^3/min and leaves at 1 MPa. The isentropic efficiency of the compressor is 78%. The refrigerant enters the throttling valve as a saturated liquid. Determine (a) the power input to the compressor, (b) the rate of heat removal from the refrigerated space, (c) the COP. The properties of R134a at different states can be taken from the following tables.

Properties of Saturated R134a: Saturation table

Pressure (kPa)	Saturation temperature (°C)	v_f (m^3/kg)	v_g (m^3/kg)	h_f (kJ/kg)	h_g (kJ/kg)	s_f (kJ/kg-K)	s_g (kJ/kg K)
150	-18.23	0.007395	0.14625	27.84	239.48	0.11315	0.9449
1000	39.37	0.00870	0.02033	107.34	271.04	0.3920	0.9157

Properties of Saturated R134a: Superheated table at 1 MPa

T (°C)	h (kJ/kg)	s (kJ/kg-K)
40	271.7	0.918
50	282.8	0.9526

REFERENCES AND SUGGESTED READINGS

1. B. D. Wood, Applications of Thermodynamics, Addison-Wesley, 1969.
2. P. K. Nag, Engineering Thermodynamics, McGraw Hill Education, 2012.
3. R. C. Arora, Refrigeration and Air Conditioning, PHI Learning Pvt. Ltd., 2010.
4. P. N. Ananthanarayanan, Basic Refrigeration & Air Conditioning, McGraw Hill Education, 2013.

Dynamic QR Code for Further Reading

1. NPTEL course on "Refrigeration and Air Conditioning", by Prof. M. Ramgopal, Department of Mechanical Engineering, IIT Kharagpur.

Scan Me

2. NPTEL course on "Refrigeration and Air Conditioning", by Prof. R. C. Arora, and Prof. M. Ramgopal, Department of Mechanical Engineering, IIT Kharagpur.

Scan Me

3. NPTEL course on "Refrigeration and Air Conditioning", by Prof. Ravi Kumar, Department of Mechanical Engineering, IIT Roorkee.

Scan Me

CO AND PO ATTAINMENT TABLE

Course outcomes (COs) for this course can be mapped with the programme outcomes (POs) after the completion of the course and a correlation can be made for the attainment of POs to analyze the gap. After proper analysis of the gap in the attainment of POs necessary measures can be taken to overcome the gaps.

Table for CO and PO attainment

Course Outcomes	ATTAINMENT OF PROGRAMME OUTCOMES (1- Weak Correlation; 2- Medium Correlation; 3- Strong Correlation)						
	PO-1	PO-2	PO-3	PO-4	PO-5	PO-6	PO-7
CO-1							
CO-2							
CO-3							
CO-4							
CO-5							

The data filled in the above table can be used for gap analysis.

INDEX

D

E

F

G

H

I

J

L

M

T

U

V